From the Parish for the Life of the World

Stephen P. Bouman

Augsburg Fortress

FROM THE PARISH FOR THE LIFE OF THE WORLD

Copyright (c) 2000 Stephen P. Bouman. All rights reserved.

First Augsburg Fortress edition, 2004

ISBN 0-8066-5176-8

The Icon of Pentecost or the Descent of the Holy Spirit pictured on the cover was written by George the Cretan in 1547 and photographed by Frederick J. Schumacher.

Manufactured in the U.S.A.

Contents

Foreword 7

Introduction 11

PART ONE: "You have made public profession of your faith...."

1. Who in the World Are We? Lutheran Nonnegotiables 19
2. Christ's Choice for Life: Law and Gospel Applied 25
3. True Confession: The Spirit of Augsburg 29
4. Rerooting in the Community:
   A Mission Strategy Grows in Brooklyn 33
5. A Lutheran Spiritual Face in the Public Arena 38
6. From Pentecost to Politics:
   How One Parish Tackled the Pornography Problem 42

PART TWO: "Do you intend to continue in the covenant
   God made with you in Holy Baptism?"

7. Life by Drowning: The Baptized Christian in the World 51
8. Children of a Greater God:
   Catechesis of the Confessional Heart 60
9. A River Runs through It: Evangelism from the Font 66
10. Bonhoeffer, Youth, and the Church:
    The Mundane *Communio Sanctorum* 72
11. Walking on Water: Mentoring the Next Generation 78
12. The Habit of Ecstasy; the Practice of Prayer;
    the Journey of Faith 84

PART THREE: "To live among God's faithful people...."

13. The Community of Grace 97
14. The Community of the Word 102
15. The Faithful Community 107
16. The Disciplined Community:
    Law, Gospel and the *Solus Christus* 113
17. Confraternities of Grace: Small Group Ministry 121
18. Family Values 125

PART FOUR: "To hear his word and share in his supper...."
19. Eating and Drinking Among the Tombstones 133
20. Full Communion on the Way Home 139
21. Embodied Ecumenism:
    The Unity of Christ's Body at the Local Level 145
22. Assisting Ministers: Identity and Function 151
23. To Carry God in the Mouth: Singing the Faith 157

PART FIVE: "To proclaim the good news of God in Christ...."
24. Bishop and Parish 165
25. The Triune Shape of the Church: *Episcope* and the Trinity 167
26. Lost and Found: Growth and Evangelism 173
27. Evangelism, Church Growth and the Swinging Door 181
28. *Hirtabrev*: Following Jesus to the Breach 185
29. *Hirtabrev*: Come to the Table:
    Koinonia as Missionary Accountability 195

PART SIX: "To serve all people, following the example
    of our Lord Jesus...."
30. The Diaconate: Consecrated DPs 205
31. Diakonia: A Mom-and-Pop Theological Store 211
32. Priests and Deacons: Earthly and Heavenly Partnership 217
33. Servants of Jesus: Diaconal People Among Us 224

PART SEVEN: "And to strive for justice and peace in all the earth."
34. Parish Schools: Christ, the City, and the Child 231
35. To Take Care of the Body:
    Social Ministry and Evangelism
    through the Parish Social Ministry Committee 248
36. Requiem 255
37. A Tale of Three Houses 257
38. Give Me That Stranger:
    The Ministry of Word and
    Sacrament Communities in the World 262
Conclusion 275

Acknowledgments and Dedications

For:

Grosspapa Henry Janson Bouman and Grandpa Victor Albert Bartling,
pastors of the Church and inspiration for my vocation,
who now serve the Church Triumphant.

Paul and Victoria: my parents,
who brought the Church to the kitchen table.

Timothy, Jeremy, Rachel: my children,
whose names appear in the book because they are gifts of grace in my life.

The saints of St. Jacobus and Christ, Woodside, Queens; Atonement,
Jackson Heights, Queens; Trinity, Bogota, New Jersey;
the Metropolitan New York Synod of the ELCA
—all partners in parish and episcopal ministry.

Pastor Glenn Stone,
who as editor of *Lutheran Forum* first published my work.

Betsy Frey, associate editor of *Lutheran Forum*,
who gave sense and shape to my manuscript.

The board members and staff
of the American Lutheran Publicity Bureau,
who have patiently encouraged me in the writing of this book.

The pastors, deacons, and lay leaders
who have been my partners in the Gospel.

And especially for Janet: my wife, friend and inspiration.

Soli Deo Gloria

Foreword

by Martin E. Marty

Those of us who think of ourselves as fanatic Lutherans will find a soulmate in Stephen Bouman. [Non-Lutherans: stay tuned, too!] To the mating of souls add the realization that he will come across as a companion to those whose resource in pastoral life, theology, family existence, and activity or activism is fundamentally in the Lutheran grasp of the Gospel.

Fanatics? They come in various breeds. A familiar definition of their kind appeared in the comment of "Mr. Dooley," the creation of a Chicago columnist of years ago, Finley Peter Dunne. He said that a fanatic is someone who knows that he's doing exactly what the Lord would do if the Lord were also in possession of the facts. We have met Lutherans of that stripe. Bishop Bouman is not one of them.

Instead, he gives evidence that his fanaticism is exemplified by reference to the etymology of the word. The *fanum* is the temple, the sacred precinct. The fanatic is someone who hangs around such a place a good deal, or, more seriously, is awed by it.

The reader can see that Bouman has done that hanging around. As one reads these columns-turned-into-a-book it becomes very clear that the Catechism, the Lutheran teaching on Baptism and the Lord's Supper, and the corollary appropriation of the "sacrament of sound waves," the Word, are available to him and penetrate his thought and action.

His Lutheran elementary school training is apparent in the way he can weave in and out of catechismal lore and reference. You do not have to picture him having to look up much of anything before he cites the Lutheran Confessions. As someone who shared the experience of parochial education from back in the days when children memorized the written teachings, I picture that one could wake the author from slumber at any 3 A.M., shake him to consciousness, and ask him to recite the Explanation to the Second Article of the Creed backward, and he could do it. This is most certainly true.

Have I turned off those who did not share his experience, do not have the teaching available, nor the way of life integrated into daily conversation? I hope not, because I want to observe and argue that because Bouman is so at home with his Lutheran sources, he is not constricted, confined.

So: those of us who think of ourselves as ecumenical Lutherans will find a spirit-mate in the author of this book. Those who think that being rooted in the Confessions must lead to dogmatic precisionism, scholastic pettifoggery, and tunnel vision will find that just the opposite is the case. Again and again, almost never by topic design but often through casual yet relevant reference, we find Bouman acting out his awareness of and dependence on the understanding that the Church is "one," just as it is holy, catholic, and apostolic.

For Bouman that oneness, that ecumenical reach, the aspiration to and enjoyment of full communion with non-Lutherans, of truly shared ministry, is rooted in an evangelical ecclesiology. In turn, that derives from St. Paul and the sixteenth-century reforms of Luther and others. Such a reach does not imply a sentimental embrace, a wishy-washy tolerance of the other. It is a strong and firm encounter with others, an invitation toward common witness and work.

Once more, those who are or who think of themselves as fanatic Lutherans, people who are nurtured by the company of fellows in the *fanum*, the organizing and sacred center, will also find affinity with Pastor Bouman when he shows that he is also profane. No, not profane as we have narrowed that concept down to phenomena that are blasphemous or obscene. Bouman has tackled debased profanity and profaneness, as readers will see.

No, what is profane is (*pro + fanum*), "outside the temple," in the streets and markets and malls, the slums and banks and hospitals. And Bouman goes to such places, not with a "wall" between sacred and profane as his metaphor, but with an understanding of the Lordship of Christ in and over history and among ordinary humans in their dealings. He moves in such places, not bragging that he does so but showing incidentally that such freedom to move beyond the sanctuary is a part of the pastoral calling. His place in the profane world, the human City, is never secure; Christians are not called to security there. But it is also not alien. He belongs and does not belong to it, which is the Pauline and Lutheran way to conceive of it.

When I first started to read Boumaniana in the various publications from which he has borrowed these chapterlets, it occurred to me that they should be collected in book form. And here they are. We have too few pastoral books that work as *enchiridia* or manuals and handbooks that teach by example. There are plenty of "how-to" instruction books, but they tend to be pedantic and in the less attractive senses of that term, preachy. There have been a few books like Reinhold Niebuhr's *Leaves from the Notebook of a Tamed Cynic* which let us look over the shoulder of someone going about, and sometimes wishing he could run away from, pastoral activity. I hope thousands of readers will share my enthusiasm for this genre.

These columns, now chapters, do not appear in chronological sequence, and sometimes one has to look at the date of an original appearance of the paragraphs to get the full sense of context. Otherwise there are moments that will seem dislocating, jarring. But I am glad the author arranged them topically, since readers who become familiar with the book are likely to revisit it by themes that meet their current sorts and conditions of life.

In some ways, the appearance of rare books like this look miraculous. When did this busy pastor, whether in the roles that demand *episcope* in parish or in synod, find time to write such reflective materials? Above, I pictured waking him at three a.m. to have him recite the Catechism. Maybe he does not retire until about that time of the night. I know how hard it is for a faithful, involved, and active pastor to find time to do sustained writing. (For eleven years I served in various sorts of parish pastoral engagements; I describe those as the years when I "worked for a living." The next thirty-five years I was a professor, and never worked so hard again.)

However he did it, I am glad he wrote this book. I have one worry and one regret. The concern: Bouman is the product of a particular generation and ethos, one that permitted him to be intensely schooled in biblical/Lutheran teaching and life and at the same time exposed to a changing urban world. Who will succeed that generation? Let us assume that similarly intelligent, experienced, consecrated people are coming along. Will their entrance to ministry upon receipt of a calling that they experience well into their lives, followed by training for ministry without all the "pre-theological" and "pre-pre" habituation that Bouman has, give them the opportunity to belong so much to the *fanum* and be so at home beyond it?

And I have one regret. This collection has to be identified as a pastoral book for pastors, and will probably be marketed that way and bought and read mainly by pastors. My regret is that lay people may not find themselves implied and addressed. Few books will give the believers who make up the priesthood of all the baptized as refreshing and empathic a glimpse of pastoral life as will this one. And since existence in parishes or such relations as chaplaincies are transactions between those "rightly called" to what we think of as ordained professional ministry and those who are "rightly called" by baptism to be ministered unto—and to minister—we do need communication across the boundaries between "lay" and "non-lay" believers.

So: read—and communicate.

Martin E. Marty is the Fairfax M. Cone Distinguished Service Professor Emeritus at the University of Chicago; an ELCA pastor; and, obviously, a friend through the decades of Stephen Bouman.

Introduction

> You shall have the trumpet sounded throughout all your land and you shall hallow the fiftieth year and you shall proclaim liberty throughout the land to all its inhabitants. (Leviticus 25:9-10)
>
> [Jesus] unrolled the scroll and found the place where it was written: "The spirit of the Lord is upon me, because he has anointed me to bring good news to the poor. He has sent me to proclaim release to the captives and recovery of sight to the blind, to let the oppressed go free, to proclaim the year of the Lord's favor." (Luke 4:18,19)
>
> For surely I know the plans I have for you, says the Lord, plans for your welfare and not for harm, to give you a future with hope. (Jeremiah 29:11,12)

What We Do

The phone was ringing as we entered the house after returning from a family vacation. "Come to the hospital. Carmine, he collapsed at the party. We're in the emergency room. He looked bad. Please come." My son, in his early teens, followed me to the car. "I'll go with you, dad." There they were in the waiting room, dressed in tuxes, suits, gowns, dressed for celebrating the fiftieth anniversary of Carmine and Dorothy. I found the room where Carmine lay, dead. I traced with oil the sign of the cross on his forehead, reading the commendation. "Into your hands, O Lord...."

Back to the waiting room, with its huddle of expectant, fearful faces. I sought Dorothy, hugged her, whispered "He died," and absorbed her shuddering tears. The waiting room became a place of dislocation and sadness. A party affirming faithful living was transformed by death.

They gathered around me in expectant silence. They sought a word from me, their pastor. I saw my own son's eyes seeking my response to the pain and death of a person he had come to love. I was not a free agent in that room. At that moment I was the voice of the Church, the Body of Christ. From Jeremiah: "Before I formed you in the womb I knew you, and before you were born I consecrated you; I appointed you a prophet to the nations" (Jeremiah 1:4,5).

And I did not know what to say. Yes, I was ordained, I was wearing a clerical collar in the black shirt tucked into my jeans. But Jeremiah had voiced my own fear: "Then I said, Ah, Lord God! Truly I do not know how to speak, for I am only a boy" (Jeremiah 1:6).

Dorothy, who had watched our children when they were babies and given them their first presents in the Christmas season, looked at me through tears and the shock of sudden bereavement. My words caught, stillborn in my throat.

I looked again at these dear faces and began to speak, for when there are no words, God gives them. "Then the Lord put out his hand and touched my mouth; and the Lord said to me, "Now I have put my words in your mouth.... for I am watching over my word to perform it" (Jeremiah 1:9&12b).

I began to speak words I know by heart: "The Lord is my shepherd...."and they spoke the words with me. "My sheep hear my voice, and I know them and they follow me and no one shall pluck them out of my hand...." "In my father's house are many rooms...I go to prepare a place for you...." "Nothing can separate us from the love of God in Christ Jesus our Lord...." We were exiles then, our faith a dimly burning wick. I opened my Bible and proclaimed Jeremiah's words of Jubilee hope to the exiled and broken-hearted centuries ago: "For surely I know the plans I have for you, says the Lord, plans for your welfare and not for harm, to give you *a future with hope.* Then when you call upon me and come and pray to me, I will hear you. When you search for me, you will find me.... and I will bring you back to the place from which I sent you into exile" (Jeremiah 29:11-13).

We prayed, I commended them to the Risen Christ, in whose presence Carmine now dwelled. And I asked them to hold on to one another, and to remind one another of the promise of the presence of Jesus. They, the people of God, would continue the words spoken by their pastor.

In the car I took off the collar and put my head on the steering wheel and cried. "So," said my son from the shadows next to me. I felt his hand on my arm. "So, this is what you do."

I told my son: "This is what you do, too."

This is what we do. We who are pastors and the baptized in the world, we who are part of a Christian parish, this is what we do. I write this introduction at this millennial moment in human history, in a world cringing in the waiting room before the advent of Y2K. I offer this book on Christian parish ministry filled with the hope of the presence of Jesus, to a world which has forgotten why we mark time the way we do. The parish, liturgically oriented around the life of Jesus, is a living invitation for the world to consider again the Incarnation of Jesus of Nazareth. A renewal of parish life and mission is how the Church on this eve of the third millennium can proclaim "a future with hope" through the death and resurrection of Jesus.

To proclaim a Jubilee is to offer the world a fresh start, even as each day we renew God's graceful embrace of us in remembrance of our Baptism.

Jubilee 2000 rests on what we do in each of the parishes of the Church: as parishes reroot in their communities, follow Jesus into the lives of people and neighborhoods, and gather around Word and Sacraments to proclaim Christ.

Pastor Dan Anderson lay in bed in a Brooklyn hospital, fighting the last stages of brain cancer. We spoke of many things, but the conversation repeatedly returned to the people and ministry of Fordham Lutheran Church in the Bronx. Dan's ministry there as an interim pastor had been a Jubilee in the life of that beleaguered congregation. By his gentle and loving pastoral presence, his patient listening, and his Gospel ministry he had proclaimed "a future with hope" for the saints of Fordham. Their recent history of conflict and heartbreaking decline had many wondering if there was any future at all for this parish. Dan's ministry provided space for healing and reconciliation, a true Jubilee fresh start. By the grace of God, Dan loved the saints of Fordham back into the confidence of their own great giftedness and potential. Their ministry today mightily proclaims to the entire Fordham neighborhood "a future with hope." In the hospital bed Dan spoke of his love for Fordham. Then I took bread and wine and shared the family meal of the church with Pastor Anderson. It was like a revelation. He ate and drank and smiled. "So," he said, "This is what I have been doing."

After several weeks at home Pastor Anderson went back to Calvary Hospice in the Bronx to die. But he did not die alone. Fordham Lutheran Church became partners with St. John's and Messiah (the Brooklyn parishes Dan was serving as pastor) in ministry to and with Pastor Anderson at the end of his life. The saints of Fordham, who had heard and believed the message of Jubilee in their parish life, now gathered frequently at his bedside to proclaim Jubilee to their interim pastor. They sang his favorite hymns, prayed with him, shared in his favorite passages from Scripture and by their faith and presence reminded him of the Jubilee called resurrection, death transformed into the fresh start of eternal life. The pastor whom God had sent to heal the heartbreak in the life of Fordham parish was now visited in his own vulnerability at the gate of death.

In the rhythm, sublime and mundane, of parish ministry the face of Jesus becomes visible among us; and in the Name of Jesus, by word and deed, we proclaim a Jubilee Future with Hope.

Every Christian parish is a gate of heaven. Remember the call of Jeremiah. "Do not say, 'I am only a boy;' for you shall go to all to whom I send you, and you shall speak whatever I command of you. Do not be afraid... Now I have put my words in your mouth." Let us proclaim a future with hope through a renewal of parish life so that the world may see the face of Jesus. It's what we do.

Reflections on What We Do in the Life of a Parish

This is the first in a regular series of columns I will be writing for *Lutheran Forum*. Their subject is pastoral theology. Their goal is singular: keep the heart in focus. The community of Grace gathered around Word and Sacraments is not just another among competing "expressions" of the church, another consumer for the myriad programs and agendas devised by headquarters, not just one option among many in being spiritual, not just another agency to make the world a little better. This column is written from the midst of a local congregation, a community of Grace gathered around Word and Sacraments, in the faith that each such community is an eschatological sign, servant, incarnation of the presence of Jesus. One of the tasks of this column will be to take up the many themes presented by life in the church and the world and illumine them from the perspective of parish-rooted pastoral theology. Through the parish perspective the Means of Grace will be the prism through which we examine the issues of our lives. I will tell brief stories from parish life, which may serve as parables of grace concerning these issues. Consider them dispatches from campaign headquarters, in the service of God's graceful campaign to reconcile all creation through the dying and rising Christ.

The above paragraph introduced a regular column, "From the Parish," in the Lent 1989 issue of *Lutheran Forum*. I recently read through the forty-some articles I have contributed to the pages of *Lutheran Forum* since my first published work for the Pentecost 1981 issue. Most of these pieces appeared in the "From the Parish" column. They are certainly not a systematic theology of pastoral ministry. They are as random and wide-ranging as parish life. Their form is not so much the theological treatise as the story, the sermon, the confirmation class, the exploration of the biblical drama, the spiritual retreat. The articles come out of the quotidian stuff of parish life.

This is a book about the parish, written from the heart of parish life. Its heart is an edited collection of the *Forum* articles, with other published work and new material adding dimension to some of the themes explored in these pages. I have chosen to arrange the chapters around the covenant for renewal of Baptismal Vows in the *Lutheran Book of Worship*. This collection is certainly not a theological *summa* about the parish and its mission. But I believe their diverse soundings of parish life in the Gospel suggest a Lutheran theology of the parish, one that I hope is accessible and relevant across the ecumenical diversity of the One Body of Christ. I believe that the commitments lifted up in these pages cut across denominational lines. I hope that this book will call our national and synodical church bodies to a

renewal of support for their parishes, as well as inspire and provoke dialogue in local parishes. Certain themes emerge with relentless frequency:
- The Word and Sacrament heart of parish life is continually lifted up.
- Confessional integrity is explicit in the day-to-day life of the parish.
- The parish is always a center for mission. There is a sustained conviction that a church which turns its face toward the presence of Jesus with the poor and the lost is always in renewal.
- There is a diaconal (servant) activism in these pages that remains linked to the altar, font, pulpit, Scripture.
- The stories of Scripture are continual sources for explicating parish ministry.
- The liturgical rhythm of the Church circumscribes the life of the parish.
- The central theological commitments of the Church are explored in the intensely local, practical life of the parish.

I am entering my twenty-seventh year of ordained ministry. The first twenty were spent as a parish pastor in New York City and New Jersey, in fairly long-term pastorates. The past five have been spent in support of the parish through synodical ministry, the past three as an elected bishop of the Church. My parish experience has always included work in the wider Church as well. Some of that work has come full circle. My commitment to church-based community organizing as a vehicle for faithful parish leadership development and engagement has continued throughout my ministry. An early meeting I convened in Brooklyn to introduce organizers from the Industrial Areas Foundation to local pastors led eventually to the establishment of the East Brooklyn Churches and Nehemiah Housing. The Diakonia program I helped begin seventeen years ago now has seven hundred graduates; its Hispanic track is central to our Latino mission strategy. Koreans baptized and confirmed in my first multi-ethnic parish in Queens are now providing leadership twenty years later for a new Korean mission start in that borough. But these wanderings in the wider Church always led back to the parish and its mission.

I am more convinced than ever that the Christian parish is the organizing form the Gospel takes in the world ever since folks gathered in households in the aftermath of Pentecost's conflagration of the Spirit's power. The parish is what we do as the Church in the world. T. S. Eliot has written: "Not only the best, but the most individual and creative parts of a writer's work may be those in which the dead... his ancestors, assert their immortality most vigorously." In "What is a Classic?" Eliot defined that word in terms of "...maturity: the maturity that grows from a knowledge of the past, so that the writer is aware of his predecessors and we in reading can hear the ancestral traits in a voice that nevertheless remains unique."

Eliot's description of the blend of continuity and creativity\originality in the arts can help us to think about the parish as well. How can we continue to tell the "old, old story" in ways which also lift up the "new thing" God is continually doing in changing settings? The parish is the setting that gathers the voices of ancestral faith in life-and-death encounters with today's gathered faithful.

As you read this book and think about the people and ministry they reflect, I hope that you will see our ancestral faith etched out in the creatively bold and new Gospel encounters throughout your own parish life. We are together part of one flock, one parish, with one Good Shepherd. By God's grace, it's what we do.

PART ONE
"YOU HAVE MADE PUBLIC PROFESSION
OF YOUR FAITH...."

Chapter 1

Who in the World Are We?
Lutheran Non-negotiables

This ministry, like all Christian ministry, finds its source and its summit in Word and Sacrament. It is unwaveringly devoted to gathering around these means of grace congregations of the poor bound by faith-filled obedience to the risen Christ...Finally, this ministry should share with the poor the best of our spiritual tradition. In preaching, worship, catechesis, music and the arts the most elevated is in order for those whom the world counts the most debased. While sensitivity to cultural differences is required, it is both futile and condescending to pretend to represent a tradition other than our own. The strength of the community is related to the distinctiveness of the community. People are attracted to the community not because it is the same as every other community but precisely because it is different.... (From the paper drafted by Richard John Neuhaus and presented at the 1986 pan-Lutheran conference in New York City on "The Church, the City, and the Poor")

A community without a good, matter-of-fact pastoral institutionalization of its ministry runs the risk of losing for good the apostolicity and thus ultimately the Christian character of its origin, inspiration and orientation—and in the last resort its own identity. Ministry is connected with the special concern for the preservation of the Christian identity of the community in constantly changing circumstances.... The community has a right to a minister or ministers and to the celebration of the Eucharist. (Edward Schillebeeckx, *Ministry* [New York: Crossroad, 1981], pp. 24 & 36)

"So tell me, what is nonnegotiable for you? Distill to its essence what Lutheran ministry means to you. Where does the heart beat?"

I am speaking to a Black pastor in an urban congregation. It is a mixed, formerly all-White parish in the midst of a Black neighborhood. The parish and pastor have listened to the people and the neighborhood. They have committed themselves to a ministry of outreach and hospitality among their neighbors. My friend's deep spiritual instincts are joined to an unromantic realism concerning the need for his people and neighbors to define their own issues, accept accountability for their communities, seek power as they organize their community, and avoid the traps of social service and partisan political co-optation that blunt the collective effectiveness of many inner-city churches and their pastors. Our conversation ranged from shared community-organizing tales from our earlier New York City days to questions of liturgy and ministry in multicultural settings. The conversation kept coming back to Lutheran identity in the midst of such issues and opportunities.

His answer to my question about identity could have been spoken by Jerome or Luther. "The Meal. The form of the liturgy. The message of Jesus. The community gathered around them. The rest is up for grabs." Amen.

Lutheran identity: The meal/the Sacraments. The form of the liturgy/the apostolic tradition. The message of Jesus/the Word. The baptized gathered around and by these Means of Grace, whereby the dying and rising Christ is present and the Holy Spirit gives faith and forgiveness and eternal life.

Let the liturgy be filled with what is "up for grabs," giving voice and sound and substance and specific density to the many cultural streams in which faith flowers. "Precious Lord, Take My Hand," "Dame la mano," "Christ der Herr ist Sonn, und Schild," or "The Church's One Foundation" can all fill the Mass with hospitable, new, or familiar praises to the living God, flowing from the heartbeat of the Gospel.

We are being offered bogus choices in the identity struggle of American Lutheranism. Before the publication of *With One Voice* I used to hear the LBW trashed at "multicultural" gatherings as something at odds with an "inclusive" church. I hear expressions of the faith that are multicultural in hymnody and style debunked by so-called "traditional Lutherans" as somehow "unLutheran." Liturgical, theological and doctrinal concerns are set against social justice concerns as if they are somehow incompatible. You are either inclusive or Lutheran; a liturgical obsessive or a mindless social activist; a legalist or a dispenser of warm fuzzies.

First Things First

The New Jersey Synod had to change the script. The script for a synod assembly video highlighting the ministry of a nearby urban congregation had begun something like this: "The Food Pantry and Shelter is known citywide for its programs of compassion and social service." Even though that was a true statement, the pastor told them the script got it all wrong. "We are not "The Food Pantry and Shelter," he insisted. "We are a church. The pantry and shelter is one of the ways we act on the faith we share as the people of God gathered by and around Word and Sacraments. It is a part of being the Body of Christ in the world." They changed the script.

It now goes something like this: "The family of believers at First Lutheran Church is known citywide for its ministry of compassion. One such dimension of the congregation's ministry is "The Food Pantry and Shelter." They finally got the script right. Lutheran identity in social ministry does not start with this or that program or human effort. This is the starting place and script for all ministry: "God was in Christ, reconciling the world to himself."

There is only one ministry. There is no such thing as "social ministry," that is, some specialized activity of the Church that is somehow different from all else which the Church does, prays, is. All ministries of mercy in our Lutheran congregations have their genesis in the Word and Sacraments. They are part of the ministry of congregations to gather around these means of grace a community of believers and relate them to Christ. All other goals, laudable and vital though they may be— social justice, economic growth, power for the powerless, partnerships for social change, ideas of liberation, neighborhood renewal— are derived from the self-understanding of a community gathered by and for the Word and Sacraments. We must always remember the script.

A Two-Handed God

The Augustinian distinction between the City of God and the Earthly City, as expressed by Luther's doctrine of the Two Kingdoms, should be taken with utmost seriousness by Lutherans engaged in faithful social ministry. Our efforts to stand with the poor, to transform systems of dominance and corruption, to engage in corporal acts of mercy are not messianic. The Kingdom comes indeed without our efforts. We are not ushering in the Kingdom of God by our activity in the world. Many of today's political and liberation theologies are flawed by such deification of human longing and efforts. All activity of the Kingdom of the Left Hand comes under judgment. It is proximate, provisional, at best a sign of the reign of God that is to come.

Yet there is much we can learn from liberation theology as we struggle to reflect Christ's presence in the midst of the Earthly City. Lutheran social ministry is a ministry of empowerment and dignity. It resists the spurious choices between transcendence and immanence, between spiritual and practical, between changing structures and renewing lives. The Lutheran catholic affirmation that the finite is capable of the infinite enables us to see sacramental possibilities in our social ministry in the world, a coherence between the Real Presence in the Eucharist and the Real Presence of Jesus among our neighbors in the world. In the words of *The Church, The City and The Poor,* "Touched by the hope conveyed in the gracious invitation to share the promises and power of the Risen Lord, people and communities are invited to break the bonds of dependency on the programs of strangers, and become artisans of their destiny in obedience to Christ."

Lutheran social ministry must help strengthen the bonds of family, parish, neighborhood and mutual help in the Kingdom of the Left Hand. Parish ministry invites people into the family of believers, where by the love of God nobodies become somebodies, pain is borne, hope is sustained, and every believer is a priest and "little Christ" to her neighbor. By God's grace the social ministry of parishes can offer signs of transcendence, activity in the midst of a suffering world where the right- and left-hand Kingdoms meet in fleeting embrace this side of heaven.

The prophet Jeremiah gives a glimpse of the two kingdoms, a modest biblical realism concerning the social ministry of the faith community. The children of Israel are in exile in Babylon, an exile of God's own design. They face an identity crisis. "How can we sing the Lord's song in a strange land?" While never allowing them to forget Jerusalem, Jeremiah yet gives this advice: While in Babylon plant your trees, have your babies, live your daily lives fully and "seek the welfare of the city in which God has placed you in exile, pray for it, for in its welfare you will find your own."

Babylon is not home. Neither is New Jersey— or California, or Illinois, or Washington, DC, for that matter. But any city can be the particular place in which the believers are to seek God's presence and live in obedience to God's commands, affirming the city while awaiting the Messiah. Social ministry can be the way that our Lutheran parishes "seek the welfare of the city," (or town or country) and affirm the carnal, intimate particularity in which God is always present in the world. Social ministry can be an affirmation and sign of the community's faith in the God of history. Such ministry places the activity of eschatological Word and Sacrament communities in the midst of this time, this place, these neighbors, these hurts, these present opportunities. It is the practical living of the implications of Baptism and Eucharist for the life of the world.

TO RE-MEMBER THE BODY OF CHRIST

Lutheran social ministry will remain rooted in the meal, the form of the liturgy, the story of Jesus, the people gathered around them, because Lutheran identity is rooted in the liturgy, Word and Sacraments and life of the parish.

After you have made the first decision, that the holy things of the church are public and accessible to everyone, then the connections between Baptism, Eucharist, and social ministry follow naturally.

Baptism: Consider how Ricky and his mother, Maria, found the font of the parish I served in New Jersey. You pull into the driveway of the motel, one of North Jersey's refugee camps for the homeless. The parish you serve has gotten the bad reputation as a place you can go when there's nowhere else to go. When you open the door people come and call. She had called. As you get out of the car this three-year-old boy comes rushing at you, shouting, "Give me the money!" Your money means another night of shelter. His mother, a young widow (whose husband had been killed in a drug fight) comes out of the room and tells her son to be quiet. He pitches a fit as you enter room #7. Every time you try to talk, or to hear his mother's story the boy shouts, "Shut up!" until finally you just lift him up, thrust his little face parallel to yours and say quietly, "No. You shut up." And you sit down with the boy on your lap. He is quiet as his mother tells you her story. He snuggles closer. Your arms become the arms of the Church, the incarnation of Jesus. Soon you get up to pay for a couple of nights. You put Ricky down.

"Don't go," he says.

"I gotta go now, sport," you say.

The social ministry committee of the church took over from there. Months later Ricky and his mother received the baptismal embrace of the Church.

Eucharist: The congregation had bought the house next door to the church and began to plan transitional housing for homeless women and children. Ricky and Maria were on our hearts. This was a matter of taking responsibility for Baptism. We don't leave children of God at the font, but follow them into the world in baptismal integrity. One Sunday, after the Eucharist, the entire congregation processed to the house we had purchased next door. We went from the Lord's table out into the street. The crucifer, acolytes, book bearer led the family of Jesus into the house next door. In groups we gathered in the kitchen. We imagined a mother and her children around the table. In the kitchen we prayed for God to bless this future ministry and to consecrate the kitchen for holy use. Group after group filed into the kitchen to visualize the future of this ministry and pray. We could almost smell the bread on the table. We then reassembled in the church for the benediction. "Go in peace, serve the Lord," echoed into our ears as we left for our own kitchen tables to continue the Eucharist. The first family to be nurtured in our shelter arrived the week of Christmas six years ago.

Since then many children of God have sat at that kitchen table to experience the grace of God's love and protection. That is what social ministry looks like as it listens to the presence of Jesus in Baptism, Eucharist and ministry.

There is a role in the Church for Lutheran social service agencies, synodical and national support and expertise. But the initiatives and the consequences are borne by communities gathered by the meal, the story of Jesus, the shape of the liturgy. These communities will define their issues and take responsibility for their mission response. Lutheran social ministry, close to the people, unashamed of the Protestant work ethic, unwilling to pose as the Messiah, clear about its identity, can contribute much to the welfare of the city by rolling up its sleeves and, brick by brick, student by student, Baptism by Baptism, Eucharist by Eucharist, share its hope for history and its faith in a gracious God who was in Christ, reconciling the world.

(*Lutheran Forum*, Pentecost, 1990)

Chapter 2
Christ's Choice for Life: Law and Gospel Applied

Birth and Rebirth

Trouble. Past due date. Why will this child not appear? Dull fetal heart tones. The doctor telling me: Stephen, he may not make it. We have to take the baby tonight. They call it a Caesarean. I am lost, so madly in love with this insistent, hidden presence, and the woman's abdomen that enfolds it, that all I can do is cry and pray. What kind of love is this, that you have no say over it, all you can do is wait with vulnerable terror?

The nurse holds this skinny, blotchy, squirming, naked human. I look to my wife: her smile is wonderful. I hold out my arms and the nurse places Timothy into their cradle. Flesh of my flesh. His little face screws up to let out another wail. I tell you, if a heart could break for love, mine was splintered all over that hospital room.

Several weeks later I hold Timothy over water in the old church. My trembling hand dips into the water. "Timothy, I baptize you in the name of the Father, and of the Son, and of the Holy Spirit." Water drips around his little bald head.

I think about the baptism of Jesus. "This is my beloved son..." As far as a human is able, I understand.

Although we held, since conception, the power of life and death over this child, the truly awesome power is the child's, a gift of the living God.

The Christian community does not worship a dinosaur. The systemic sexism of the Church, its exclusion of women from the ordered ministry of Word and Sacraments in many communions, and from due recognition and respect in the Church's language and thinking, ought to be fossilized remnants of the past. The Church does not worship a dinosaur of gender-based domination. But the Church also does not worship a "reimaged" invention of the heart's desire, be it liberation, feminist, or any other projected deification of human longing. Rather, the Church worships Jesus Christ as Lord, foolishness to old male hegemony, stumbling-block to new rising spirits.

The debate on abortion is littered with sexist, feminist, class-based, political and other ideological mines, ready to explode when one steps into the conversation. The terms "choice," "life," and "pro" have been stripped of their primal, sturdy meanings and have become decals of identification in a polarized cacophony of anger, resentment, mistrust, and politicized rancor. The tension is too easily resolved by alignment with one camp or another. Instead, the tension— not the noise and slogans— ought to be heightened, especially within the Christian community so that true debate and conversation can help clarify what is at stake in the abortion controversy. Heighten the tension! Yes, a woman has a right to her own body, especially in the most personal and sensitive areas of sexual activity and reproduction. But yes, we are all bodies within a Body, the Body of Christ, and together we are Body within the body of all humanity and creation. Yes, autonomy. But autonomy within community; the Christian community would extend this freedom to all outsiders, vulnerable ones, including that burgeoning life drawing sustenance from its mother's autonomous body. No more worship of ourselves. What we need is a real debate, especially among those of the community that believes that Jesus is Lord.

Heightening the Tension

Time to step on some mines as I make my own modest contribution to heightening the tension on the issue of abortion.

I believe categorically that abortion, the taking of an innocent life, is tragic.

I believe that sometimes, in certain instances, abortion may be the lesser of two evils.

I believe that all such decisions stand under the grace of a forgiving God.

I am skeptical of governmental intervention in this area.

I believe in a consistent ethic of life— something like the late Cardinal Bernardin's "seamless garment" of opposition to capital punishment and the war in Vietnam as well as abortion on demand— though I see the world as grayer and more inconsistent than he seemed to.

I long for the strident single-issue polarization to evolve somehow into a deeper dialogue about the kind of people we are, and the kind of a community we want to become. I wish the Church would exemplify such a dialogue concerning our individual and corporate character before one another and God. We need signs that such a respectful, prayerful conversation is possible in the Church.

Would it be possible to ask for silence from so-called "pro-life" groups unless they are also actively involved in some ministry that supports or enhances life after birth? Housing, easing hunger, employment, education, health, day care, adoption services, foster care, advocacy concerning issues of human dignity and life come to mind.

Would it be possible to ask for silence from so-called "pro-choice" groups unless they are also involved in some ministries that really help a person to make a choice, such as counseling that includes identification of adoption or foster care agencies, as well as acknowledging public opposition to abortion as birth control? We need to move beyond the caricatures that "pro-life" concern ends with the fetus, and that "pro-choice" is another term for evasion of individual and corporate responsibility.

I would like to see all sides of the debate focus together on the role and responsibilities and presence of the fathers of these unborn children caught in the tug-of-war between life and death.

I would like mutual recognition that a woman's right to her body, and a man's right to sex without consequence, are not the highest morality that we seek.

But finally more important than what I think, or what you think, is what the Church thinks, believes, teaches, and confesses, as the bearer of God's Word and Sacrament presence in the world. Stanley Hauerwas put it bluntly: "The Church is my social ethic."

GRACIOUS LIFE, GRACIOUS CHOICE

Women, men, and couples do come to my office, and those of pastors everywhere, as they seek from the Church guidance, permission, confession, absolution or a sympathetic ear over the decision to terminate a pregnancy or bring it to full term. These encounters range from casual disclosures of taking care of some birth-control "loose ends" to year-long counseling for grief over a life lost twenty years ago. The Church is involved in this issue because it cares and loves, and finds its life among people for whom Christ died. But it is primarily involved because it is the bearer in the world of the Word of God and the presence of Jesus.

It is from the midst of communities of Jesus that we can begin to recapture some of the meaning of terms like "choice," "life," "pro-."

God is pro-life, as the community confesses weekly in the First Article of the Creed. All of life is gift. And God is *pro, for* this gifted life, not against it.

And *God is pro-choice*, as we confess weekly in the Second Article of the Creed. God chose to speak Christ. And Christ did not regard equality with God as something to be exploited, but willingly chose to empty himself and take on our human form, become a fetus in the womb of a woman named

Mary, and in obedience go the way of the cross, where pro-life and pro-choice came together for our redemption. Jesus was pro-choice in his ministry, choosing to touch lepers, give hope to the poor, recognize and lift up the dignity of women, children, and outsiders everywhere. And in that touch Jesus was pro-life, offering living water, living bread, eternal life. Pro-choice, in that he never forced or conned anyone into his fellowship; pro-life, in that in his lifting up on the cross, all humanity is drawn to God.

The Church is the community of that story. A community of Jesus that baptizes is pro-life. Yet the process of spiritual formation in a Christian community, that growth in the community's story we call character development or identity, is pro-choice in that it is the community's fervent prayer that the baptized one will identify with God's gracious choice of her in Christ, and participate in the community's mission to the world in Jesus' name.

There is a continuum between counseling sessions in the pastor's office and the pastor's presence at the font, at the altar, in the pulpit. Ministry seeks to help believers identify with the story of God's creation and redemption, and its authority in the life of the people of God. In the pastor's office the hunger of God's people for the assurance of God's presence and forgiveness is disclosed. Again and again people caught in the tension between a permissive, autonomy-obsessed society and the Law and Gospel message of the Church pour out their grief and thirst for grace. Mothers and fathers who chose an abortion, even for reasons of the mother's health, yet cry out in sorrow over the ending of a life. People who have not been able to bring their grief to words over a period of many years suddenly blurt out their sense of loss and guilt. And in the gracious words of absolution the healing power of God's forgiveness in Christ is spoken and believed.

The greatest contribution the Church can make to the conversation concerning abortion and other communal issues is to live out the implications of her identity. A Church that knows, teaches and lives by what it believes untiringly includes the outsider; combines confessional integrity with radical compassion; and demonstrates the primal meaning of a person's autonomy through baptismal inclusion in the community of a gracious God. So it discloses the presence of Jesus in the mine-filled, naked public square.

Would it make a difference in the abortion controversy if the Christian community helped us remember, every time it eats and drinks in communion with the living and those recumbent around the throne of the Lamb, that we are all as fetuses before God, branches on the True Vine, utterly dependent on the Gracious Choice?

(Lutheran Forum, Advent 1989)

Chapter 3
True Confession: The Spirit of Augsburg

> As they gave witness to the Gospel, the confessors at Augsburg believed they were not only standing before emperor, empire, and world, but also before God...For them and for their heirs, confessing Jesus Christ and His unconditional Gospel is the way of life. (Robert Kolb, *Confessing the Faith: Reformers Define the Church, 1530-1580* [Concordia, 1991], p. 140)
>
> The Christian faith naturally flows into a confession of the faith. As at Augsburg, so in the daily life of the Lutheran Christian, confession of the faith was a gift from God, an opportunity to serve Him and to love the neighbor, an expression of the trust binding the believer to Christ. (Kolb, *Confessing the Faith*, p. 115)

In 1569 the University of Erfurt, controlled by the Roman Catholic church, elected its first Evangelical rector, Johann Gallus, an Erfurt pastor. Then, as they say, the stuff hit the fan. The office of rector was traditionally bestowed with much ceremony, including a faculty breakfast, a clergy procession through the streets of the city, and a Mass in the cathedral. Gallus considered these ceremonies mere formalities in which he could participate while maintaining his confessional integrity. He accepted the appointment. His Gnesio-Lutheran colleagues split over the issue, some agreeing with Gallus, others saying that confessional integrity prohibited any form of public participation with Roman Catholic colleagues.

As I read about this controversy it was for me, as Yogi Berra might say, "déjà vu all over again." The confessional moment of Augsburg had deteriorated by 1569 into "confessionalism," bringing memories for me of my Missouri roots, with its appeals to confessional integrity triggered by a proposal of Eucharistic sharing between Missouri Lutherans and those who belonged to the then-ALC.

On the other hand, the Gallus incident also illustrates how profoundly the spirit of public confession of the faith was embedded in the Lutheran ethos among the first-generation pastors of the evangelical reformation. The spirit of confession reclaimed at Augsburg is instructive for our confessional movement today as a Lutheran communion. What follows are some of the salient features of the Augustana, and what they could mean to confessional integrity in parish life and ministry.

Augsburg is catholic. It stands in the apostolic tradition of the three great ecumenical creeds. With them it became a dogmatic standard among Lutherans, a secondary authority for teaching and confessing the faith. Robert Kolb, in his 1991 study of the Augustana, quotes Werner Elert: "With the Augsburg Confession began a fresh assumption of form by the Christian church. The binding together of the many in a community of hearing is form. The chorale is form. The confession is form. Proclamation itself is form. Each of these is a shaping of the many into a unity." (p.15) Moreover, what is catholic, apostolic, faithful to the Word, is also ecumenical. In contemporary confessing situations, the spirit as well as the confession of Augsburg provide firm ground as Lutherans witness to the catholicity of the church.

Augsburg is evangelical, Gospel-centered. At the heart of the confession is Christ, through whom a gracious God embraces fallen creation and a sinful humanity. There is in the Augustana a winsome weighing of words, a deep concern that the confession of faith affirm what can be affirmed about the confession of other Christians, and yet effectively proclaim Christ crucified and risen for the forgiveness of human sins. The confession of faith is meant to help draw all humanity to Christ. As the Lutheran communion confesses Christ in these latter days, what difference would it make in every program, outreach, theological statement, division, board, task force, if the evangelical heart of Augsburg beat at its core?

Augsburg is the deepest expression of the common witness of pastors, theologians, and laity. It was the princes of the German states who made the open confession of faith, who took the risk in the public forum. Their confession was, however, informed, animated and largely written by their theologians and pastors. What a tremendous parable this is for an ELCA riven by false divisions between clergy and laity, and between pastors and teachers. The work of the pastors and theologians of Augsburg inspired and informed the witness of the people of God in the public arena— what we, echoing Paul, call equipping the saints for the work of ministry. At Augsburg, the whole people of God gave voice to the *viva vox Evangelii*, each part of the Body sounding its proper note in praise of God and confession of the Gospel.

Augsburg spoke a precise word against heresy. What strikes me about the Augsburg Confession is its modest and judicious refutation of error. Melanchthon did not submit a negative embodiment of "confessionalism," but an earnest engagement with those issues of the day that hindered or denied the Gospel. The Augustana evoked the approbation in Proverbs— "A word fitly spoken is like apples of gold in a setting of silver." An example: issues of language in relation to God are deeply felt among us today. It is an issue that I believe needs deep exploration. Idolatrous images of a male God, women's experiences of paternalism and prejudice in the Church, the proper uses of inclusive language, deeper insights into the mystery of a God who loves us as a mother hen are all issues which deserve discussion, clarification, and the pooling of the Spirit's gifts. But in the spirit of Augsburg the Church must say a clear No to proposals such as those that would discontinue Baptism in the Name of the Father, Son and Holy Spirit. I am amazed at how little comprehension there is among some of our churchwide leaders about what our people really want from their Church. It is not mainly quotas or finances, or this or that program, that really disturb our people. It is the perception that we are losing our perspective, our center, our evangelical heart. The clear confession by the ELCA's Conference of Bishops on this issue — "A Statement on Trinitarian Language" — is close to the heart of Augsburg. We need to learn that we do not have to choose between being faithful or living in caves.

Augsburg is an act of confessing. Augsburg was public. The Gospel's case was made before the emperor, in the public square, so to speak. The Augustana engaged the lives and decisions of the confessors. It was much more than a static document or moment. As the heirs of the confessors, we should regard issues of theological education, moral formation, and social ministry within this rubric of confession as a total act. All are disciplined and shaped by the evangelical and catholic core of Augsburg. The Word is believed, taught, confessed in the totality of our life and action.

In 1992 there was a meeting of Lutherans in San Antonio about community organization. One evening those attending the conference went to a public "action" of a local community organization based in the Hispanic churches in San Antonio's poor neighborhoods. In the members' pursuit of justice they met with the mayor and some of the highest authorities in their city and state. Their articulation of the issues was clear, responsible, and effective. Their ability to achieve justice and participation in decisions reflecting their communal values was an example of a confessional moment. Confession is public. It is action as well as speech. One of the issues in San Antonio was the willingness of the member parishes of the organization to spend some time during Lent to study the Word of God together in a disciplined way. I experienced the meeting as a breath of the spirit of Augsburg, an undertaking in the public arena in which values and beliefs are declared, evangelical outreach is intentional, and activity is grounded in the Word of God.

Augsburg is an act of teaching as well as a document. The Augsburg Confession presented the teaching of the confessors so that God might be honored and the Gospel might have free course to illuminate the presence of Jesus. As a document the Augustana is an expression of God's revelation, a *norma normata* in the technical phrase, because it flows directly from God's Word. Each year during Lent, in one parish that I served, we returned to the text of the Augsburg Confession and from its depths we explored together the faith we share with one another and the Church catholic. We made a special effort to invite the unchurched and lapsed Christians to these classes. As the community of Word and Sacraments confesses its faith in Augsburg's spirit of teaching, and in our use of the document, the Holy Spirit works to strengthen the faithful and embrace those without the Gospel.

Finally, *Augsburg is eschatological.* Let the last word be Luther's as he wrote about confessing the faith:

> I desire with this treatise to confess my faith before God and all the world, point by point. I am determined to abide by it until my death and (so help me God!) in this faith to depart from this world and to appear before the judgment seat of our Lord Jesus Christ. (From *Confession Concerning Christ's Supper*, quoted in Kolb, *Confessing the Faith*, p. 27)

I have been a pastor and bishop for twenty-five years, in one parish for over ten of those years. There are advantages to a long pastorate. On the first Sunday of Lent in 1992, I began instructing a group of children in preparation for First Communion. They were of varying ages — I share the belief of Eastern Christians that they really should be fed from the moment of their Baptism — but the one thing in common is that they had all been baptized during my ministry. Because we did not abandon our children at the font the ministry of this parish was also deeply involved in community issues that included education, poverty, housing, substance abuse, and being present with children at risk. We followed their parents into issues of employment and economic justice. We created institutions and ministries to nurture children and educate adults. Some of our public witness was controversial. We sinned boldly and made mistakes. I see all of it as confessing the faith, a full engagement of the life of the body of Christ with the life of the world for which Christ died. This parish is not singular. Every Baptism, every Eucharist, every cup of cold water in Jesus' Name, every hospital visit, every effort for justice informed by the Gospel and the Ten Commandments is a confession of faith. For Lutherans, the form that the Augustana takes above all others is the local parish. The life and mission of each faithful parish, confessing its faith for the life of the world, is an ongoing miracle.

(*Lutheran Forum*, Reformation, 1992)

Chapter 4
Rerooting in the Community: A Mission Strategy Grows in Brooklyn

The Spires of Brooklyn

Southwest Brooklyn is the motherhouse of Scandinavian Lutheranism in New York City. It was the church which accompanied the immigrants as they made a stand in the new world, helping people find jobs, housing, hearth, community. Brooklyn is known as the borough of churches and as you drive along the Gowanus Expressway the sky is pierced by their steeples erupting from the working-class streets. The spiritual hunger of a people longing for and creating a home was answered by the spires of Brooklyn.

Southwest Brooklyn is still a staging area for immigrants. Now, however, the Lutherans of Bay Ridge and Sunset Park are surrounded by new neighbors speaking Arabic, Spanish, Russian, Mandarin, Cantonese and Amharic. When Olson's Bakery closed on 8th Avenue, it served as a visual rite of passage for a neighborhood that has changed. In the midst of that change Lutheran congregations and institutions have experienced difficult times as they struggle to sustain their life and mission. In many ways Southwest Brooklyn is a bellwether place for Lutheranism — a place where the choices are stark, survival is at stake, community change is gripping and sweeping. This area's struggles and opportunities are, or will be, played out throughout the nation's metropolitan areas in the years ahead. It was in Southwest Brooklyn that the Metropolitan New York Synod's "Rerooting in the Community" mission strategy first hit the streets.

Invitation to Reroot in the Community

The Synod was invited by pastors and leaders of the Southwest Brooklyn Conference to explore with them opportunities to do some strategic planning about the future of the Conference's mission. I had recently joined the Synod's staff, with particular responsibility for developing a mission strategy process that reflected my experience of twenty years of parish ministry in contexts of change, struggle, and renewal.

I had been involved in a mission strategy process in the Meadowlands Cluster of the New Jersey Synod while serving in my last pastorate. It was a sturdy process that helped our congregations decide on some long- and short-term mission goals. What seemed to be missing, however, in the gathering of data and the convening of leadership around its implications was *a relational dimension* — a compilation of living testimony to breathe life into the statistics and demographic data. The invitation of the Southwest Brooklyn Conference to engage in a study of mission provided *the first opportunity in our Synod to add the insights of relational community organizing* to the creation of an area mission strategy. Eighteen years of involvement with church-based community organizing, in which I saw indigenous leadership flower, communities transformed (such as the creation of Nehemiah housing in Brooklyn and the Bronx), and congregations strengthened as they reroot in their communities, convinced me that we could develop a mission strategy that would do more than add another fine-looking report to dusty bookshelves.

In retrospect, it is somewhat ironic that the first meeting took place in the basement of Salem, a Danish congregation. As the mission strategy unfolded this struggling congregation with a part-time pastor has become the host and partner with a new outreach to the Arab community. Here is what Lutheran re-rooting looks like in Brooklyn: Salem begets Salaam.

A Narrative Description
of the Mission Strategy Process

Brooklyn was the first. There are now more than thirty strategy processes that include inner city, town and country, urban, suburban, and ethnic-specific. Leaders have emerged who are training and consulting with others across the synod. The mission strategy has been a work in process, leaving plenty of room for the wind of the Spirit and the gifts of local leaders.

A description of the process is fairly simple: The congregations, schools, social ministry organizations and other Lutheran institutions join together in a discipline of prayer, listening, training, and relationship building as they do strategic planning for mission.

These are the building blocks of the process:
- This process is shaped by the presence of Jesus in Word and Sacraments. The initial training sessions lift up this centrality of Word and

Sacraments, and stories from the Biblical drama that illuminate listening, mentoring, building community, leadership development, and public mission. The participants in these sessions covenant to join together in the process.
- Training in conducting one-on-one interviews and small group "house meetings" leads to a disciplined listening presence in parish and community. *This listening presence is the heartbeat of the process,* as living testimony is shared by member and neighbor, grassroots ownership of proposals is developed, real issues are identified and addressed, and the church is exposed to potential new leaders.
- Strategic "Dream Teams" for the area and each institution lift up issues and implications for mission by analyzing the interviews and collected demographic and statistical data.
- Several area-wide consultations wrestle with these issues and implications as mutual support and solidarity in mission emerges.
- Each institution and the area as an entity draft a mission statement.
- Concrete proposals for the mission of each institution and the area are developed.
- Throughout the process training sessions are held in evangelism, leadership development, Word and Sacrament-centered mission. Worship and prayer keep us focused on the centrality of Christ.

These are some of the initial goals of the process:
- To fish and to feed
- To secure the future of our institutions and turn their lives toward the poor and the unchurched as they reroot in their communities.
- To raise up a cadre of indigenous leadership as agents for a renewal of mission.
- To develop concrete proposals for mission out of the listening process.
- To make tough institutional decisions leading to an area-wide strategy.
- To link social ministry organizations and schools to communities of Word and Sacrament.
- Wherever possible, to link with existing church-based community organizing and diaconal ministries to enhance the public nature of the Church's witness.
- To strengthen the faith of the faithful through prayer, worship, and action/reflection Bible study.

The area mission strategy process will take from eight months to a year or longer. The Synod offers continuing support, resource development and training as the proposals for mission are enacted in the coming years. This

process mirrors the twin mandates of Jesus to Peter:
"Follow me and I will make you fishers of people." Mission.
"Feed my lambs. Feed my sheep. Feed my lambs." Nurture of the faithful.

REROOTING IN BROOKLYN

There were many questions and a healthy dose of cynicism at that first meeting in Salem's basement. Churches across the street from one another were struggling for survival. Aging leaders were weary and discouraged. Good things were happening as well, but the balkanized nature of Lutheran life in Southwest Brooklyn made it difficult to gain mutual strength from the sharing of either successes or burdens. These were stewards of a magnificent legacy with their backs to the wall.

But what a gathering in Salem's basement! The riches of Lutheranism in Southwest Brooklyn were well represented and passionately engaged. Every congregation was represented, including the two Chinese parishes and one Spanish-language ministry. Lutheran Medical Center— with its network of neighborhood-based health facilities— and the Augustana Home for the Aged were represented. Parish schools and early childhood centers were represented. In each of the mission strategies we attempt to build on existing strengths and gifts already present. Each institution caucused and voted an affirmative recommendation to their respective councils. A table was under construction for the communal mourning, comfort, agitation, and renewal of mission in Brooklyn.

At the next meeting the strategy process was enacted, a team of pastors and lay leaders was chosen, and a time line was established. The strategy team oversaw the process. The high degree of lay ownership and leadership helped make our work together credible and effective. Over the next months the congregations completed the listening process in congregation and community. As they reported on what they heard there was a sense of excitement which put me in mind of the Seventy returning to report to Jesus after their encounters (Luke 10:17). The strategy team collected and analyzed the demographic data and the reports of the interviews and house meetings. They conducted two conference-wide consultations on the implications of the reports. Issues, trends, directions began to emerge. Lutheran Medical Center's demographer and planner conducted a consultation on present realities and future trends. Training events for developing mission statements and team building were conducted.

Undergirding the process was a *cantus firmus* of prayer, shared worship and Bible study, strategic episcopal visits, and exploratory initiatives conducted by congregations working together. Mutual accountability, consistently high levels of participation, and unflagging passion have energized the process. The strategy team drafted mission proposals that were studied by each institution and ratified. The proposals included authorizing an outreach in the Russian language in the conference; exploring the formation of a multi-parish school; cooperation in existing programs; and many other short- and long-term strategies. The conference institutions appointed a Mission Council to state priorities and oversee the implementation of the proposals. The Synod will continue to offer consultation and resources as future mission unfolds.

What is going on here? In a sense we have been improvising as we go along. Ascension Eve, 1995, helped put this process in perspective for me. The conference held a dinner at Good Shepherd in Bay Ridge, followed by a liturgy at which Bishop Sudbrock presided and preached. In the past, an event like this could have been held in a phone booth. But this dinner and liturgy overflowed with people from all the institutions of the conference. What the Holy Spirit had been doing over the time of the strategy process was leading the people of God to fall in love with one another again. The deepening *koinonia* of the Church gave hope for the future. Dreams of new schools, new ethnic outreach, parish\social ministry organization partnerships, renewed life among cooperating congregations began to seem plausible as the Spirit's tether drew us closer to Jesus and to one another. God's people were finding a way to say "thank you" to veteran leadership even as there emerged a collective gladness to hear and learn from new voices.

The jury is still out in Southwest Brooklyn. Synods and denominations must continue to learn ways of servant leadership, finding their mission in support of local grassroots mission. But synods and strategies can only do so much. The Lutheran faithful of Southwest Brooklyn have enacted bold and broad proposals for future mission. Now they must continue to seek the will and the courage to act on them. Change and new mission is risky business. But the viability of Lutheran ministry in Brooklyn can only be secured by going back to the future, to a time when the spires of Brooklyn welcomed the stranger in the Name of Jesus.

(*Lutheran Partners*, 1995)

CHAPTER 5
A LUTHERAN SPIRITUAL FACE IN THE PUBLIC ARENA

> No, I have not lost my faith. The expression "to lose one's faith," as one might a purse or a ring of keys, has always seemed to me rather foolish. It must be one of those sayings of bourgeois piety, a legacy of those wretched priests of the eighteenth century who talked so much. Faith is not a thing one "loses," we merely cease to shape our lives by it. (Georges Bernanos, *Diary of a Country Priest* [New York: Macmillan, 1965])

SPIRITUAL HUNGER

"Faith is not a thing one 'loses,' we merely cease to shape our lives by it." Well, yes and no. I am thinking of standing on the grass in front of the town hall with a group seeking to shape their lives by faith. The occasion is a ceremony and welcome for a group of Native Americans and their friends who were marching across the country to remember what they have lost here in North America, but also to lift up opportunities for healing drawn from the remembrance. I was glad to be a local sponsor for the event. Most of the speeches and ceremonies were fine, drawing all of us into wider worlds and mutual, if cursory, understanding. Then a medicine man, standing by a tree and evoking the mystery and grandeur of creation, asked us to consider participating in a ritual of Native American spirituality. Next he invited folks to come forward, to touch the tree, and to pray to it. Up filed some of my neighbors, many of whom had not gone near a church for years. With emotion, with tears, they touched the tree, spoke their prayers, seeking to shape a small part of their lives and longings around this faith that had deified creation. There was nothing beyond, in, with, or under either the longing or the tree. It was faith in faith. And it is that subjective cul-de-sac that characterizes much of the striving toward "spirituality" these days. The search is private. It has become a matter of technique, mediated by experts. And, like my neighbors' stretching out of the longing for faith toward God's creation, it touches me deeply.

So I think the Bernanos quote gets us down the road a piece. I would, however, add two words to it. It is not naked faith by which we seek to shape our lives, but faith *in Christ*, in the *solus Christus* that shapes us and all creation. Faith shaped by Christ is not private, nor does it draw the believer away from creation or the public arena. The *eikon Christi* is the very fullness of God, pleased to dwell bodily in this world, this history. Christ is the *anakephalaiosis*, the "one who heads up" all cosmic reality. Our faith is not shaped by creation, or by humanity, "the crown of creation," but by Christ of God, the Word made Flesh, by whom all things are made. Such Christ-centered spirituality shapes us in community by promised presence in Word and Sacraments, in the midst and for the sake of all creation.

AN ANGRY SPIRITUALITY

I recently attended one of the most spiritually fulfilling retreats in which I have ever participated. Its announced purpose would seem to promise the opposite of a personal experience of "spirituality." It was entitled "A Lutheran Face in the Public Arena" and was meant to introduce the discipline of church-based community organizing to Lutheran pastors in the Metropolitan New York Synod. Far from being an activists' playground, the retreat was an experience of deep exploration of the shaping power of the *solus Christus*. The retreat was framed by evening and morning corporate prayer and culminated in Eucharistic praise. The meanings of ministry and mission were explored through the stories of Scripture that give shape to both. At the heart of the retreat were conversations about the spiritual power of relationships, the spiritual dignity of people's participation in their unfolding history, the public implications of communities of Word and Sacraments.

Organizers helped put us in touch with the spiritual dimension of anger. Anger in the sense of the Norse word *angr* means "to grieve." *Angr* is the anger of the prophets who are grieving the distance between what is and what ought to be. It is Jesus before the tomb of Lazarus, moved in his entrails at the death of his friend. It is the grief of friends who rip a hole in the roof to bring their paralyzed friend before the healing power of Jesus. *Angr* is that which propels faith to be active in love, "in word and deed." In the retreat we wrestled with the implications of a spirituality that will not anesthetize believers against their grief, but help them get in touch with it and draw them through it toward their neighbors. The story in the Gospel of John about the pool of Bethesda was front and center in some of the conversation. Jesus asked the man lying beside the pool, "Do you want to be healed?" He recognized the stasis of the status quo, the collusion in powerlessness in the situation. The ritual of powerlessly sitting by the pool at Bethesda was a privatized spirituality confirming dependence. The command, "Stand up, take your mat and walk," was a template of a spirituality centered in Christ that sets one free. The man walked away from Bethesda with his mat on his back, a reminder of his wounded past. Jesus allowed him to "walk angry," to be able to grieve the distance between dependent apathy and spiritual freedom. "If the Son of God makes you free, you will be free indeed."

Memory and vision are central to an angry spirituality. Within relationships people can act in the world in the Name of Jesus, their anger informed by their values, their beliefs, their baptisms, the Eucharist.

A Public Spirituality

Liturgy is public. Its extension into the world is the goal of a spirituality which is shaped by Christ in Word and Sacraments. Recall the public drama of the stories of Moses and Jesus. The Exodus drama between Moses and Pharaoh was a public drama. We do not leave our babies at the font when we baptize them. We do not eat at the table and then ignore those around us who have no food or who eat alone. The goal of a Christ-centered spirituality is to stretch, to extend the font and table into creation.

Come with me to a public liturgy in the Bronx, fueled by an angry spirituality. It is the dedication of the Bronx Leadership Academy, a public high school which is the creation of a church-based community organization called the South Bronx Churches, in partnership with the New York City Board of Education. The creation of this school was the product of a lot of hard work, tension, conflict, and negotiation, out of which new relationships were formed that broke through the public apathy of a school system that had failed its children. Parents and church members were carrying their mats on their backs, angry over schools without toilets; schools with a history of four principals sent to jail in a two-year period; schools that were fiefdoms of corrupt local school boards; schools in which children's lives were endangered, where they could not learn. Anger outside of relationships can become the rage of the powerless. Within relationships, however, anger can be the grieving shaped by memory and vision that can get things done. This intervention into the stagnation of the school system has produced a brand-new school with academic rigor, a program that also trains leaders for the community, a program that offers pre-law instruction, a healthy place where students and teachers respect one another, where parents have a "hands-on" relationship with the school, where the public and private sectors have been drawn together for the sake of the community's young people. In the midst of it all was the public spirituality of the churches of the South Bronx.

The Bronx Leadership Academy is a brand-new building on Webster Avenue, in the midst of a very poor neighborhood. Students in uniform escort the seven hundred-plus guests to the auditorium. The young woman who escorted me is a junior who will go to law school when she graduates. The public liturgy was dramatic. Public officials and private friends were thanked. Congregations came forward, one after another, to give their pledges of money for the school. Three Lutheran congregations and their leaders were at the heart of the dedication. One, New Hope, is a mission congregation, yet has several of its children in the school and several of its parents are key leaders. Pastor Heidi Neumark of Transfiguration summarized the history of the school in ten minutes— in Spanish and English!— wrapping the story of its genesis around the story of Daniel in the lion's den. There was anger at the meeting, as fifty leaders pledged to register one hundred voters each to unseat the corrupt school board at the next election. St. John's Church's leaders were at the forefront of those making pledges.

The dedication of the leadership academy was framed by prayer, by songs of faith, by biblical stories. It was powerful public liturgy as the congregations of this hard-pressed community put legs on their prayers and flesh and bone to their spirituality. At the center is Christ, shaping a sign of the Kingdom in the Bronx.

"Faith is not a thing which one 'loses,' we merely cease to shape our lives by it."

(*Lutheran Forum*, Advent, 1996)

Chapter 6
From Pentecost to Politics: How One Parish Tackled the Pornography Problem

As I stood in front of Judge Bruce Wright in Manhattan District Court twenty years ago, I was probably as nervous as I had ever been in my life. "Turn 'em loose Bruce" was a judge with a reputation for outspoken feistiness and libertarian leanings. Standing next to me were the high-priced Madison Avenue lawyers representing the management of the "Adult Fair Theater." For the first time the insulting hulk in the midst of our community—a place featuring "live acts," free booze (liberally dispensed to minors), a center of drug traffic and staging area for muggings and assaults, with cubicles for a brothel and a "cruising area"—had taken on flesh and blood. After almost two years of continuous research and pressure we were having our first up-front and personal confrontation with anyone connected with the theater. I was not alone in the courtroom. Behind me, filling the room to overflowing, were 50 fellow members of the Queens Citizens' Organization—a coalition of 26 Protestant and Roman Catholic churches. My fellow members were Blacks, Hispanics, Irish Catholics, German Lutherans. Their presence gave me courage.

The outward issue before Judge Wright was a motion by the attorneys of the Fair Theater to dismiss summonses for fire violations due to "selective enforcement" (harassment) by city officials. We were given permission to file a "friend of the court" statement, giving testimony to the effects of this theater on the community, and encouraging the city to do whatever it could within the limits of the law to deter "business as usual" operation of the theater. The real issue went much deeper. It had to do with a war over values being fought in our community and communities all over the nation. It had to do with the sustaining of human community and a willingness to be the subjects of our own history. It was an issue of power, control, and the beliefs of our people.

The New "Lower East Side"

In the 1970s I lived in and pastored a parish in Jackson Heights, in the New York City borough of Queens. Nestled in the northwest section of the borough between the East River, Shea Stadium and LaGuardia Airport, Jackson Heights is also the approximate home of the mythical Archie Bunker. Only Archie was getting a lot of new neighbors. Our part of Queens had replaced the lower east side of Manhattan as the true melting pot of New York City. Archie had been joined in our neighborhood by an unprecedented flow of immigrants: Blacks from urban America and the Caribbean, Hispanics from Central and South America, Asians, Greeks, Italians, and Eastern Europeans. Archie was joined at the altar rail of Atonement Lutheran Church by fellow worshippers from 29 different ethnic groups. He rubbed elbows with Jamaicans, Puerto Ricans, Colombians, Koreans, Romanians, East Indians; with welfare mothers and German widows. In many ways, these changes made Northwest Queens a place of diverse excitement and vitality. The life of our Lutheran churches and the school we sponsored together in this area was energized by our new neighbors. But the changes had not brought only good things to the community.

The other side of the vitality brought by newcomers was the cycle of exploitation and deterioration that accompanies rapid and unaccountable change in our large cities. This devastating cycle tore at the fabric of our homes, our streets, our values, and our faith itself. The change was reflected in blockbusting, redlining, misuse of buildings, deterioration of housing stock. As banks and local institutions made long-range investment decisions, some areas of Jackson Heights and Northwest Queens began to take on the tawdry look of a community starved for financial credit. One week, five moving vans showed up on my block. The cycle of exploitative change produces fear and sometimes racism. We fear our new neighbors, rather than those who exploit us both.

A crowd of porno shops and theaters had moved in among our homes in the wake of this rapid change, which led people to call our area the "Times Square of Queens." People openly sold dope to our kids, charged us debilitating insurance rates, and sneered at those values we hold dear but felt powerless to defend. Politicians pitted us against one another, played one area off against the other. The cycle produced a feeling of isolation. It made some of us dream about moving away from the area. Deterioration, fear, unaccountable change, exploitation, and racism lead to frustration. And frustration leads to apathy. And too often that apathy is reflected in the listless singing of hymns and payment of lip service to values that seem difficult to articulate or defend. One such value is the dignity of the human person that is undermined by pornography. It is important that we see pornography not only as an isolated moral issue. Pornography embodies values alien to the human communities caught up in the cycle of rapid social and economic change. The commercial exploitation of human sexuality is ultimately a community issue.

More Than Dirty Pictures

On February 27, 1978, the Queens Citizens' Organization turned out 2000 people to a public accountability session with New York City's mayor, Edward I. Koch. Each of the parishes represented by the QCO brokered local issues through this large public meeting. One of Atonement's salient concerns was the proliferation of sex theaters and cabarets in Jackson Heights, which also contributed to a growing drug (especially cocaine) and crime problem. The commercial sex establishments were stark symbols of how little control the residents had over the forces acting on their community. Further, the net effect of these places operating with impunity in the midst of the community was debilitating. Our research showed a pattern of declining or closing businesses and resident flight. The theaters and cabarets contributed to a sense of topophobia. Along with abandoned, burned-out and deteriorating buildings, they added to a landscape that accurately reflected people's inner sense of dislocation and loss of a sense of place.

Our research also revealed that the owners, operators, managers, and patrons of the sex theaters lived outside the community for the most part. An insight began to dawn on our people. Too often we see crime, building deterioration, real estate or banking credit decisions, and the operation of "adult entertainment" facilities as the inevitable *results* of rapid neighborhood change. Yet many neighborhoods undergo transitions and stabilize quickly. That has been the ongoing history of New York and of many other metropolitan areas. We need to see such things as pornographic theaters, growing public drug trade, redlining, and real estate scare tactics not only as the effects of change. They also cause it and spur it. The real obscenity in Jackson Heights was that a neighborhood was being pimped for profit.

The Fair Theater, standing in the midst of a residential community—literally in the shadow of the cross on a Black Pentecostal storefront church next door, and three blocks from Atonement—came to symbolize our frustration. The Fair was indeed a wretched place. Two business near it had folded. Young people of our parish were attacked by the theater's employees and patrons. Children were given pornographic literature. There was a steady sexual harassment of women and girls in the neighborhood; direct threats to one young woman of our congregation; men exposing themselves publicly. For a long time neighbors and members of Atonement had approached our church asking us to please "do something about it." We decided to try.

In the past petitions had been signed, the place picketed and several desultory attempts made by folks running for office to mobilize the anger of the people for their own advantage in election campaigns. The theater's presence fed its neighbors' growing apathy and feelings of helplessness. The Fair was symptomatic of many things in our town that seemed impervious to community pressure. People were walking around with a lot of unfocused anger. Because the causes of the spreading blight seemed so amorphous, people began to accept the situation with a fatalism—"I guess this is just the way things are and nothing can be done about them"—which approximated the torpor of the powerless peasants described by Paolo Freire in *Pedagogy of the Oppressed*. It is important to see pornography, its insulation by money, its objectification of human beings, and its embodiment in neighborhoods, as landmarks in what Freire describes as the "culture of silence," the worldview of the resigned.

THE FAILURE OF INSTITUTIONS

People have traditionally looked to the institutions of church, government, and family for support of their individual lives and ordered life in community. There is a growing sense among many people that their institutions are failing them. As the members of Atonement, with the Queens Citizens' Organization, engaged in a two-year fight against the Fair Theater, we naturally looked for allies. We found, too often, that indeed the institutions of government were unwilling to deal with or even regulate the manifestations of pornography and drug abuse in our communities. (In fact, our frustration with continuing drug sales on the corner of a local school prompted one of our members to make a banner for a meeting at the precinct which said, "If a ten-year-old can find the pusher why can't the cops?") Too many times we found the churches unable or unwilling to help their people struggle in the public arena. I detected a fear among some pastors that they would be perceived as inelegant or reactionary if they were identified with the effort to close the theater. This is a fear too often written large in the bureaucracies and judicatories of our churches, who confuse public relations with hopeful engagement in the public arena for the positive shaping of our communities.

I am proud of the people of Jackson Heights. In two years they learned more about the way our city works than in a hundred years of civics classes. They learned more about their values and beliefs than in a month of Sunday School classes. They discovered who owned and operated the theater. They met with the landlord. They participated in two meetings with the mayor, meetings with the lieutenant governor (Mario Cuomo), the district attorney, the captain of the morals squad, consumer affairs people, the state liquor authority, local politicians, the borough fire commander, the leaders of the Hellenic-American Neighborhood Action Coalition (the operators of the theater were Greek immigrants) and civic judges. They persuaded—or forced—the institutions of civic and neighborhood government to do all within their power to close the theater: indictments, fines, summonses, inspections, undercover investigations, arrests. We discovered for ourselves the fact that pornography is big business, bankrolled by organized crime, and almost impervious to community pressure. We uncovered payoffs, bribery, and the fact that this theater received a large easement in assessed valuation, saving the owners thousands of dollars in taxes.

Our efforts received sympathetic and extensive press coverage. All the pressure finally led us into the offices of the theater's lawyers. We offered them a deal. We would sell blocks of tickets in our churches for family entertainment if they would change their format. We guaranteed them $50,000 in advance sales. Meanwhile it was "business as usual" at the Fair and other places in the "Times Square of Queens."

Getting At Our Values

I have tried to show that pornography has effects on a community far beyond intellectual debates about censorship or fears about the "Moral Majority." The Bible suggests a healthy and joyful attitude concerning sex. But the Bible also speaks about sex in the context not only of individual relationships but also of family and community. The sixth commandment is not given only for the moral protection of the individual, but for the protection of the family and the extended community as well. It is an expression of God's covenant love toward creation. Just as sexual irresponsibility can cripple a family or shatter a community of faith, so also its institutionalization in the midst of our communities can tear away their very fabric of dignity. Pornography was not a victimless crime in Jackson Heights.

Pornography is an incarnation in our midst of the prevailing values of the culture. It represents easygoing acquiescence to "doing your own thing," whatever the cost. It represents a pursuit of pleasure that disguises a struggle for power and psychic survival. It represents—in a culture in which our collective myths are collapsing—getting the better of someone else as the only way to survive. It is a visual aid in the war of all against all. The violent, sexualized language of the ghetto came out of survival conditions and has become coin of the realm in the rest of society. What the Fair Theater finally says to our community, in its subtle but relentless echoing of our collective psyche, is "Every mother for himself!" Those of us who gather together around Word and Sacraments believe, teach, and confess other values: not the nihilism of mutual exploitation but the Reign of God.

Another theological issue that community organizing raises for the Church is what might be called the "ethics of inaction." If our use of power in the public arena must come under close moral and theological scrutiny, then our inaction must also be judged. In our churches and families we teach that our bodies are the temple of the Lord, that it is sinful to use the bodies of others or exploit them. We attempt to teach our children to live in the world, to be an agent of its transformation if possible, to find God in it. These are values basic to our understanding of what it means to live a hopeful, Christian, human life. But what happens when we see things introduced into our communities over which we have no say? A cluster of pornographic bars and theaters operated with impunity all around us. Pushers openly sold drugs to our children right in front of the local public school and in the park around the corner. Further, the cocaine traffic in Jackson Heights and its attendant robberies and murders made our neighborhood into "Coke City, USA" on network news and in *Time* magazine.

These things were direct embodiments in our community of individuals and interest groups that openly spit on our values. What does it say to our children if we do nothing about these crimes and offenses? What does our inaction say about our values and beliefs? That they are only for rhetorical practice in the pulpit? That we don't really believe them? That they cannot take solid shape and form in any way in the community? What does that do to our understanding and public hopefulness about the incoming Kingdom of God? In our inaction, do our children begin their tutelage in powerlessness and resignation?

ONE ISSUE AMONG MANY

I believe that the QCO's method of using community organizing to get at the issue of pornography and other problems in our neighborhood is a good one for churches elsewhere to consider. The Queens Citizens' Organization (still going strong twenty years later) is multiracial, ecumenical, cutting across class, and working on many different local and city-wide issues. Thus, Atonement's involvement in the pornography problem in Jackson Heights was only one facet of our ongoing public witness in the community. That track record kept this issue in perspective, as one of a host of public questions that affect our lives. It kept our concern from degenerating into a one-issue movement that becomes a panacea for the "ills" of society.

Our organization was built on a series of victories won in other areas: drug arrests at a local park; a borough-wide anti-arson campaign that gained national attention and lowered the arson rate; repaved streets; new jobs; and many others. It was built in the seeking of allies, in the *quid pro quo* relationships that cracked our isolation and enlarged our solidarity with others. Blacks from Jamaica were in Judge Wright's courtroom with us because Hispanics, Asians, and whites from Jackson Heights were in Jamaica helping register voters and fighting for York College. We developed leaders, insights into the ebb and flow of power in our city, and widened the context of the living of a Christian life. In the process, this activity was also evangelical. We became known as a church that could get things done in the community. Many people were happy to join a church willing to live its values.

Perhaps the reality of pornography among us has made us aware of one of our dearest Christian values. Humans are, by creation, political people. That is, we are community builders who are subjects rather than objects of history. One of the fundamental facts of creation is that we do not live in a herd, but in community with mutual responsibility to one another. We need to see the political implications of our prayers, liturgies and sacraments, and we need to see our witness in the public arena as a way to live sacramentally, as signs of "shalom" in a culture of death.

One more thing needs to be said. Taking active responsibility for the shape of our communities can be one way of nurturing our children and the values we teach them. In an age in which celebrity based on image has replaced real heroism based on actual accomplishments, can parents and elders be heroes and heroines for the next generation? Moreover, living responsibly in community can be joyful. That, finally, is what our congregation was saying in its confrontation with this issue.

The faith and strength of our people is nurtured at the altar. We live in the time of Pentecost; the Spirit of God has been let loose in the world. Our future is not in the hands of the mayor, the governor or the President. Nor is it at the mercy of an economic cycle that debases our cities, our communities, ourselves. Our future is in the hands of God. Tomorrow belongs to the One who loves each of us, dearly and completely. It is in that genuine love and compassion of God that we confront the illusions of pseudo-love and self-loathing in pornography, our communities, and in ourselves.

(*Lutheran Forum*, Pentecost, 1981)

PART TWO
"DO YOU INTEND TO CONTINUE IN THE COVENANT
GOD MADE WITH YOU IN HOLY BAPTISM....?"

CHAPTER 7
LIFE BY DROWNING: THE BAPTIZED CHRISTIAN IN THE WORLD

> If, then, the holy sacrament of baptism is a thing so great, so gracious and full of comfort, we should pay earnest heed to thank God for it ceaselessly, joyfully, and from the heart, and to give Him praise and honor. ("Treatise on Baptism," *Works of Martin Luther*, American Edition, Vol. 36, p. 70).

> This message should have been impressed upon the people untiringly, and this promise should have been dinned into their ears without ceasing. Their baptism should have been called to their minds again and again, and their faith constantly awakened and nourished. ("The Babylonian Captivity of the Church," *Works of Martin Luther*, American Edition, Vol. 39, p. 59).

OF DEATH, SMALLMOUTH BASS, HELEN OF TROY, AND A GRANDFATHER'S LOVE

The task of Christian ministry is to represent Christ and the church in the world. The true vocation of God's people is Baptism: to invite to Baptism, to pray for the baptized and the unbaptized, to recall to Baptism, to bring for Baptism, to witness Baptism, to live the implications of Baptism, to struggle for justice in the world as a sign of Baptism.

It was my mother who, before my first date reminded me, "Stephen, remember your Baptism." (I usually did). The Sunday School teacher who made Jesus stories come alive, the seminary professor who taught me to love more deeply the same stories, the usher who greeted me ... there has been a great cloud of baptismal witnesses in my life. But of all the ministers of Baptism in my life, Grandpa Bartling was one of the most vivid. He was a pastor and a theologian. He taught New Testament in college and seminary (Concordia, St. Louis) for most of his years as a pastor. He was passionate about three things above all: the Greek New Testament, fishing, and Baptism. It was Grandpa Bartling who would send me letters written in the Greek alphabet and then a beginning Greek grammar when, as a boy of nine or ten I expressed an interest in the ministry. As we fished together in the sweet lakes of northern Wisconsin, he would recite parts of the *Iliad* and the *Odyssey* and talk to me about my Baptism. His profound understanding of the Scriptures and theology combined with simple, childlike faith mesmerized me, caught me in the mysteries of my baptismal faith.

Years later, on the night of Grandpa's wake, I gazed at his features etched in death within the casket. Someone had put in his hands his Nestle's edition of the Greek New Testament. It was tattered, worn, familiar. Family and friends gathered from all over the country. An uncle read from Scripture and prayed with us. In that moment with family around the casket in the St. Louis night, I have never been clearer about my identity. The baptismal faith we shared bound us together. My tears were for Grandpa, because no one would ever again take me fishing and fill my world as vividly with Hector or Helen of Troy, bass and perch, Saul of Tarsus or Jesus of Nazareth. But my tears were also tears of recognition for the gift of this very human family; for the biblical drama which had shaped our lives; for the love of Jesus Christ made flesh in Grandpa, friend, loved one. God was not far off but as familiar as the runny noses, glistening eyes, and mute embraces of these very ordinary people of faith trying to make sense of the place where life and death transform one another. To know that Grandpa is baptized, and what that means, gave incredible comfort and hope.

At the funeral liturgy the following day we lost ourselves in the music and Scriptures of joy and resurrection. At a time when there are no words, the Church had words to say and sing. I remember singing "For All the Saints" with such intensity that I must have thought I could sing my grandfather into heaven. One of the speakers recalled some of Grandpa's words about Baptism. Among them was this sentence, heard first by me with a fishing pole in my hand: "In your Baptism the only death you need fear is behind you."

Grandpa's Baptism was finally complete.

> The sacrament, or sign, of baptism is quickly over, as we plainly see. But the thing it signifies, the spiritual baptism, the drowning of sin, lasts so long as we live, and is completed only in death...therefore this life is nothing else than a spiritual baptism which does not cease till death...("Treatise on Baptism," *Works of Martin Luther*, Vol. 1, p. 58).

THE ICON OF THE INVISIBLE GOD

> He is the image of the invisible God.... For in him all the fullness of God was pleased to dwell, and through him God was pleased to reconcile to

himself all things, whether on earth or in heaven, by making peace through the blood of his cross. (Colossians 1:15-19)

Grandpa was right. Baptism is about death: the death of the crucified Christ, the death of the old Adam, our own death, a great drowning. We learned about this death early in the nurture of our baptismal faith as Lutherans, in the cadences of Blessed Martin Luther's catechism.

> What does such baptizing with water signify? It signifies that the old Adam in us, together with all sins and evil lusts, should be drowned by daily sorrow and repentance, and be put to death; and that a new person should come forth daily and rise up, cleansed and righteous, to live forever in God's presence. Where is this written? In Romans 6:4, St. Paul wrote, "We were buried therefore with Christ through baptism into death; so that as Christ was raised from the dead by the glory of the Father, we too might walk in newness of life." (*Small Catechism*).

Death. Drowning. Crucifixion. We prefer a cover-up, a spiritual Watergate. The carnal, earthy particularity of Jesus' dying offends us. So we spiritualize the earthy and, as today's counterfeit theologians call it, we "reimage" God in our own likeness. Which renders baptism harmless.

As St. Paul has put it, we exchange the truth of the cross of Jesus for a lie. Drive through the South Bronx and you will see what I mean about a cover-up of reality. Decals of windows with potted plants and curtains cover up shards of broken glass in the abandoned buildings and shattered windows looming on the horizon of that place of the poor. A bogus image of well-being and domesticity camouflages the reality of human misery and suffering. "Good for the image we need to attract business to the city," says the government that shelled out hundreds of thousands of dollars in the mid-1970s for that insulting cover-up, an insult still visible today.

But you cannot mask the Christ of scripture, or sweep the quotidian, intimate particularity of Jesus under the rug, or cover it with a decal of piety or ideology. Scripture, in the letter to the Colossians, claims about Jesus that "He is the image of the invisible God...in him all the fullness of God was pleased to dwell..."

The true meaning for image in Greek, *eikon*, is a lot different from the meaning we usually give it. We tend to think like the followers of Plato among the Colossians, that an image of something is an abstraction, an evocation of the real, a dead thing, a shadow. We must get beyond the image to the "real" or "ideal." So, according to this thinking, Christ is just a way of talking about God, or justice, or peace, or whatever else those who manipulate the image want to emphasize. So if Christ is no more than an image, we can strip that image of its specificity: the humanity of Christ, or the divinity, or his maleness, or his Jewish mother, or his persistent companionship with the "least of these," or his cross, or his death. He's just an image of a great ideal. God in our own image.

And the trivialization of Baptism follows from this misunderstanding of Christ's imaging of God. I think that the laziness so many parishes slip into, the stilted habits and survival mentality, the casualness about frequency of the Eucharist, prayer, the study of the Word, the lack of excitement about the Jesus story, the fear and paralysis which stunts the Church's ability to act in the public arena on the great issues of the world around us, the Church's shyness about evangelism, is somehow related to avoiding the implications of Baptism, of avoiding the *eikon Christi* and the death implicit in it. Baptism becomes instead something cute and trivial, something for the family picture album, a "christening" that measures out God's grace in niggardly fashion in drops of water, done on the side in the afternoon after the faithful have gone home from Mass. The way we cheapen Baptism is a mirror image of the culture in an age of ironic detachment devoid of mystery. Nobody gets drowned any more.

But this is what the Greek term *eikon* means. The icon is filled with the presence of what it represents. When we view the icon we are confronted with the reality that permeates it. In the *eikon Christi* we are confronted with the reality of the invisible, dying, and rising God. In the image, the icon of Christ, the fullness of God was pleased to dwell. Jesus of Nazareth is not an analogy of God, or a copy, or merely "like God." Nor is he a clone of the Father, produced by a divine version of genetic manipulation. The *eikon Christi* that confronts us is the Lord of creation, participant in our created world and its history, reconciler of all creation by death and by the blood of his cross. We do not cover over or explain away that image. We worship the *eikon Christi* as our very salvation. And it is into Christ's death and resurrection that we baptize.

Nothing could be more misleading than to associate the baptizing of children with what we do in any launching or naming ceremony. In Baptism, we do not receive our given names, the names that identify us among humans. In Baptism we are "Christed," "christened." In our Baptism in the Name of the Father, Son and Holy Spirit, we receive the *eikon Christi*, and in such reception we become an icon of Christ. And that is the mystery of a Christian's vocation and ministry in the world.

We avoid the reality of Baptism because deep down we know what it means. We see Jesus immersed in the waters of the Jordan. His will is no longer his own. It belongs to the One who sent him. From the waters of baptism we see him hungry in the wilderness and assailed by Satan. His journey of faith from the devastating waters of Baptism led him inexorably to Jerusalem, to the cross, to his death. We avoid the true meaning of the act of Baptism, as we avoid the *eikon Christi* because drowning scares us. We are afraid to die, because we are afraid to really live. We know that Luther is right— that this drowning is a daily one, and that it is in the waters of life that we must daily live our Baptism. The *eikon Christi* is real, the fullness of God. The world is real. Death is real. Baptism brings them all together in the embrace of a gracious triune God.

LIVING AS ICONS OF CHRIST

> For Baptism is administered for the very purpose of taking away sin that a person may now become pious and increase in good works...we may now lay aside these vices, pray a Lord's Prayer instead, and henceforth earnestly strive to be obedient, patient, kind... (*What Luther Says*, p. 57).

The cemeteries of this world are appropriate resting places for countless Christians who spend their live waiting for clues that never came and summonses that were never delivered. Why should rank-and-file Christians, in the last years of the twentieth century, beg a theologian or a bishop to furnish them with their Christian responsibility? God encounters each person individually to seek a personal response. Our world is a gift and task from God. The initiative is ours. (Ed Marciniak, from *Initiatives*, a newsletter of the [Roman Catholic] National Center for the Laity).

Two things become ours in Baptism. We receive a name, an *identity*. To be baptized into the name of God, to receive the *eikon Christi*, is to be grasped by the being of God, the purpose of God. Your name, your story, your identity, your reality and destiny, is washed and drowned in the story of the death and resurrection of Christ, the fullness of God. You are initiated into that story which belongs to the messianic community, the Church. You become somebody! You belong to Christ, to Christ's body, the Church, the people of God's new future.

In our baptismal identity we each receive a *mission*. The voice of God at the Jordan echoes around our own baptismal font. "This is my beloved son, daughter...." The voice is a call to mission. If we are clear about Baptism, then we could clear out much of the confusion concerning ministry in our Lutheran communion. The mission of the Church and of each baptized member is to represent the dying and rising Christ, to be an *eikon Christi* or as Luther put it, "little Christs"— in the world. It is a matter of being as much as doing.

The Church does not exist primarily to make its surrounding neighborhood a little better, to provide an array of services to its neighbors. Where this social improvement attitude exists, Baptism itself as well as Christian marriage and burial and the Eucharist all become services which people contract to have provided for them. On the contrary, the Church exists to incarnate in the midst of the world communities of Jesus who, through Word and Sacraments and ministry—which will, God willing, make neighborhoods better—confront the world with the *eikon Christi* so that all may be reconciled to God by the blood of the cross.

Baptism is the ground of both ordained ministry and the ministry of all the people of God. By ordination, which repeats the baptismal actions of the laying-on of hands and invocation of the Holy Spirit, the ministry represents Christ to the Church. As *eikon Christi* the ordained minister presides at the Eucharist, baptizes, proclaims the Gospel, publicly absolves sin, and oversees communities of Jesus. In such communities the people of God reaffirm their identity and mission through encounters with the dying and rising Christ in the Word and Sacraments. Hearing a fellow baptized member exhort them to "go in peace, serve the Lord," they go out into the world, continuing the liturgy, representing Christ and the Church to and in the world.

As the baptized people of God represent Christ in the world, they do it through what Luther calls their *Amts* or routines of daily life: as mother, aunt, teacher, plumber, barber, citizen, neighbor, father, husband, fisherman-theologian-grandfather. This does not mean that we necessarily call everything we do in the world "ministry." It *does* mean that in all we do we are bearers of the *eikon Christi*; we are representatives of Christ and the Church.

As icons of Christ in the world we are people of prayer. Martin Luther dedicated *A Simple Way to Pray* to Peter Beskendorf, his barber. He encouraged Barber Peter to reflect on the Lord's Prayer, the Psalms, the Ten Commandments, parts of the Catechism, or other parts of Scripture. Centuries ahead of his time, Luther encouraged his barber to reflect on the meaning of everyday life and the world situation in the light of such reading, meditation and prayer. Today liberation theologians call this approach "praxis." Luther encouraged an openness to the leading of the Holy Spirit so that formal prayer should be postponed if the Spirit leads us to situations awaiting our presence in the world. As a continuation of one's private prayer Luther concludes, "Then go about your work." His is an earthy, baptismal spirituality. Ministry is not so much a matter of what we happen to be doing at the moment as it is who we are—and Whose we are—as we do it.

Such ministry in the world obviously will include doing. The hungry will be fed, the lonely will be visited, justice will be sought for and with the poor, the sick will be healed and comforted, the homeless will be housed, the spiritually hungry will be sought out and fed. But in all of it the touchstone will be Baptism and the ministry of the Church. We are not working out our salvation, adding to our Baptism, or representing ourselves. We are living out the implications of our baptismal call to ministry. We are a part of what the Church is doing in the world to confront it with the presence of Jesus so that all might be reconciled to God. For too long we have separated the social ministries of our Church from their genesis in and relationships to communities of the baptized gathered around Word and Sacraments. We become technicians of the pain of life, taking our place alongside all the other "experts" of this world, rather than living as icons of Christ.

All of our ministry of prayer, baptismal identity, and service will seek to invite the dying world to the Church, to Baptism or its remembrance, to the family meal. Churches I have served have had wonderful ministries, especially on the part of those who are always bringing people to the church, inviting, living a life of baptismal and Eucharistic hospitality.

A friend of mine, a Carmelite priest in my neighborhood, told me one day of his ordination. He told of expecting this special day to be one filled with transcendence, of wonderful, holy evidence of the power of the Holy Spirit. He expected a "burning bush," a divine "zapping". Now there is one part of the Roman ordination rite in which the ordinands lie prostrate on the floor in a position of symbolic service and obedience. My Carmelite friend recalled lying there thinking that this would surely be the moment in which the ecstasy of the Spirit would fill him. Instead three things went through his mind as he lay on the cold stone. First, he had worn a pair of cut-off shorts under his vestments, and he was worried that his legs were showing. Second, he was worried that one of the photographers roving about the sanctuary would step on him. Finally, he was worried that he would forget when to get up, afraid that the bishop would hover over him impatiently while he lay there in ignorance of the next part of the ritual.

In place of intimations of divinity and immortality, this apprentice priest experienced instead the all-too-human emotions of vanity, vulnerability, and insecurity. Yet we have a parable here about the ministry to which God calls all the baptized. Ever since the Word became flesh, *eikon Christi*, it is in the very vanity, vulnerability, and insecurity of human life that ministry takes place, that Christ is present in the baptized children of God.

The liturgy of the "Affirmation of the Vocation of Christians in the World" ought to be familiar and used often in our parishes. At one point a representative of the laity says the following: "Through Holy Baptism our heavenly Father set us free from sin and made us members of the priesthood we all share in Christ Jesus. Through Word and Sacrament we have been nurtured in faith that we may proclaim the praise of God and bear his creative and redeeming Word to all the world."

That is the life by drowning to which we are called in our Baptism.

THE FLICKERING CANDLE

> When our last hour comes, we intend to clothe ourselves in the vestment of baptismal grace and hear the absolution of faith and pass away. (*What Luther Says*, p. 61).

The call came in the night, "Come quickly, please hurry." I went to Cumberland Hospital in Brooklyn, where a newborn babe fought for life, little chest heaving in the incubator. After an embrace with the parents and a prayer, I donned surgical mask, gloves, in order to do what I was born to do. A nurse produced a basin filled with warm water and the miracle began — in the Name of the Father, Son and Holy Spirit. Figures in crisp white uniforms bowed their heads. In the corner an intern mumbled "En el nombre del Padre, y del Hijo, y del Espiritu Santo." The timeless, life-giving drowning commenced, water from a dropper three times on the tiny forehead, the sign of the cross lovingly traced on the wet forehead and heaving little chest. And God claimed a child. And we knew it. And we were still. Silence filled the room full of machines and charts and tubes. Silence filled in where medical science could only wait. Silence and the vision of water and the cross filled beating hearts, screaming dread, smoldering anger, heartbreak. And with the silence and the water and the Word came hope. And so we waited....

Two days later the child died, and yet still lives on in the bosom of God. And our hope does not go away, and all whose hearts are touched with hope and water and Word and the *eikon Christi* are God's gift to a hopeless world.

In the remembering of our Baptism all the other remembering of our lives takes shape and meaning. Each year, the mother and father of the child that I baptized that night light a candle on the anniversary of their child's Baptism. There are other children for them now. Life goes on. Precisely! That is the hope and the promise of this sacrament. In our Baptism the only death we need to fear is behind us. My friends light the candle for what might have been. They are human. But in the flickering light of the candle their longing is tinged with hope and yes, even joy. True, their arms never encircled the child, but the everlasting arms enfold their loved one. That is the life we gain by drowning.

Today we live in a age of parentless chaos. People drift and wander, seek and latch on to the latest fads in ideas as well as clothing. Our society teaches our children that success and meaning beckon in the next purchase, the next plateau of achievement, the next adjustment of our looks or surroundings. In the midst of the uneasiness fostered by contemporary myths of meaning, our extended family gazes into the light of a flickering candle, lit at the anniversary of each of our Baptisms. We speak the Creed. We use the language of the rite ("Anniversary of a Baptism" from the *Occasional Services*, LBW). In the light shed by the small flame the chaos of our age receives new form and definition. We are not tossed adrift in the swirling maelstrom of life. We are people of God!

(*Lutheran Forum*, Reformation, 1988)

Chapter 8
Children of a Greater God: Catechesis of the Confessional Heart

> So Philip ran up to the chariot, and heard the eunuch reading the prophet Isaiah. He asked, "Do you understand what you are reading?" He replied, "How can I, unless someone guides me?" And he invited Philip to get in and sit beside him. (Acts 8:30, 31)

Finding a Language for Grace

When Erik confessed his faith the full, yet silent church vibrated with his eloquence. The family of believers watched and strained to hear in the wonder of this pristine moment of explicit confession. His chubby fingers were surprisingly dexterous as he signed the words. His attempt to speak the words he was signing burst through the silence of his deafness. We heard this dear brother. This is what he said on the festival of Pentecost, on the day of his confirmation:

"For God so loved the world that he gave his only Son, that whoever believes in him should not die but have life forever."

He paused for a moment, fished a card from the pocket beneath his robe, glanced at it and replaced it. He continued in a combination of sign language and garbled verbal speech:

"What does this mean to me? It means that Jesus died for my sins. It means God loves me. It means when I die I will go to heaven."

He gave us a nervous smile and returned to his place in the line of confirmands in the chancel. As one of his classmates began her verse he looked at me, passed his hand over his head and rolled his eyes in a "Whew, what a relief!" signal and smiled again.

The ministry behind this wonderful moment bears mighty witness to the grace of a God who brings, in the words of the Eucharistic prayer, "Light from darkness, life from death, speech from silence."

We call the process of forming Erik's faith *catechesis*. The partnership between the home and the church, the sheer effort by all involved in Erik's catechesis is a parable of confessional witness in our neo-pagan age.

There was a time several years ago when it seemed that Erik would slip into a lifetime of silence. He had attended our Sunday School for awhile but became progressively sullen, morose, and then combative as his isolation from the social and pedagogical life around him deepened. His mother began to fight for her son, first against a local public school system that takes a cookie-cutter approach to children; then the county; then the state. She could teach our church body something about the true and primal meaning of the term "Advocate." She fought for her Erik and won on many fronts by her sheer persistence. Through her dogged effort Erik entered appropriate programs and began to learn. She learned sign language. He learned to read.

She was also an advocate for Erik's soul. She enrolled him in a Sunday School for the deaf in a local Episcopal church. She found materials that gave appropriate sign language for religious concepts and vocabulary. Erik's family also continued to worship in our hearing congregation because of their strong attachment to their Lutheran identity. Erik's older brother made his confirmation among us.

When it was time for Erik's catechesis his mother approached me, once more an advocate. We worked out a weekly home tutoring schedule. Each Wednesday Erik, his mother, and I sat around the dining-room table and worked together to entrust to Erik the substance of his baptismal faith. His mother interpreted. I learned some sign language. The first day I showed up Erik was very uncomfortable. We worked on that. We both love the New York Knicks. I told him I was Patrick Ewing. We got easy with one another. We worked hard together to find a language through which we could both communicate the chief parts of Luther's catechism. We had to match Luther's concepts to Erik's signs. Our catechesis was filled with analogy, story, wild gestures, his mother's manual continuo as she worked to translate our mutual efforts into Erik's language. I read our progress on Erik's face, tracing the looks of consternation until they reflected the brightness of recognition. When he grasped a concept he would read it back to us in sign and agitated verbalizing. Sin was translated as "bad things," or "bad relationship." I finally taught the Sixth Commandment as "Don't have sex unless you are married." (That's how I teach it to my kids also!) The Ninth and Tenth Commandments became "Be happy with what God has given you." You get the idea.

Erik's mother worked hard with him. By the time we were finished he had memorized and "recited" most of the Small Catechism. Erik's catechesis was a communal matter of greatest importance. His father would come home from work, join us at the table, and get a report of his son's progress. His brother would watch the dog and do his homework while we worked together. He and the dog greeted me at the door each Wednesday. On Erik's big day his extended family, Sunday School teachers, and neighbors were present at the Pentecost liturgy.

The catechesis of Erik, and of the other eight young people who made their confirmation that spring day, is a living example of the activity of what Stanley Hauerwas calls a "truthful community" or "community of character;" a community capable of hearing the story of God, willing to live faithfully by it. Catechesis is immersion in the narrative that shapes the life of the church. It is separate from the world, albeit for the world, with its own integrity. The story of Israel, the story of Jesus, and the story of the church became Erik's story.

What is instructive here is the passion of those involved. Our church needs to see itself in the role of Erik's mother, a relentless advocate for the faith formation of its people. I think of the pastor in Jersey City who walked the streets of his neighborhood before the opening of his confirmation classes to visit the homes of the children and their families. One child never showed up for liturgy and Sunday School. But he did not cut the child loose. He went to the housing project where the child lived. When he walked into the entrance he interrupted a dope deal going down. One of the men whirled, pistol in hand, ready to shoot. He saw the pastor's collar and blurted out, "Jesus Christ, Father, I almost killed you!" The pastor nodded, walked up the stairs, and completed the call. We need to believe once again that the upbuilding of the faith of the people is a task worthy of giving our lives.

Pious Pagans

The neo-pagans among us are a religious lot. Even if the self or the things of this world have taken the place of God, the search for the aura of religion and the longing for meaning are very much in evidence. Couples who have already planned self-indulgent wedding festivities still search for the pastor willing to add a dash of God to the proceedings. "We always wanted a church wedding, Father." A child's baptism has become a rite of passage for extended families who attend the party but not the liturgy. Folks go to the neighborhood church or the church of their youth to "get the kid done." "Spirituality" has become another addendum to the dreary litany of self-help projects, a matter of technique rather than immersion in the Word. We worship our pain, our ideologies, our identities, our anxious self-scrutiny.

There is much to be learned about the primal hunger for God expressed in a world where Jesus shows up in the spaghetti of a Pizza Hut billboard in Atlanta, the windshield of a car in Queens, the bark of a tree in New Haven, or the vision of a Madonna in Medjagorje. The hunger of Adam and Eve, which is still our own hunger, is a hunger for God. In the beginning God filled the hunger with all of creation. In the beginning, humans were created to be priests and priestesses, called to bless all creation by acknowledging the Creator, by partaking of creation as life from God. To bless, to name, to take responsibility in obedience to the Creator, to eat and drink and partake with reverence and thanksgiving—that was the eucharistic life of those made in God's image in the midst of Creation.

And this is the form of our pagan life: Eating and drinking and partaking are now ends in themselves and not sacramental means of life with God. The transparency of creation as a medium of communion with God has been lost. Creation is now a mirror reflecting back on us hungry humans ourselves and our needs. The things of this world are sought for their own sake. We are no longer priests and priestesses of the sacrament of life, but consumers of desacralized objects. Our eating and drinking and partaking do not give us life, do not fill us or satisfy us, except for a time. The worship of ourselves and the things of this fallen world will not keep us from death when we see only food but not its Creator. The paganism of our time treats religious things as it treats everything else—as something to reflect us and fill us. And so we worship.

Centered in the Word

It is through the Word that we are offered God's reconciliation. Catechesis is rooted in God's Word and leads the hungry sinner back to a gracious God through the atoning death and resurrection of Jesus. Consider a few of the many catechetical encounters in Scripture:
- The Shema in Deuteronomy and the injunction to teach it.
- Jesus and a woman at a well in Samaria.
- Jesus interpreting Scriptures to the disciples on the way to Emmaus and to the Eleven before his Ascension.
- Philip and the Ethiopian eunuch.
- The catechesis of the newly baptized Paul by Ananias.

One of the chief responsibilities of the ordered ministry is the work of catechesis. These are just a few of the many opportunities in our parish ministry. You have your own list.
- The obvious opportunity given by a church's Confirmation and First Communion ministries is supplemented by home visits and family meetings.
- When I worked with couples desiring marriage my preparation included a thorough study of the wedding liturgy, followed by a time of instruc-

tion on the basics of our faith as expressed in our confessional identity. The first meeting was usually over a cup of coffee after the Sunday liturgy.
- Families seeking baptism were also instructed in the Baptismal liturgy and the basics of our faith. When the baptized child reached two years of age I made a home visit during which I brought a book of Jesus stories for the child and engaged the family in conversation about the faith.
- Once a year I taught a course on our confessional identity.
- Sometimes the most effective catechesis takes place over lunch, in the home or the workplace. Here connections can be made between the faith and a person's situation. Catechesis happens over a period of time during the course of a pastoral relationship.
- Each year for five years I mentored a pastoral intern.
- In the evaluation sessions after every public action of our church-based community organization opportunities arose to reflect on our faith as we attempted to live it in the public arena.
- I am impressed by the renewal of the communal and prayerful process of the "rite of Christian initiation" and extended catechumenate lifted up by the recent ELCA study on the use of the Means of Grace.

Pastors and other leaders of the church must be relentless in their pursuit of the ongoing catechesis of the People of God, using every available opportunity to teach and image the faith we share so that people may be drawn closer to Jesus.

Some Lutheran Emphases in the Faith We Teach

1. *Lutherans are called.* Being a student, a friend, a worker, an adult member of a congregation are all vocations, or callings. The doctrine of the priesthood of all believers strengthens the fundamental dignity of the rhythms of our lives as our respective fields in which to praise God and love our neighbor. To help flesh out the specific vocation of church membership I stress five tangible things:
- Regular worship and reception of the sacrament.
- A regular money offering.
- Participation in a specific piece of the congregation's ministry (taking an elderly neighbor shopping; teaching Sunday School; sharing in the ministry of music, etc.)
- Some form of continued growth in the Word (home study, Bible class, etc.)
- Daily prayer for the ministry of the Church and those in need.

2. *Lutherans are ecumenical.* We share common ground with the whole body of Christ. Every community of believers is a microcosm of the whole.

3. *Lutherans are evangelical.* Our life together is grounded in grace. Catechesis is a part of God's gracious invitation to encircle each human with unconditional love and acceptance. Because of Christ, a person does not have to earn her existence as a member of the parish. Ministry includes credible invitations to deeper ties in the parish or to join in its life.

4. *Lutherans are apostolic.* We stand on the faith of the ages— "the democracy of the dead," in Barth's words. The Story of Israel, the Story of Jesus, and the Story of the Church are our stories. We teach them as we have received them.

5. *Lutheran identity is communal.* We see the Church as the community gathered around and by the Word and the Sacraments. Luther's emphasis on nurture in the family and home translates well into contemporary ministry. For many people—especially children—in our atomized society the only sense of family they may ever have is among us in our parishes and their programs. We will continually find ways to increase our people's growth in faith through appropriate ritual, and root their rites of passage in the liturgical life of the church.

6. *Lutherans are sacramental.* The things of this world convey the presence of Christ. Water, bread, wine, the poor, children, a teacher become signs of God's ubiquitous grace. Teaching the faith means being stewards of these mysteries of grace, and enabling baptismal and Eucharistic communities and insights to be born.

7. *Lutherans take education seriously.* Luther's catechetical pedagogy, rooted in Jesus' rabbinic question-and-answer style of teaching, is a foundation for our own efforts. We teach because we baptize.

8. *Lutherans are rooted in the proper distinction between Law and Gospel.* We are not naive about sin and its consequences. We teach and embody a theology of the Cross as opposed to a theology of glory. We are communities of forgiveness.

For Erik, and for each of us children of God, catechesis is not an event that took place once in our lives, but a continuing process of baptismal consciousness and growth, as the Holy Spirit kindles in us the presence of Jesus, leading us faithfully past all deified pretenders to our home in God's gracious love.

(*Lutheran Forum*, Reformation, 1991)

Chapter 9
A River Runs through It: Evangelism from the Font

"Baptism, proclamation, and Eucharist are at the heart of healthy evangelization." (Thesis Three, *The Grace-full Use of the Means of Grace.*)

"I asked, 'How many of you are dads?' and only three hands went up. That didn't sound right to me. So later on, I asked, 'How many of you guys have kids?' And almost every hand went up. These guys made a distinction. Fatherhood meant taking responsibility, providing security and affection, being there, which they'd never seen. Having a kid just meant they'd had sex with a girl, and she had a baby." (Charles Ballard, speaking to a roomful of teen-age boys at a Cleveland High School, quoted in the *New York Times.*)

"The child is father to the man." W. B. Yeats

In This Room

Three years ago I watched my oldest son walk into Newark Airport knowing I might not see him again for two years. He went to the Ukraine with the Peace Corps. Letting go was the hardest act of love for this father. We were together in this Ukraine (literally, "borderland"), father and son, in our baptismal journeys. I read so many Jesus stories with new eyes after he left. As I watched the strong back of the young man disappear from view I remembered the scrawny child he once was and thought of Jesus, about to take leave of his disciples before the Ascension. It was the disciples— it is Timothy— who are launched. Walking on water. Rattling around inside him were two births and two homes: his family in the birth of blood and water; his family in the water of Baptism. It gave me comfort.

The evening after I saw Timothy off I was standing in a room and I filled up with gratitude. The room was the undercroft of Atonement Lutheran Church in Jackson Heights, Queens, where I had been pastor and my family had lived from the altar and font and its community for almost ten years. We were meeting together— pastors and leaders from northwest Queens congregations— struggling like so many between survival and mission, seeking a strategy to strengthen these communities of Jesus. I think about the strengthening of his baptism that Timothy received in that congregation and of its power in forming the Jesus-shaped space in the young man now out in the world. What had been imparted to him seems like a sound mission strategy issuing forth from the waters of Baptism.

In this room he had learned Jesus songs, said his first public prayers, learned Jesus stories by heart, and participated in his first expressions of Christian community beyond the family. His attendance in this room of Sunday School, nursery school and kindergarten, had given him his first mentors in the teachers who shared in his growing baptismal faith.

In this room he had eaten kimchi with Koreans, curried goat with West Indians, had sung songs in Spanish, and played with children from India, Brazil and Romania. With them he learned the liturgy and sang "This Is The Feast" and other songs at worship with the school and Sunday school choir.

In this room he had watched the adults from his church and neighborhood plan for a meeting with the mayor and learned that his faith has implications in the public arena.

In this room he had shared food for homeless families, and from this room he ventured out with his father to deliver gifts to the homebound and food for the shelters.

In this room he had learned the Creed, the Lord's Prayer, the Ten Commandments, and prepared to receive his First Communion.

In this room I thought of the gifts of the Spirit which sank deep in the soul of my son, at that point somewhere in the Ukraine. His two families were with him, and in that presence Jesus was surely abiding with one christened Timothy Paul.

ANOTHER ROOM

On the eve of Father's Day, the second Sunday of Pentecost, I am in another room, leading the liturgy for about thirty homeless men at the Franklin Avenue shelter in the south Bronx. Assisting me is a team of deacons from a nearby parish. In this room we share in the ancient Eucharistic liturgy of the Church, in the key of gospel and soul. When the liturgy was ended I asked how many of the men were fathers. Two-thirds of them raised their hands. I asked them to rise. I had a blessing for them. We then prayed for their children and their mothers. The men added their own petitions, several in eloquent cadence for minutes at a time. The longing, sorrow, and heartache were palpable. Two left the room. Several wept. I reminded all of us of the power of Baptism, of the love of Jesus from which nothing can separate us, of the dignity of the unconditional grace of our heavenly Father.

The deacons and I spent a lot of time after that liturgy in one-on-one conversations. The men also encouraged one another. The message of the Gospel was crowding in on all of us. This is evangelism, I thought in that room: relevant baptismal witness and encouragement. There are not a lot of facile happy endings in that place. The knots of pushers wait just across the street from the shelter. The racism and economic deprivation of the neighborhoods where these men live will continue to bear down hard on them. But relentlessly, on each Lord's Day and in midweek Bible studies, the presence of Jesus will continue to create communities of Biblical virtue through the evangelical witness of the Church. A room in a church basement, a room in a shelter, a room somewhere in the Ukraine: a river runs through it.

WATERY STRATEGIES

The evangelism strategy of the ELCA, ELCIC, LC-MS, the Holy Spirit, is the Church. As I read the responses to the symposium on "The Graceful Use of the Means of Grace," I was struck by two major themes. Some seem to think that God's Word drops out of thin air. No. It is made incarnate in the life of the Word and Sacrament communities that are the Church. Others seem to think that the Church and its liturgy need to be protected from too much passion in missionary fervor. Certainly if that passion for mission causes some to trash the Church's liturgy and its traditions, then that misdirected passion needs to be resisted. But a Church that lives only for the cultic life of the ninety-nine is unfaithful to the passion of the Good Shepherd who left the ninety-nine and untiringly pursued the one who was lost. But the Church, with its cultic life, is the only evangelism strategy given to us by God.

As Lent approached several years ago the leaders of the parish that I served in New Jersey were wondering where so many of the recently baptized and their families had gone. At that time we were baptizing about twenty people a year. We decided to use Lent as a season for reconnecting with the baptized. A team from the parish visited the homes of every person and family that had been baptized in the past ten years. They invited them to a baptismal reunion. Bring the baptized, they said, bring pictures of the baptism, family pictures of their growth. Just come. Many did. We went through the baptismal liturgy, especially the promises. We talked about worshiping with children in church. We began a conversation on the nurture of children that grew into a parents' support group, to which we invited the parish school, the Sunday School, and the community. The baptismal reunion became a port of entry into the life of our parish. Every one who did not come to the reunion received another personal visit and we distributed the materials we had shared. The reunion became an annual event. When we began to see Baptism not just as an event that happens "'cause Granny wants us to get the kid done," but as a lifelong process, we began to understand the evangelical power of this watery witness. A river runs through it.

COVENANTAL STRATEGY

We found that when we began thinking about baptism as a lifelong process rather than a one-time event, we also began to see and act on Baptism's evangelical power. With annual baptismal reunions we stayed in touch with the gracious invitation embodied in the covenant for the renewal of baptismal vows in the *Lutheran Book of Worship*. In the Metropolitan New York Synod we often use this covenant as we plan congregational and area mission strategies.

"You have made public profession of your faith...."

The mission of the Church is public. Such activities as the creation of parish nursery schools, latchkey programs, church-based community organizing, and other programs that institutionalize exposure of the life of the parish to the life of the community are all part of the corporate baptismal witness of the Church.

"Do you intend to continue in the covenant God made with you in Holy Baptism?"

The key word here is *continue*. We must stop performing pastoral acts as events and begin to see them as processes of the Holy Spirit's activity. Marriages, funerals, baptisms, confirmations are all abiding opportunities to stay in touch with people in the Spirit's power. The Occasional Services are untapped resources for enclosing life's passages within the evangelical arms of God.

"To live among God's faithful people..."

The biblical term for what is intended in this part of the covenant is *koinonia*. It means to participate in, to belong to one another and to Jesus. It is the *koinonia* of the cup and the loaf incarnate in human community where we bear one another's burdens. It is an evangelism strategy in the Bronx as Spanish-speaking leaders begin support groups and communities centering in prayer and Bible study in the midst of the neighborhoods of unchurched people.

"To hear his word and share in his supper...."

The heartbeat of the evangelical parish will always be the Book, the Bath and the Meal. Jesus invites in some mission strategies building by building as children in the city are invited to Sunday School. In a former parish that I served, homeless men who were members of the parish would take the palms from the Sunday of the Passion liturgy and distribute them, along with my name and phone number and that of our congregation, to residents of the welfare motels nearby, inviting them to church.

"To proclaim the good news of God in Christ through word and deed...."

The mission statement of Trinity, Lower East Side, is derived right from the baptismal covenant and Eucharistic liturgy: "In Word and Deed." The recent groundbreaking for Trinity's new building was held on the streets of the surrounding neighborhood and witnessed by hundreds of folks, from the Bishop of the Synod to the local street people. The building incarnates in bricks and mortar this "Word and Deed" strategy of evangelism. On one floor is the soup kitchen and shelter. Another houses the sanctuary for worship and Christian education. Another floor provides parsonage space for the pastor and family. With structural integrity a river runs through the baptismal vision of Trinity.

"To serve all people, following the example of our Lord Jesus, and to strive for justice and peace in all the earth."

The biblical word that is relevant here is *diakonia*, or service. The mission strategies of our synod are undergirded by a cadre of deacons available to the bishop, the contributions of such social ministry organizations as Lutheran Social Services and Lutheran Medical Center, and participation in church-based community organizing. Nehemiah housing, adult day care for Alzheimer's patients, summer programs for youth are not just do-gooder activities patched on to the life of the Church, but central to its baptismal covenantal mission.

A Dispatch from the Baptismal Front

It had been two weeks since my son had left and I had heard nothing from Timothy. Prayer kept us close but the heart sometimes also looks for the occasional burning bush. Staring at the computer screen one night, I saw this message jump out at me. Our Huck Finn was surfing the cyberspace of the Internet.

"Greetings from Lutsk in Western Ukraine! I'm alive, well, and living with an old lady who cooks me a lot of food and doesn't speak a word of English. Unfortunately, she has no phone and public phones can't call internationally, so I had a friend send this message for me. Everything is fine. I've mailed you a long letter. Miss you all! You'll hear from me soon.

Tim

PS. Ever go to a nice hotel and find that they have index cards for toilet paper? You've never been to Ukraine!"

As Luther put it, "Baptism is the one-time event that takes your whole life to accomplish." From birth, through life's passionate adventure, to death, to new life ... a river runs through it.

(*Lutheran Forum*, Reformation, 1995)

Chapter 10
Bonhoeffer, Youth, and the Church: The Mundane *Communio Sanctorum*

> Our question is not, "What is youth and what are its rights?" but, "What is the congregation and what is the place of youth within it?" (Dietrich Bonhoeffer, "Eight Theses On Church Youth Work")

Reflections from the Undercroft Floor

Every great vision, every worthy organizing effort eventually deteriorates into work, including the building-up of a Christian congregation. And it was tedious business to be lying on the church undercroft floor, still shaking in fury and frustration. It was five in the morning at the Youth Group "lock-in" on the Sunday before Thanksgiving, and I had just scared the hell out of the kids in the basement, their chaperones, and most of our North Jersey neighbors. Kids shrieking and laughing had awakened me from a deep sleep and I had leapt up like the hound of heaven, vaulted over several sleeping bags and charged the party going full blast in the kitchen: "That's it! Knock it off! Go to sleep! Now!" I was one step away from throttling a particular child of God who had relentlessly made my life miserable all evening and now into the morning. In several hours the family of God at Trinity parish would be gathering in the sanctuary on the Lord's Day to share the Word and Sacraments. The pastor lying on the floor would be expected to lead them in the liturgy, preside at the Eucharist, and proclaim the Word of God from the pulpit.

"Am I nuts?" "I'm too old for this," were some of the thoughts bouncing around my tired and hassled head as the young people hushed and silence descended on the undercroft. All I could do was stare at the ceiling and wait for the dawn, feeling guilty for my outburst.

So-called "youth ministry" has been both the downfall and great joy of many a parish pastor. "Let's get a vicar\associate pastor\deacon(ess)\youth staffer!" has been a frequent response to the challenges of this ministry. My fervent prayer on that hard stone floor on that particular night was, "Never again." Ministry to youth, Yes! Overnight lock-ins with my aging bones sprawled on the undercroft floor, No!

Soon the brightly shining Lord's Day took on its own rhythm, a rhythm in which we basement denizens and all the people of God at Trinity were always caught up. All proceeded to the liturgy. We gathered around the Word and Sacraments. Twenty dazed and exhausted teenagers sat in the back and endured the liturgy, paying about as much attention to my sermon as they had to my instructions the night before. During the offertory they trudged in a desultory manner to the altar, bringing the Thanksgiving baskets containing items they had made and collected and gathered during the lock-in, everything from freshly baked bread and preserves to handwritten notes. They knelt at the altar and ate and drank the Family Meal of the Church with their brothers and sisters of every age, every time, and every place. When the Assisting Minister rang out the dismissal, "Go in peace, serve the Lord," the chorus of "Thanks be to God" to which the young people added their voices was accompanied by the shuffling of their feet as they joined the recessional, following the cross, carrying their baskets into the narthex, out the door, into the street, and toward their destinations of hospitals, nursing homes, and homes of the parish homebound.

Like the seventy who had been sent out two by two they returned after the second liturgy. We spent a few moments together, praying for those the young people had visited. They spoke of their visits, of their impressions, of their feelings in the presence of the children of God with whom they had shared food baskets and conversation. We briefly related their experiences to some Scriptural references to aging and to ministry. We spoke of the Baptism they had in common with the people they visited. We said the Lord's Prayer. And then we all returned to our respective domiciles and went to bed.

It had been a quirky event, this youth group "lock-in" and its aftermath, but it had been informed by a vision of the wholeness of the Church. On Saturday night, besides crafting Thanksgiving baskets and having lots of fun, we had studied Scripture, the youths had spent time with adult mentors, and sometime long after midnight we had gone to the chapel together and prayed Compline. All our activity pointed toward the reunion on the Lord's Day around Word and Sacraments, and all subsequent activity flowed out of it. This "lock-in" was not a "youth event" sideshow, but a part of the ongoing life of the whole congregation centered in the Gospel.

Within the congregation, generational tension is overcome. Youth has no privileged place. Youth serves the congregation by listening to the Word, learning it, and doing it.... Church youth work is only possible if it constantly reminds young people of their baptism, and if it has as its only purpose that they may hear the Word of God. Youth work remains the action of the congregation on behalf of its members. Every infringement of this principle is a betrayal of the congregation of Christ. (Dietrich Bonhoeffer, "Eight Theses On Church Youth Work")

THE MACERATED PARISH

Joseph Sittler once wrote about "the maceration of the minister." He spoke of how the pastorate was being divided, sliced and diced into separate guild worlds, each with its own agenda. No longer simply priests of God, pastors were now expected to be counselors, community organizers, social workers, advocates, participants in "healing teams" and other worthwhile vocations. Today we might add "church growth experts," "media consultants," "chief operating officers," and "market analysts" to the list of roles that pastors are expected to fulfill. Some pastors want to take their place in the world on the world's terms, seeking its approval, forgetting that they were ordained to be priests. It has, however, been given to pastors, in the power of the Holy Spirit, to preach, teach, baptize, celebrate the Eucharist, forgive sins, and build up the Body of Christ. With priesthood— Ministry of Word and Sacrament— at its center, the macerated vocation of the ordained finds its essential unity given by God. All other important tasks and areas of service find their rightful place in support of this priesthood.

I believe that today, we also are finding too often that macerated parishes accurately reflect their macerated pastors. They also reflect their macerated denominations, which sometimes seem to be a collection of competing interests better served by the *Federalist Papers* than by the Nicene Creed. We have youth ministry, social ministry, older adult ministries, advocacy ministry, women's and men's ministries, Sunday School, singles' ministry, church-based community organizing, homeless ministry, and more. To the extent that these specialized programs reflect the ministry of the whole community of Word and Sacraments to and with these groups, they are wonderful and necessary things. But when these worlds compete, when they spin off into their own enclosed cliques, when they each claim to be the Church, when they are organized as groups of consumers to be "serviced," then we have a macerated parish.

Just as there is only one priesthood, so there is only one Church. There is no such thing as "social ministry" as such but rather the ministry of the whole Church centered in Word and Sacraments to the brokenness of humanity, serving corporal needs, forgiving sins, and inviting the broken into the community of believers. There is no such thing as "pastoral counseling" in isolation, but a particular ministry of the whole Church centered in Word and Sacraments that offers the cure of souls as part of its one ministry of the Gospel. No parish ought ever to be simply a cell in a church-based community organization, but if it organizes, it does so in order to extend its altar and font out into the world. Hear the words of our brother Bonhoeffer to our macerated parishes as he speaks of "youth ministry:"

> As a matter of fact, a "church organization" as such is impossible, there is only the Church. The youth of the congregation is not made up of the church youth club, but of all baptized young people who belong to the congregation. All church organizations as such deny the very essence of the Church. They can be regarded only as a temporary measure, and therefore as having some relative meaning. (Dietrich Bonhoeffer, "Eight Theses On Youth Ministry")

So the ministry to youth in the parishes I have served has been anchored within the whole ministry of the parish. It includes, of course, meetings of the "youth group" and events like the "lock-in insomniac Thanksgiving basket caper." But ministry to youth also includes visiting the baptized at the youth correction center; encouraging and training youth to teach in Sunday School and Vacation Church School; connecting young people with spiritual mentors; counseling them in times of stress or temptations to substance abuse; or making appointments with all the baptized young people in the parish to spend a moment in my office over a Coke and to ask, "How's your soul?" Youth ministry includes involving young people in leadership of the Church's liturgy, in evangelism to their friends. It seeks their regular presence at the Eucharist. It is a part of "being with" all the baptized of the parish in the Name of Jesus.

From the Files of a Parish Pastor

The "Eight Theses On Church Youth Work" reproduced below have been in my files since the early years of my ministry. I don't know how they got into my possession or whether they were excerpted from a larger article, book, or speech by Pastor Bonhoeffer. I only know that their vision of ministry has informed my priesthood from the day I first read them. I have kept the theses in the form reproduced in this article because they reflect in a small way how great visions deteriorate into work and are lived out in the small details and private dramas in the life of a parish and its pastor. As you read them you sense the great themes of Bonhoeffer's thought that are illuminated in discussions of ministry: the *communio sanctorum*, the *theologia crucis*, and a certain modesty about what specialized ministry can accomplish juxtaposed against the backdrop of the centrality of the congregation. Read them and follow their progression, and you have the framework for a durable and faithful vision of parish ministry.

Eight Theses on Church Youth Work
by Dietrich Bonhoeffer

1. Since the beginning of the youth movement, church youth work has often lacked the Christian realism which would have made it realize that the spirit of youth is not to be identified with the Holy Spirit. The future of the Church lies not with the youth, but with Jesus Christ alone. The task of the Church is not to win youth, but to teach and proclaim this Word of God.

2. Our question is not, "What is youth and what are its rights?" but, "What is the congregation and what is the place of youth in it?"

3. A congregation is a company of people who have been saved from the power of death and evil through the power of the kingdom of God on earth, who listen to the message of the building of the kingdom of God in Jesus Christ, and who gather around the Word in obedient faith. A congregation is the living presence of Christ as true Lord and brother. To be in Christ is to be in a congregation. Confession, intercessory prayers, and the making of offerings are brotherly acts of a congregation. A congregation can only be judged from within itself. It is the nature of a congregation that there can be no criticism from the outside.

4. Within the congregation, a generational tension is overcome. Youth has no privileged place. Youth serves the congregation by listening to the Word, learning from it, and doing it. God's Spirit within the Church is not to be confused with criticism of the Church by youth, the radical demands which God makes on people have nothing to do with the desire of youth to create a better world. The phrase "Christian youth" is a false juxtaposition of words, not because it is modern or old-fashioned, but because it is contrary to the teaching of the Church.

5. The biblical attitude to youth is very realistic, for example: Genesis 8:21; Isaiah 3:5; Jeremiah 1:6; Ecclesiastes 11:10; 1 Peter 5:5; 2 Timothy 2:2.

6. Church youth work is only possible if it constantly reminds young people of their baptism, and if it has as its only purpose that they may hear the Word of God. Youth work remains the action of the congregation on behalf of all its members. Every infringement of this principle is a betrayal of the congregation of Christ.

7. Youth may have the right to protest against adults. Such protests can be genuine only when youth recognizes its identity with the congregation, when it carries the burden of love, and bows in penitence before the Word of God.

8. As a matter of fact, a "church organization" as such is impossible, there is only the Church. The youth of a congregation is not made up of the church youth club, but of all the baptized young people who belong to the congregation. All church organizations as such deny the very essence of the Church. They can be regarded only as a temporary measure, and therefore as having some relative meaning. ("Dietrich Bonhoeffer Werke," monograph, vol. 12, Berlin, 1932-33 [ed. Carsten Nicolaisen and Ernst-Albert Scharffenorth; Gütersloh: Gütersloher Verlagshaus, 1997])

FOR THE PARISH

Did you know that at the Lutheran church in Narrowsburg, New York, along the Delaware River, children visiting on Sunday mornings are invited by the pastor to help ring the old church bell? It is an evangelism strategy known throughout Sullivan County. And did you know that in our Lutheran parishes in the South Bronx strong young mentors are trained to hit the streets and meet the youth of the neighborhood, inviting them to programs and liturgies that must have elements of food and safety to speak at all to the needs of these children of God. All ministry, whether churchwide, synodical, institutional, or congregational, finds its heartbeat on the floors of church basements at five in the morning, in Thanksgiving baskets, in ringing bells and encounters on the street, in the ebb and flow of the people of God gathered around and by Word and sacraments. There is not a confusing multiplicity or pecking order of "church organizations"; there is only the Church.

(Lutheran Forum, Reformation, 1993)

Chapter 11
Walking On Water: Mentoring the Next Generation

Of Mop Handles and Bowstrings

For more than a year I had no idea that the parish sexton was a musician and a poet. William Garcia cleaned the church on Saturdays, a quiet and competent high-school kid. He came to church each Sunday with his sister and sat near the back. He never said much. He was as reliable in his churchgoing as in his cleaning. He and his sister were from Colombia, like so many new Latino neighbors from Central and South America who were transforming the Queens neighborhood surrounding our parish. A year into our perfunctory and polite relationship we finally had a real conversation. Our church was thinking of starting to celebrate the liturgy in the Spanish language. I began trying out the idea on some of our Hispanic members. One day I finally mentioned it to William Garcia.

We sat for over an hour in the church undercroft and I listened as William told me about his passion for the violin, his love of language and poetry, the jumble of his family life, his effort to extract an education and musical excellence from the local school system. Looming over our conversation, as it does for all city kids, was the street. There were certain things he was not ready to talk about. I asked: Will you play the violin in church sometime? He smiled.

The next Sunday he played "Beautiful Savior" and made a lot of people cry. His rendition was neither mawkish nor sentimental, but played with lyrical grace and the confidence of faith. He had contacted the organist during the week and he was ready for his debut in church. During the offertory he played the Air from Bach's Suite #3 in D. His large brown eyes shone as he played and his face radiated the joy of the music. After that he played often in our church. He played like an angel. It turned out that William was one of the better violinists in the city's student orchestra. He played more Bach and more hymns and accompanied the choir's soloists. When we began using our liturgy in the Spanish language it was William who accompanied us on the hymns. It was William who wrote the prayers for that liturgy in language of poetic splendor and deep faith. He played, he prayed, he led— because one day I stopped ignoring him and listened. And called forth his competence. And helped him find his way into our community to share his gifts.

To listen. To challenge. To invite into community. These are three ways in which we can mentor the next generation. And your local congregation can be your ally. The acolyte with the "Church Reeboks" peeking out under the white alb; the eighth-grader helping with the summer Vacation Church School program; the young hand ladling the stew at the homeless shelter; the voices singing Christmas carols at the nursing home; the lectors and choir members and Sunday School teachers; the sextons and the neighborhood kids who just drop in— all are present in our churches. In an age of chaos and confusion, of absent or uncommitted or self-absorbed parents, the local parish, rooted in the Word of God and the language of faith, can be a mentoring presence by listening, challenging and creating human community for young people.

Let us examine three Scriptural stories to help congregations mentor young people by listening, challenging, and including.

MARY AND MARTHA AND JESUS: A LISTENING PRESENCE

> After three days they found him in the temple, sitting among the teachers, listening to them and asking them questions. (Luke 2:46)

> She had a sister named Mary, who sat at the Lord's feet and listened to what he was saying. (Luke 10:39)

Until I listened to William he had never played his violin in church. Refusal to listen goes back a long way. Mostly, in Luke's Gospel, people don't listen to Jesus.

- He reads the Scriptures from the lectern in his home church in Galilee, connecting his mission with the Servant Song in Isaiah. The hometown crowd won't listen. "Isn't this Mary and Joe's kid? Who does he think he is, anyway?" And then they try to throw him off a cliff. His own people didn't listen.
- But some people begin to notice and flock to him as he preaches, teaches and heals in his home region of Galilee. Then they send the church

leaders and high muckymucks up from headquarters in Jerusalem to check out this Jesus. "Who does he think he is? The Almighty?" His own co-religionists didn't listen.

- At Caesarea Philippi he thinks finally his disciples have been listening. Peter has just said: "You are the Christ, the Son of God." He begins to tell them about the cross. They can't handle it. Peter cries out, "Forbid it, Lord, that you should go and die!" His closest friends don't listen.
- Near the end, on the Mount of Transfiguration, as he sets his face toward Jerusalem and his passion, he gets Moses and Elijah to come to his meeting. Now his closest disciples will understand. But instead of being willing to follow him down the mountain and toward the mount of Calvary, they want to stick around and build a Day's Inn! They still don't listen.
- In the Garden Jesus pours out his heart's desire in bloody sweat against the silence. "Father, if you are willing, remove this cup from me."
- And on the cross it finally seemed that even his own Father wasn't listening. "My God, my God, why have you forsaken me?"

Yet, from the very beginning, as a twelve-year-old in the Temple, it was always Jesus who was listening to others. Drawing out their spiritual hunger, responding with love and grace and the truth. And one day, like a small miracle, Jesus dines with friends and someone just sits down and listens to him. Mary listened, and her listening enabled Jesus to speak of the Kingdom, to unfold his story to another human being. Martha, like the busy pastor rushing around the church and the neighborhood, had important things to do. But maybe, like Mary's listening ministry to Jesus, the most important miracles in that parish had their genesis in the silence and attentiveness of human conversation—and the receptiveness of a good listener.

The most effective ministers to and with young people I have known are not the most hip human beings; but they are the ones who really care, who create space and hospitality for the stories of the emerging generation. My own children have been blessed by mentors in church and Lutheran school who listened to them, who asked for their developing stories and treated those stories with respect. Where are the listening posts in your parish? Bible study, Confirmation\First Communion preparation, and discussion groups can be places where the Word and world converge in the questions and issues in the lives of young people. These groups can be support groups where burdens are borne, doubts entertained, and support given by adult models of integrity. The pastor's office ought to be a welcoming place for young people of the parish and neighborhood. We ought to be asking young people often: How's your soul? And listening to what they say.

Walking on Water:
A Mentoring Presence

> Peter answered him, 'Lord, if it is you, command me to come to you on the water.' He said, 'Come.' So Peter got out of the boat and started walking on the water. (Matthew 14:28-29)

We listen in order to enlist. I have recently begun to read the story of Peter's walking on water as a mentoring story. Jesus was grieving over the death of his cousin John. He tried to withdraw to a lonely place to mourn. The crowds were so needy and so persistent that Jesus had compassion on them. He listened to them and healed their sick. But they were hungry at the end of the day. He called forth and accepted the loaves and fishes of the boy and used it to feed the five thousand hungry bodies. In all of this I believe Jesus was teaching his disciples, mentoring them in their own nascent leadership. Don't be afraid of the crowds. Attend to their great hungers of body and soul. Don't deny them their competence. Help them to understand that their loaves and fishes count for something. Ask for what they have to offer. Then it was night and the hunger in Jesus cried out for a hearing.

> "And after he had dismissed the crowds, he went up the mountain by himself to pray. When evening came, he was there alone." (Matthew 14:23)

So here he comes on the water in the night, in the fourth watch— a technical term in Hebrew, the witching hour, a time when all that we fear and can't control is running amok. Peter is ready to leave the boat. Jesus is never more a mentor than when he invites Peter out of the safety of the boat. "Come!"

Who is inviting this next generation out of the boat these days? Who is pressing for their spiritual maturity, their human competence? Do we know how many sextons are poets and violinists? Or, for that matter, how many violinists can fix the boiler? Is church a place where the development of faith and competence is the highest mission? Is your church a place that represents the safety of the boat or the scary, exhilarating invitation to walk on water? Will Christian parishes begin to be organized around the spiritual gifts of the people of God?

There was an outstanding group of young people in the New Jersey parish I served. After Christmas one year I invited them to a meeting in which they were asked to plan and implement a summer program around their gifts and interests. I invited them to bring along their friends. The youth were involved in the planning, marketing and implementing of the program. Workshops in drama, sports, music, art, and storytelling were built around their talents. In effect they were creating both parish outreach and their summer jobs. They learned about accountability, economics, organizing, teaching, and the practical application of their respective talents. The program was as quirky yet as joyful as they were. The combination of listening, invitations to share competencies, and community building helped mentor these young people as they mentored others and shared their varied gifts in their church's outreach. The community response was overwhelming as networks of relationships emanating from the church wove a widening web of young people and their families.

Sometimes churches can organize in a more extensive way to invite young people out of the boat. Urban school children often begin their high school years with attitudes of resignation and defeat resulting from their experiences in the schools of our cities. But in one case, churches who were part of grassroots community organizations in urban north Jersey helped negotiate a positive collaboration among banks, school administrations, employers, colleges, and local parishes to create the PASS Plan (Passport Awarded for Staying in School) in Paterson, Passaic and other cities. Five hundred high school students per year are guaranteed entry-level jobs or college tuition scholarships if they meet grade-point average and attendance requirements in their junior and senior years. The key ingredients here are the PASS Plan meetings, mentoring sessions run by over two hundred and fifty trained adult sponsors from the local churches. Here the students receive training, mentoring, and conversations about values and identity that foster hope and dignity for urban young people. Over the years hundreds of urban young people were guided into hopeful engagement with the future by their spiritual mentors.

"And Jesus said to Peter, "Come."

MOSES LOOKED THIS WAY AND THAT: A COMMUNAL PRESENCE

> One day, after Moses had grown up... he saw an Egyptian beating a Hebrew, one of his kinsmen. He looked this way and that, and seeing no one he killed the Egyptian and hid him in the sand. (Exodus 2:11-12)

The traditional interpretation— the one I learned in Sunday School— of this story is that Moses' looking around was motivated by the desire to avoid detection. On this reading, when Moses saw that the coast was clear he went ahead and killed the oppressor of his people. But Hillel, a rabbi and contemporary of Jesus, offered another opinion. He said that Moses was looking for help. And looked left and right, this way and that, and when he saw that he was alone, he reluctantly fought the bully. Hillel believed that the rest of the Hebrew Scriptures are about this story, about the building of community so that Moses and Israel would never again be in the position where "[they] looked this way and that, and there was no one..."

How many of our young people are in the position of Moses, or of the one being oppressed? Many of the young people in your church or school will find with you the only family they are going to get. We listen, and we call forth the gifts of young people for one purpose: to include them in the Family of Jesus, the church. One of the few multigenerational opportunities for community left in our world is the church. The Body of Christ is the hands and arms of Jesus in the world. Our schools, Sunday Schools and parish ministries are the points of entry into this family. They are extensions of the baptismal font, the Word of God, and the altar in the midst of the world where William Garcia and the others wait with their music inside them.

In the upper room Jesus looked this way and that. The Twelve were around him. They were listening now. "Take and eat, this is my body... take and drink, this is my blood..."

As he washed their feet and gave them a new commandment, as he shared the bread and wine and finally his own broken body and shed blood, Jesus was always listening to the Father, was the mentor *par excellence*.

(*The Good Shepherd Magazine*, Spring 1995)

Chapter 12
The Habit of Ecstasy; the Practice of Prayer; the Journey of Faith

In the life of a parish a powerful partnership is forged between the home and the congregation for the nurture of faith. The baptismal mandate to "continue in the covenant God made with you in Holy Baptism" takes on flesh and blood in that partnership. This chapter explores three aspects of the post-baptismal nurture of young people through the dynamic partnership of home, congregation and Holy Spirit.

The Habit of Ecstasy

> Peter went up on the roof to pray. He became hungry and wanted something to eat; and while it was being prepared, he fell into a *trance*. He saw the heaven opened and something like a large sheet coming down, being lowered to the ground by its four corners. In it were all kinds of four-footed creatures and reptiles and birds of the air. Then he heard a voice saying, "Get up, Peter; kill and eat." But Peter said, "By no means, Lord; for I have never eaten anything that is profane or unclean." The voice said to him again, a second time, "What God has made clean, you must not call profane."...Then Peter began to speak (to Cornelius), "I truly understand that God shows no partiality, but in every nation anyone who fears him is acceptable to him...." (Acts 10:10-16,34)

Up on the Roof

Long before The Drifters sang about it, people have been going up on the roof for rest, refreshment and escape. Until our recent move to Riverside Drive, our synod office was on the seventh floor of an office in midtown Manhattan. Sometimes between meetings I would take the elevator to the top floor, climb up some fire escape steps, and step out onto the roof. It was escape, new perspective, a bit of peace in the midst of the city. Peter was in the home of Simon the Tanner in the city of Joppa in the early Pentecost days of the Church. He goes up on the roof to wait for lunch. He goes into a trance.

Up the coast in Caesarea Cornelius, a Roman general and a Gentile, is also hungry. He is seeking God. He sends for Peter, whose fame as a spiritual leader is growing rapidly. Will Peter, a Jew, come to see this Gentile spiritual seeker? Cornelius wants to know if the God of Peter and Abraham and Sarah and Isaac also loves Gentiles.

In his trance Peter sees all kinds of food descend on a tablecloth. He is hungry, but the food is not kosher. He would dishonor God by eating what is ritually unclean. God speaks. "If I make something clean, it is truly clean. *Bon appétit.*" Strangers knock on the door. Peter comes out of his trance. Messengers from Gentile Cornelius want Peter to come with them and teach them about the true God. Peter goes. In the living room of a Gentile in Caesarea the first words out of Peter's mouth are these: "God doesn't play favorites. Everyone is acceptable to God."

STEPPING FORTH IN ECSTASY

This remarkable story of God's grace going across boundaries turns on the trance of Peter the daydreamer on the roof. The English word *trance* is inadequate, suggesting a kind of woozy reverie. The Greek word for trance is *ek-stasis*, a dynamic word from which we get the word 'ecstasy.' *Ekstasis* means, literally, "to step forth." It is the shift in consciousness of Peter hungry on a rooftop, who in a moment of *ekstasis* was made vulnerable to the imagery of the sheet full of animals, unclean as well as clean. The insight about God's inclusion of the Gentiles, which had been repressed and resisted by his everyday consciousness and worldview, overwhelmed him in the state of openness and receptivity that is ecstasy, *ekstasis*.

What rooftop ecstatic visions does this emerging generation receive from their elders? We live in a state of hunger for ecstasy, for the kind of experience that is open to the urgent interior word of the living Christ who dwells in each of us. Life in Christ asks us to step out continually into wider worlds, deeper spiritual insights, passionate engagement with the calling each of us has from God. Do our children see us wrestle honestly with our faith, ransack the Scriptures for meaning, listen to those who are different, explore worlds other than our own? We live in a culture of too many trances and reveries that are only celebrations of the self or of a received tradition. We are balkanized, walled off from one another.

Tactics of Ecstasy

There are simple ways to help the next generation step away from the wall of mirrors. One path is story. In the contemporary climate of fearing and blaming immigrants for current social ills, tell your children how your— and their— own family came to this place. Who helped them? Where did they land? How did they get started here? What role did their church play in welcoming your kin when they were strangers to the United States? Let our Sunday Schools and vacation church schools be stewards of these stories as teachers and students share ancestor stories from the Bible. Take a book out of the library that describes a different world, perhaps a biography or a poem or a piece of fiction. I remember gaining a curiosity about the world of music by reading biographies of great composers written for young people. Tell stories from Scripture, stories of Jesus, Israel, the Early Church, stories that push the boundaries of human identity and acceptance.

The visual and performing arts are another wonderful way to help young people explore the wideness of the human condition. Trips to the Art Institute in Chicago put me in touch with the souls and surroundings of great artists. Music or dance of all kinds and traditions widens our angle of vision. Drama suspends reality in order to lead us to experience it on a deeper level. Even musicals like "The King and I" and "West Side Story" made a big impression on my youthful view of the wideness of the world and my place in it.

Example and experience are other doorways to ecstasy. Tell your children when you have been moved by an experience of sorrow or joy or beauty or the need of another. I remember the big snow of 1975. The day before Christmas I put my two sons on a sled and walked to the apartments of the homebound of our parish, bringing Communion and Christmas gifts made by our youth group. Hosting dinners for the homeless in our church basement caused several of our young people to make long-term commitments to neighborhood programs of mercy and outreach. The ethnic parades of New York, as well as street fairs and free concerts, were all fertile ground for ecstatic growth.

Ecstasy begins by listening and noticing. When we really listen to another, we step outside of ourselves and attend to the other. People rarely listen to one another, let alone really listen to this emerging generation of Christians. Without experiences of being heard by others, folks cannot know the grace of the gift they could offer by listening to others in their turn. How can we learn to listen more grace-fully? The greatest act of noticing and listening is intercessory prayer. When we pray for others, they are fully present in all their unique humanity. When we take the time to pray for others by name and situation, when we step outside ourselves to attend to others before the God whom Jesus called 'Father,' we know that the genesis of ecstatic love is the living God of all creation.

On the mountainside, in the great sermon in Matthew's Gospel, Jesus was pushing those who follow him toward ecstasy. "Blessed are the peacemakers, for they will be called children of God." It is on rooftops, then and now, that peacemakers continue to step forth.

The Habit of Prayer

> He was praying in a certain place, and after he had finished, one of his disciples said to him, "Lord, teach us to pray, as John taught his disciples." He said to them, "When you pray, say: "Father, hallowed be your name…"

"He was praying in a certain place…"

Prayer is taught. Jesus taught his disciples to pray not only by the words he gave them, but also by his example. Prayer for Jesus was a regular discipline, carried out in a certain place, in public and accessible to his disciples. It is no different between parents and children today. It is as important as it was to Jesus' disciples that our children see us pray, that the discipline of prayer is accessible to them.

My parents surrounded us with song and prayer each evening in a bedtime ritual familiar to many. We would pray together the Lord's Prayer, then "Now I lay me down to sleep…"; then we would go through the "God bless" petitions remembering everyone and everything possible (sort of like the *Goodnight Moon* book). Prayer before and after meals was taught. When Janet and I had children of our own we continued these and other practices of prayer. In the season of Advent we would light the candles, open the Advent wreath, sing songs and have a time of devotional reading and prayer around the supper table. It is amazing to me that our children would come home from college and still be comfortable with the rituals of their childhood. Prayer at times of birthdays, anniversaries, illnesses and other events would link the times of our lives with the providence of God. Especially in our transient and overstimulated world times of prayer and reflection are a gift across the generations, a centering in the presence of God.

One can think of the Church as a linking of these kitchen tables at the table of the altar. The teaching of prayer is a great partnership between Church, school, Sunday School and the home. Scripture gives us a picture of a Jesus who was continually at prayer:

- in homes and in public places;
- in the wilderness after his baptism;
- in mourning after the death of his cousin John;
- in public before the raising of Lazarus and other miracles;
- at the Mount of Transfiguration before the journey to Jerusalem;
- in the Garden on the night of his betrayal;
- on the cross.

Jesus was a teacher of prayer, not only in the words he taught, but also by enacted example. "He was praying in a certain place...."

"Our Father"

His disciples asked of Jesus: "Lord, teach us to pray."
Jesus answered: "When you pray, say: 'Our Father'..."

Prayer is the exercise of a relationship with God. Our *Father*. Prayer is the exercise of the family and the church community with God. *Our* Father. Prayer is taught by Jesus Christ. Parents, in the place of Jesus, are instructors to their children in the art of prayer.

My middle child, Jeremy, was hurting the deep hurt of a second-grader. He was in the school play, a production of "Bambi" more vivid and lavish to a child with imagination than any Cecil B. DeMille production. He had the part of Thumper, the rabbit in the story, and he took the role as seriously as anything in his young life. He would come home and fill us with tales of the rehearsals and our home would ring with songs from the play.

The week of the play our little Thumper got the flu. Each day he spent in bed, missing rehearsals, made him more morose. Even second-graders get the blues. "They're counting on me," he would say, "I can't let them down." At each meal and at night he would pray for renewed health.

"Help me get better for the play, Lord. Amen." It sounded as much like a subpoena as a prayer. The morning of the dress rehearsal he came downstairs, throat still raw, face still flushed. He was frustrated. I will never forget the look he gave me when he said: "Dad, I've prayed and prayed to God to make me better and it hasn't worked!" He was angry. His look said, "What kind of a line have you been giving me about God all these years?" In that look I recognized the deep feeling of disappointment and doubt that I have seen, as a pastor, in the eyes of so many others— the eyes of those who have lost loved ones, who have lost jobs, whose children have gone astray, whose marriages have broken, whose friend or relative is chronically or terminally ill. In Jeremy's eyes I saw my own heart which has been weighed down by prayers seemingly unanswered; situations which, put into God's hands, did not immediately resolve themselves. But I also had had the example of parents and elders who continued steadfast in prayer even in the midst of disaster. I had acquired this habit, you see, this ritual of communication with God.

Were the wounded eyes of my son also mirrored in the eyes of Jesus who prayed three times, sweating blood, that he be spared the bitter cup of the cross, and who received in the stillness of the Garden only silence? What do you say to a second-grader who has been initiated into the mysteries of disillusionment? I offered my own silent prayer for wisdom and answered something like this: "I am your father and I love you. Before you became sick I was your father. I am still your father in your illness. And I will be your father when you get better. You are, maybe, never more my son than when you tell me how you hurt and ask me to share it. Maybe that is something like praying. God is like a father or mother to you. God cares about you and loves you. When you are hurting God hurts with you, just like I do. When I talk to God in prayer I feel a certain comfort, like I hope you feel now talking to me. I trust that God is my Father, no matter what happens. The same goes for you. The answer to your prayer will come. Until then we just trust our Father loves us and that all of our moments are in his hands."

And Jesus said, "When you pray, say: 'Our Father....'"

Jeremy was still angry, but later it seemed to help. He didn't stop praying. There was more to say that I did not think of at the time. For one thing, God's answer to life's disappointments and tragedies is Easter—eternal life. It is still God's final answer, final victory and joy behind the door of life's greatest disappointment, death. In Easter faith we endure, connected by prayer, as do children who talk to their parents in trust and faith.

And what about Thumper? The fever broke the day of the play. With raw throat Jeremy croaked through his part. Through it all a precious child taught me a little more of the incredible love between parents and children, of the Father's love for each one of us, and of the power of prayer.

THE JOURNEY OF FAITH

"Civilization is going to decay. Children no longer obey their parents." (Carved in hieroglyphics on an Egyptian stone over 6000 years ago).

Help! My Son's on the Beach in Fort Lauderdale and I'm Feeling Blue! Some Stories From the Home Front

"Mom, dad, I'll be fine. All my friends are going. You trust me, don't you?" Sound familiar? When do you say, "OK, go"? "I trust you." When do we begin to realize that our children can only grow into themselves when we can begin to let go? What is this ministry of nurture that can only accompany the emerging generation in the inevitable conflicts of growth with the gifts of faith and presence, not control? There was a time when my sons were twenty-two and twenty respectively, my daughter sixteen. That means they had all been teenagers at once in our home. Sometimes I believed that the teenage table grace was literally true: "I thank the Lord for preparing a table before me in the presence of mine enemies."

Nothing remains the same between the ages of eleven and fifteen. There is a tremendous spurt of physical tension and energy. The walls and ceilings of our home track the development of our children, smudged as they were unable for years at a time to pass through without jumping and touching— higher, higher. I watched them strive to be independent even as they remained very much children. They balked at going to church even as they asked questions about the homeless. I tracked their search for identity in their dress as their peers transformed them from "nerds" to whatever was lately "fresh." They became capable of philosophical reflection, of creative output, of idealistic outreach.

It was not only as a father, but also as a pastor that I have been a part of the fragile ministry of nurturing adolescents (from the Latin, "to grow up"). In ministry in both inner-city and suburban congregations I saw an emerging generation "at risk," growing up earlier and earlier as the choices became more confusing, with potentially lethal consequences. I watched as a generation of adults began to abandon its children, even if there were elders at home.

The kids have names, and even if what you experience in your home or church may not be exactly the same as mine, common issues emerge from their stories. And ever since the Word became flesh as Jesus "grew up" in this world, these issues have spiritual significance. The maturation of our children matters greatly to a God who "grew in wisdom and in stature..." in the home of Mary and Joseph.

Roberta is an immigrant from Brazil, a high-school student who teaches in her Sunday School. Among the decisions forced on her this past year are: what college to apply to; possible career decisions; whether to have an abortion; and what songs to choose for the Sunday School Christmas pageant.

One of the tasks of adolescence is to establish identity.

Kenny is a junior-high student with no father at home. He comes to church periodically, mainly to check if a friend has come or to knock on the pastor's door and talk about nothing in particular. He is shy with girls, unhappy in general, and can't stay out of fights. He's just gone off suspension at school.

One of the tasks of adolescence is to expand one's social life.

Jean is in the seventh grade. Each day she comes home from school and lets herself into an empty house. Her folks must be at the Hunts Point market in the Bronx by 4 AM to get produce for their fruit stand; they won't return until 9 PM. As they chase the American dream Jean is being parented by the kids on her corner, by MTV, and by the programs at her church.

One of the tasks of adolescence is to exercise independence.

June is in high school and thinks she might want to be a teacher, or "do some kind of work with children." She is a leader of the youth group and volunteers in the church's nursery school. She is frustrated from time to time by the lack of involvement of so many the church's kids in the youth group and their inability to take it seriously.

One of the tasks of adolescence is to examine the future.

During adolescence the emerging adult is involved in these four tasks, indeed *must* be involved in them:
- establish identity
- expand social life (dealing with emerging sexuality)
- exercise independence
- examine the future

It is important to remember that each of these tasks involves inherent conflict. (I was dependent and now I must be independent; I played only with members of my own sex, now I must interact with the other half of the human race; I lived only for today, now the future is shoved on me; once I was safe, now there are rules for telling me who I am that I don't understand.) These four tasks, accompanied by rapid physical and psychological changes, lie behind that defiance, that recklessness, that morose and sullen withdrawal, that unease the kids slip into around you. If your adolescent is wrestling with these four tasks, then you know that there is normal and healthy growth taking place. Normal rebellion is essential to the emerging generation.

Our children need us now as much as they ever did. But we must begin to let go of some of the control, start trusting that good stuff we tried to put inside them, and be willing to accompany them on the journey. We need to continue to say "No" when necessary, while expanding the opportunities to say "Yes." They are exploring, not abandoning the values and faith we nurtured in them at home and church.

Shaping the Jesus Space

In the best of all worlds Christian nurture is a partnership among family, church, school. The greatest thing you can give the child is two strong parents with whom to fight, and many mentors across the generations. Often, sadly, that does not happen. We live in a society that is abandoning its children, even if there is nominally someone at home. Langston Hughes, in *Simple's Uncle Sam*, says: "I have been in so many empty houses full of peoples that I do not want to live in no crowded empty house no more..."

For many children, their only experience of family or of human nurture may be in our churches and schools. Shaping the Jesus space, and accompanying the children in their adolescent journey to responsible adulthood has become the ministry of us all. As our children grow, they mature in faith as well as in body and psyche. The journey of faith begins in Baptism. In the power of the Holy Spirit we grow in the faith into which we were baptized. As our vocation to follow Jesus deepens and our faith journey takes us into all walks of life, we can see how the gift of faith develops in us. It is a matter of the senses, the heart, the mind, and the will.

Faith through the Senses

In the first years of our lives we observe, mimic, and copy what we see, hear, feel, and taste. Children brought to the liturgy as infants, although they understand little on the cognitive level, can watch those around them pray and worship. They experience an awareness of transcendence, the mystery of faith which stays with them all their lives. Little ones learn to pray, not just through repeating the words, but by seeing others pray and sing. They imitate. Faith comes through all the human senses, as Luther frequently remarked.

Faith of the Heart

As we grow older we learn to participate in a family of believers and feel a sense of belonging to it. We internalize the songs, liturgies, arts, prayers, rhythms of the community. The story of our shared identity and its authority for our lives is asserted. The stories of Israel, the Church and Jesus must be told and heard as ancestor stories. When my kids would say, "Everyone is doing it," we would reply, "That's not the Bouman way," undergirding an identity that claims a story, a way of life that is ours. The way of Jesus. This is the Bouman way. This is who you are. As ushers, acolytes, choir members, as family members seated around the kitchen table, and in many other ways our faith is nourished by being given something to do, a piece of the action. Faith of the heart belongs to the community. It is not yet one's own. It is, unfortunately, the level of faith of most adults in our churches. Their pilgrimage ends here, with some form of identification with the community. To them, confirmation means graduation.

Adolescence is not a stopping point but a time to continue to grow and live this faith in all the circumstances of our life's routines, relationships and opportunities.

Faith of the Mind

Let's call this searching faith. This is faith on a vision quest, of readiness to act in the world. It is a faith at home with questions, doubts, a willingness to be present in the ambiguities of life. We begin the painful process of carving out our identities. We assume a questioning posture toward all we have been taught and given. "Why is my way the Bouman way?" We are not always at home with uncertainty, tension and doubt. So also the Church. We're always giving apologies to folks whose lives are being torn apart. Instead of taking them by the hand and going into the deep darkness, as the Psalmist said, into the depths of Sheol, where God waits for them and for us, we quickly want to get them back on track with the faith. Adolescence is a place of great light and deep darkness, where God waits to join those willing to search and grow.

This searching faith is congruent with the four main tasks mentioned above that adolescents need to complete. They need to widen their social relationships, their ability to include more and more people in their circle of work and play. The peer group dominates for a time, as a sense of generational kinship develops and is expressed in shared dress, language, music, heroes, causes. They're figuring out who they are. Second, young people need to confront their sexuality. Third— and at a time when they are least equipped to do so— they are forced to look toward the future, to make their first decisions about jobs, education, vocations. Finally, they need to wrestle in a healthy way with the authorities in their lives and come to some sense of who they are and of what will be important to them in later life. Any youth programs that overlook or ignore these basic tasks will be irrelevant, or even in danger of stunting the development of young people.

Faith in the Will

On the other side of the tension, doubt, and questions of searching faith there is owned faith, religion situated in the will. It is a matter of claiming an identity for oneself (the Baptismal identity given by God). A person can act, can stand up to the world. One is possessed by faith. Mature

Christian faith, nurtured on Sunday and lived on Monday, is the process described in Ephesians, "growing to mature personhood, to the stature of the fullness of Christ."

It is, finally, a matter of faith for the parents and elders as well as for the children becoming men and women. It is a baptismal journey that ends in life eternal. Along the way we have been privileged to give shape and form to the Jesus space in the hearts of our children. Essential to that nurture is the abiding love and acceptance which takes its strength from the Word of God: "Train children in the right way, and when old, they will not stray."

(This chapter is based on writing that first appeared in *Good Shepherd Magazine*).

Part Three
"To live among God's faithful people...."

Chapter 13
The Community of Grace

> ...his voice, though halting, was strangely distinct. "Does it matter? Grace is everywhere..."
> I think he died just then.
>
> (Bernanos, *Diary of a Country Priest*, p. 255)

Hungry Hearts on Broadway

You walk across the George Washington Bridge and onto the streets of Manhattan, turning south on Broadway. On the left is the old Loew's Theater at 175th, now converted into Reverend Ike's community temple. Reverend Ike is the one who packs them in with promises of wealth and riches if you follow Jesus. The sign on the marquee says, "Come on in, or smile as you pass by." Around you are mostly poor streets with the sights and sounds of Dominican, Caribbean, and vestiges of Old World Jewish cultures. You pass an old Methodist church with steel doors and barred windows.

What makes people "come on in" to our religious assemblies, you wonder, and others just "smile as they pass by?" What is the human heart reaching for when a person writes a check to the 700 Club, walks into a candlelit church once a year at Christmas, listens to Reverend Ike spin his dreams, drags a baby in for baptism or a fiancée for a "church" ceremony, carries in the dead for a proper send-off, or in the midst of a crisis mutters "God help me?" What do they need from me, you wonder about those to whom you are traveling? You think about the Augustinian hungry souls as you plod down Broadway.

You look across the street at the empty lot where the Audubon Ball Room used to be, where Malcolm X was gunned down, then enter the Columbia Presbyterian Hospital. You enter the intensive care unit for infants with your heart in your throat. You see many cribs with bars and infants lying in them. You see and hear machines of many sorts, you notice tubes and hovering parents and green-clad staff.

They direct you to a crib in a corner where a mother rushes out to greet you. You hardly know her but she hugs you. She holds on to your arm and says, "When the nurse told me you were outside the door, I could hardly believe it! You have no idea how much your being here means to me. Come and see Andy." She tightens her grip on your arm.

You had met Andy and his mother a week ago at the urging of one of their neighbors, a member of your parish. "Go see them, pastor; they are having a rough time. The kid is having an operation that might kill him."

Andy had one of the most generous smiles you had ever seen. He is a happy baby. But he is six months old and he is no larger than a two-month-old child. He has heart problems—leaky valves—and he has almost died more than once. This operation is risky, but it is his only chance. His mother, long absent from participation in the life of a church, has already lost one infant, and she is now barely hanging on to faith. You were there to listen to her fears, to sit with her as she groped for assurance that there could be a God, to hear her speak of her little Andy, already a fixture in her own heart and home.

You sat and listened and prayed with these children of God and put your hands on Andy's head and asked God's mercy. Kyrie Eleison.

Since the operation he has lain in this crib, each day a little stronger, but by no means out of danger. Now you stand over the crib and look down at Andy. His little chest heaves up and down, struggling with a partially collapsed lung. He is attached to machines and tubes that feed him and give him fresh blood. You see the rhythm of the heartbeat on the monitor. His narcotized eyes are closed, his little body battered, but as you lay your hands on him to pray and anoint with oil, he looks awfully good to you, alive and giving so much hope to those who wait. Above the crib his mother has taped a picture of Andy blazing in the most radiant smile you have ever seen. Beneath it she has typed: "With God nothing is impossible."

Then neither of you speak. You hear the sound of machines whirring, children crying. You hold the mother's hand and gaze at Andy. He is so vulnerable, his hands stretched out as he lies in his crib. She says the obvious: "I think of Jesus when I see him lying there, stretched out like he was on a cross."

Andy's mother tells you that they allowed her to put one thing on the stretcher with Andy when they took him to surgery. She says that she took a miraculous medal which had been in the family for years and wrapped it in the visitor's sticker with your name on it which you had left as a little reminder of the prayers of your parish. You and your church were in the room with him, she said. You don't know much about miraculous medals, and you usually leave the hocus-pocus to Reverend Ike and your buddy Oral. But you do know something about presence. And about the poignant ache in the human heart not to be left desolate and alone. The impulse which caused a mother to stretch out her hopes for her baby by wrapping a precious medal inside the sticker of a visitor and send it with her little one into his own valley of the shadow of death is a glimpse into the spiritual hunger of all to whom Christ gave himself on the cross. It is a cry for the assurance of Grace.

FOR YOU AND FOR ALL

What was I doing in that hospital room? Why was I there? If you read the plethora of books linking theology and psychology, you might think I was there as a "caregiver," or a pastoral counselor, or a member of some healing "team," or a participant in Clinical Pastoral Education using this encounter for my own growth and self-awareness. And each one of these roles might be authentic and appropriate at a given time. But they are not the reason I was there.

I was not there to help Andy's mother put her ultimate trust in the personal transformation she was undergoing in her suffering.

I was not there to help her put her ultimate trust in either supernatural miracle cures or the power of the technology of the healing arts.

I was not there to anchor her hope in her own techniques of "spirituality," her tenacity as a good mother, or notions of a pervasive and formless spirituality inhering in all of life.

I was there as a pastor of a church, a leader and representative of a graceful community of Jesus. I was, by the fact of my presence and my prayers and pastoral encouragement, a means of linking these isolated and vulnerable sufferers to the presence and promises of a gracious God, through the presence of the dying and rising Christ incarnate in the life of the parish community of Grace. I was there to put her trembling hand and her wounded child into the hand of God, who loves them unconditionally for Christ's sake.

I have been a pastor for twenty-five years and yet I still must take off my shoes at the mystery and wonder of the eucharistic communities of Grace before which I have stood holding bread and wine; at the gratitude in my heart that the Holy Spirit of God would call me to serve such families of Jesus as pastor, presiding at the Family Meal of the Body of Christ. I believe with all my heart that each Baptism, and each Eucharist, and the life of the community that flows from such miracles, is the most prodigious revolution that can ever happen. It catches up fearful mothers and vulnerable children in the graceful embrace of the crucified and risen Christ.

The community of Grace gathered around Word and Sacraments is not just one among competing "expressions" of the Church, another consumer of the myriad programs and agendas devised by headquarters, not just one option among many in being spiritual, not just another agency to make the world a little better. Grace alone! Christ alone! Through faith! "I believe that I cannot by my own reason or strength believe in Jesus Christ my Lord or come to him, but the Holy Spirit has called me by the Gospel, enlightened me with his gifts, sanctified and kept me in the true faith..." Remember? The Holy Spirit is the presence of Christ in the Church, working faith through the means of Grace. The Word and Sacraments are: proclaimed in Scripture, in service to others, in visits to hospital and homebound, in ministry in the neighborhood and world community; sung in cadences of Teutonic chorale or Hispanic *choritos*, taught; received in Eucharist and Baptism, Confession and Absolution; signed by the life of the community of Grace. Word and Sacraments, Christ among us, through communities of Grace.

A week after she brought her baby home from the hospital, Andy's mother brought him to a Sunday morning liturgy of our parish. During the time we call "Concerns of the Church" she showed us her smiling child, and thanked our community of Grace for waiting with her. She said, "You reminded us that no matter what happened, Jesus loves us forever." Then Andy and his mother joined the Family at the altar. "For you and for all..."

Ubiquitous Grace

After twenty-five years of pastoral ministry I am still in awe of how desperately believers hang on to the narrowest shred of grace. The connection between the public and objective Means of Grace in Word and Sacraments, and private and subjective moments of grace in beleaguered hearts is often revealed in the everyday struggle of parish life.

He sits across the table in my office. He stares into space, his eyes red and puffy. He takes deep breaths and lets out sighs that come from the bottom of his torpor. Ken is forty years old. My small talk is finished. I am worn out with it. The coffee is cold. He lights the fourth cigarette and cries again. And for twenty minutes, a half hour, sometimes almost an hour he is unable to say a single word. Depression. Life's cupboard is bare. Like Elijah of old, he is in the cave. "I alone am left, only I..."

The phone rings. Ken's voice is not the listless, smoky monotone I have come to expect. It is bright, matter of fact.

"I'm sorry, Steve, I can't make our appointment today."

I ask if everything is all right.

"Not really. I just cut my wrists."

The last time it was pills, a coma, Levine tubes, shock treatments. I call his wife, then the police. Together we enter the cave again to pull out one who believes with all his aching heart "I alone am left, only I..."

He sits across from me at the table in my office. He is trying again. I ask: Is there anything that gives you a small measure of hope?

"The Eucharist," he says. He tells me he understands about Thomas who wanted to believe but could not until he could see the wounds of Jesus. He tells me that when I consecrate the Host, and then elevate it, he always says under his breath, "My Lord and my God."

"Grace is all around us," gasped the dying priest in Bernanos' novel. When the center holds then baby Andy, his mother, morose Ken, and all the world's hungry hearts will be enfolded through Christ in the arms of a gracious God.

(*Lutheran Forum*, Lent, 1989)

Chapter 14
The Community of the Word

> We shall now return to the gospel, which offers counsel and help against sin in more than one way, for God is surpassingly rich in his grace: First, through the spoken Word, by which the forgiveness of sin (the peculiar office of the gospel) is preached to the whole world; second, through Baptism; third, through the holy Sacrament of the Altar; fourth, through the power of the keys; and finally, through the mutual conversation and consolation of the brethren. (Martin Luther, "Smalcald Articles," *Book of Concord* [Philadelphia, 1959], p. 310)

The Great Thirst

> As pants the hart for cooling streams
> when heated in the chase,
> so longs my soul, O God, for you,
> and your refreshing grace.
>
> (Nahum Tate and Nicholas Brady [LBW, Hymn 452])

There comes a time when the thirst for the Word of God is the deepest reality in this parched human life. The wake had ended. The immediate family sat or stood around the casket in desultory conversation or numb silence. I just stared into the casket, trying to will a movement of life from the stone-cold visage of the remains of our loved one. It was a moment of overwhelming dislocation. Where is he now? Where am I? And the haunting question death always brings: Is this it? The preacher entered and we shuffled to our seats. I was grateful for the appearance of the person in the black suit and collar, a messenger of God's Word. Expose the lie of that damned casket! Please, just give us the Word, pastor!

But the preacher had another agenda that night. Let's have an Irish wake, he said. It will be good for you to talk about your feelings, to say something about our departed friend. Who wants to go first? Silence. Our feelings could lead us only to the casket. In that silence was a pervasive dread and sadness. The silence was an expression of our great thirst for a Word from beyond the casket. After a time a few of us mumbled a word or two, in deference to the preacher, a good and compassionate man. Finally, he left. To hell with "grief management."

An uncle then brought out a Bible. He began reading from Romans, chapter eight. And the Word again became flesh as the dying and rising Christ embraced the living and the dead in that funeral home. "In all these things we are more than conquerors through him who loved us. For I am sure that neither death, nor life, nor angels, nor principalities, nor things present, nor things to come, nor powers, nor height, nor depth, nor anything else in all creation, will be able to separate us from the love of God in Christ Jesus our Lord."

This broken, thirsty hart craned his neck over the cooling stream. And was refreshed by grace. *Sola Scriptura.*

Or let the following story disclose the thirst. Two sisters and a brother spend all their waking hours together in the nursing home room of one of the sisters. They are old. They have survived much, both in Czechoslovakia on the other side of the Atlantic, and in northern New Jersey on this side. They alone are left, and each day they give themselves to one another. The one sister's illness renders her helpless. She cannot eat or move or bathe without assistance. Her sister and brother, members of our parish, arrive early in the morning to clean and bathe and feed her. They leave late at night after tucking her into bed. There is a sense of joy to their life together. Once the stricken sister told me, "From the moment I open my eyes in the morning I look forward to seeing the faces of my brother and sister. Then my day begins."

When I visit we share the family meal of the Eucharist. The sister and brother go around the nursing home and gather the hungry and thirsty, those whose parishes have forgotten them. In the crowded room the presence of Jesus, the Good Shepherd, fills thirsty harts. Given and shed for you.

In the sister's room are icons of identity, remembrances of things past: pictures of family; letters from loved ones; Confirmation certificates; cards with Confirmation verses handwritten in German *Schrift*; old crosses; devotional booklets; Mass cards marking their dwindling earthly fellowship; an ancient picture of the Good Shepherd holding a sheep, beneath it flowing the words of the twenty-third Psalm; an old family Bible. One day the sister took the Bible and brought it to me as I was preparing for the Eucharist. "Pastor," she said, "Please read to us before the *Abendmahl.* When my sister was in a coma we read to her for hours every day." She gave me the Bible as if she were conferring on me this world's greatest treasure. They looked at me in joyful expectation, with thirsty eyes. What should I read? "From Romans," she said.

Word and Sacraments. Christ, the Word made flesh in the revelation of Holy Scripture. The Word in the breaking of the bread and the sharing of the cup. The Word written, remembered, studied, read, and proclaimed. The Word in Eucharistic invitation to thirsty souls in a nursing home. The Word in loving human service to a sister. The Word in the eating and drinking of the Eucharist. The Word in the assurance of the forgiveness of sins spoken by the pastor in the Absolution, and in the mutual consolation of the brothers and sisters. In all of it, *sola Scriptura*. The Church is the community gathered by the Word of God, servant of that Word, faithful to the Word.

Of course the first great thirst is God's. Holy Scripture is the witness to that thirst which desires to forgive, to embrace in covenant love, to reunite the broken pieces of creation. In covenant fidelity, God spoke Christ. And the Church is the witness and sign that even now, in funeral home or nursing home, God continues to speak Christ.

HIC

> I say of the right hand of God: although this is everywhere, as we may not deny, still because it is also nowhere, you can actually grasp it nowhere, unless for your benefit it binds itself to you and summons you to a definite place. This God's right hand does, however, when it enters into the humanity of Christ and dwells there. There you surely find it, otherwise you will run back and forth throughout creation, groping here and groping there yet never finding, even though it is actually there; for it is not there for you...He himself gives meaning to the bread for you, by his Word, bidding you to eat him. (*Luther's Works*, vol. 36, 68-69.)

Verbum caro factum est. "The Word became flesh." I saw those words carved into an altar in Nazareth, the place where Mary heard that she was in the family way. I noticed one other little word that almost gave me a heart attack. *Verbum caro hic factum est. Hic.* Here! Thus! The Word was made flesh here! Here, the fullness of God was pleased to dwell! The explosion of love and compassion from the thirsty heart of a gracious God came *hic*, here, to this woman Mary, in this Arab town, in this world, a family to include all the world's orphaned, thirsty children. "*Hic.*"

We must insist with Luther that the finite is capable of the infinite. But we must also insist that the infinite is the generator of such condescension. The encounter of God and humanity does not flow from human thirst, human questions, human desires or feelings. God discloses. *Sola Scriptura.*

Two of my pastorates were in New York City and nearby New Jersey in congregations serving neighborhoods of incredible diversity. On Sunday mornings, with little Lutheran ethnic base from which to draw, the only thing we had in common is that we were all washed in the water of Baptism, fed at the altar where we receive the body and blood of Christ. We paid common attention to the witness of Scripture, and reached out together. People in kimonos, dashikis, turbans, leisure suits, and shirts with little alligators on them know each other as brothers and sisters in Christ. We have not been gathered by lowest-common-denominator liturgies, human ideologies, ethnic bonds, or church growth principles of homogenous unity. In Word and Sacraments, people have heard the invitation of a gracious God, and they have become bearers of that invitation to the neighborhood around them. As long as the center of *sola Scriptura* holds, and that evangelical heart beats, everything else about such gatherings can be strange, fragile, jarring, and yet remain intact.

Which is to say that the only church growth principle that has theological integrity is *sola Scriptura*.

"Here." The Church's activism in the world, and its ministries of mercy and service, will flow out of its gatherings around Word and Sacraments. They will be offered as signs of the Kingdom, activations of God's presence, not substitutes for it. I am an activist, and have been for the quarter century of my ministry. Too many people seem to think that one must be either an activist or a confessional Lutheran; obsessed either by liturgical precision or by evangelism; holding primary allegiance either to the Word or to the Sacraments—as if they were not the same thing! *Sola Scriptura* unites these polarities and others, not in some bland unifying abstraction, but in the dying and rising Christ.

One of the greatest joys of my ministry came during a Bible study with leaders from a variety of community organizations based in local congregations. From Newark, the Bronx, Paterson, suburban Long Island and New Jersey, Harlem and Union City they came: middle-class and poor; African American, Hispanic, and Caucasian; Protestant and Catholic. We studied together the story in Mark's Gospel of the paralytic let down from the roof to be healed by Jesus. We looked at signs of paralysis and healing in our own lives, neighborhoods, churches. These dear people were hungry and thirsty for the Word. Our activism was anchored in the Christ of the Gospels, in whom the ultimate victory over the paralysis of sin and death has already been accomplished by the cross and the empty tomb. We were able to see our activity— some of it controversial— in the light of *sola Scriptura* as signs of the Kingdom, as service to our neighbor, as efforts toward proximate justice in a fallen world, as activity that must be accountable to God's

word and open to extending and receiving forgiveness. *Sola Scriptura* sees activism for social justice as extending the activity of the Church into the middle of the world in which the incarnate Christ died, and in which he is even now present—the world of doubt and struggle where the mass of unchurched people can be touched by the love and concern of the people of God.
   Hic!

(*Lutheran Forum*, Reformation, 1989)

Chapter 15
The Faithful Community

> With extended arms true faith joyfully embraces the Son of God, who was given into death for it, and says, "My Beloved is mine, and I am His" ... therefore this "for me" or "for us" constitutes true faith and differentiates this faith from every other faith which merely hears the facts of history. (*What Luther Says: An Anthology*, vol. 1 [Concordia, 1959], p. 470).
>
> Faith is a mode of life ... all life becomes a hearing, a listening for permission to go on; faith is this listening— to the Gospel. (Eric Gritsch, *Fortress Introduction to Lutheranism* [Fortress, 1994], p. 41)

WAITING

Waiting.

Her name is Victoria. The doctors called it a "secondary viral infection." That means they did not know why she had gone into a coma. They did not know what to do anymore. They were just waiting. Each day the family waited. Mother and father waited in her room, talking to her, singing to her, bathing her in sounds of love and familial voices. Each day they came and gave themselves to Victoria. Her four brothers and sisters also waited. They visited and made her tapes of their voices, pleading with her to wake up, singing songs they had learned in Vacation Church School, taking turns pouring their hopes into the microphone. And Victoria's community of faith, the members of her church, waited also. The cards, the meals for the children at home, the prayers flowed continually. Yet sixteen-year-old Victoria would not wake up.

Parish ministry is the sum of such waiting. It is after the precision of the chancel rituals, at the narthex door in the back, that the waiting discloses itself to the pastor. Those who shake your hand, who smile or frown, who look you in the eye or avoid your gaze, are involved in the great human dramas of waiting. Waiting for the diagnosis of the lump. Waiting for the routines of quotidian living to make sense. Waiting for a job or a promotion. Waiting for answers. Waiting for grief to recede. Tired of being alone and waiting for a friend or lover. Waiting for the paycheck at the end of the month. Waiting for someone to die. Waiting to stop drinking. Helplessly waiting for a marriage to slowly dissolve. Waiting for a prodigal to come home. Waiting for forgiveness or a chance to say, "I'm sorry." Waiting and straining at the limits sin, death, and the Evil One place on human living. Waiting for a young woman to awake from a coma. Fearing, doubting, yet waiting for the presence of a gracious God.

And the pastor waits alone by the narthex door after they have all gone home. Waiting for those who were not present at liturgy. Waiting for the right Word to hurl against all the waiting of the beloved faithful community. Waiting for signs that the speaking and hearing of parish ministry has been faithful. Waiting with, waiting for, waiting in ... Christ.

The waiting members of Victoria's church needed comfort. They asked their pastor to help them pray together. So we gathered in our home, about fifty of us. At the same time Victoria's family joined hands around her bed.

What to say and do? What sound and content should the pastor and people give to the *viva vox evangelii*? Too often we make of things like this a matter of technique. Too often we raise expectations only to be jolted and disappointed later. It is such a temptation to anchor the faith of the people in the details of a situation, to say "This or that is God's plan," to assert that God is sending signals if thus and such happens. But then, which details are God's plan? Which can be ignored? Faith is not simply about pat answers. Or believing hard enough. Or crossing our fingers in blind optimism. How is a pastor to care for the hope and longing and confusion and faith of the faithful community? What is the meaning of *sola fide* in the midst of the waiting parish?

Asphalt Leah

In the prologue to the Gospel of Luke/Acts, the Third Evangelist speaks of his desire to write an ordered account concerning the life, ministry, and teaching of the dying and rising Christ, and the birth of the Church as the embodiment in the world of Christ's new life.

Two Greek words in the prologue can direct our thinking about "faith alone." The first is *pare'dosan*, as in "just as they were *handed on* to us by those who from the beginning were eyewitnesses..." The Greek *paradosis* means something like "handed on" or "handed down," as in the baptismal dress which makes the round of the generations, or the Yankee sweatshirt worn and handed down from older brother to younger brother to little cousin. This word is central to Luke's concept of continuity. The *Paradosis* is the Tradition from Adam and Eve to Paul and Priscilla and beyond, which sums up the continuity of God's salvation. The great "hand-me-down" of the Gospel moves all our waiting moments into the stream of Biblical faith, into the journey of all of God's faithful people. Others have waited before us. Our baptismal incorporation into this journey of faith gives depth and content to our longing for faith. The tradition of the Gospel is the promise of God to love us unconditionally through Christ. This *Paradosis* is conveyed through the power of the Holy Spirit in Word and Sacraments. The Church is the Community gathered by and around the Gospel.

The second word is *aspha'leian,* as in "that you may know the truth (or "have *assurance*") concerning the things of which you have been instructed." It names what we are waiting for in faith. *Asphalia* doesn't mean clinical proof, or a strangely warmed heart, but something more like assurance or comfort. *Asphalia.* As in that old hymn, "Blessed *asphalia,* Jesus is mine." *Asphalia,* assurance, is based on the great *paradosis* hand-me-down of Lucan continuity, hinging on Christ, reaching back to Abraham, Sarah and Hagar, centering in the womb of Mary, exploding through the power and preaching of the Church in the Spirit to Jerusalem, Samaria, Rome, and even North Joisey. And how can we know that this *asphalia*— in North Jersey dialect, Asphalt Leah— this hand-me-down will fit Victoria, her family, the faithful community gathered in our home for prayer? Such *asphalia,* such faith, is the work of the Holy Spirit, anchoring us in the presence and promises of a gracious God. *Asphalia* is the total dependence of the believer— not on the events of the proximate moment, rational understanding, correct prayer, pat answers, imminent healing, or anything else but this: that the dying and rising Christ lives for us eternally and is with us in every waiting moment. Romans 8— "Nothing can separate us from the love of Christ"— is not about coping, but of turning all things into praise of God. Asphalt Leah.

> "Victoria, I anoint you with oil in the Name of the Father, and of the Son, and of the Holy Spirit."

So we were gathered in our living room to pray for Victoria. It was for the pastor to link the faithful community with the *paradosis.* It was not my words alone that were called for, but God's promises. Not just my hope to be articulated, but the hope of the waiting people of God through the ages. Not just my *asphalia* to be shared, but the Church's reminders of the surety of Baptism. We made our own prayers, making our hearts' desires known before the throne of Grace. Then I referred to the rite of "Laying On of Hands and Anointing the Sick" from the *Occasional Services.* I placed oil before us, a sign and symbol like the oil of Baptism that the promises and love of God are not ethereal but carnal, earthy, touching. I read the Scriptural instructions of Jesus to the disciples to touch and heal. This oil, I said, will be used to make the sign of the cross on Victoria's head, a cruciform tracing like she received in Baptism. I will do it at ten in the morning. Wherever you are in the world at that moment, stop and pray with us.

And so I anointed, and so the faithful community was present, as well as the *asphalia* of the Church through the ages in the Word always made flesh, present, human and touching. Our faith is anchored in Jesus, who is God's unconditional acceptance of us and of all our waiting moments.

Well, Victoria began coming out of the coma the day of her anointing. There had been several weeks of waiting. We know that not every answer to prayer comes as it did for Victoria. Some never wake from their sleep, and there will be that moment for each of us when we will no longer wake up in this life of waiting. That is all in the hands of God. Yet in her Baptism the only death Victoria ever had to fear was behind her. Asphalt Leah.

THE RHYTHM OF THE FAITHFUL COMMUNITY

Luther's Reformation began as a crisis in pastoral care. It was animated by a concern that humans not seek to escape from confrontations with sin and death. In facing them we are confronted with the dying and rising Christ, so that even the confession of sin becomes not a condition but a consequence of God's free grace. All of parish ministry becomes a midrash on this text: "God was in Christ, reconciling sinners to Himself." The life of the parish is centered in the Word and the Sacraments because it is through them, in the power of the Holy Spirit, that a parish remains in continual existential dialogue with the presence of Jesus in the "hand-me-down" of the Gospel. That dialogue is called faith. It involves a continual breaking-down and a continual building-up. Parish ministry of Word and Sacraments takes people where they are waiting and builds them up when they are broken down and rid of the last of the idolatrous rationalizations that would place conditions on God's free grace through Christ. Or it takes people where they are waiting in puffed-up self-righteousness and breaks them down to where the Spirit can enter and they can see Christ alone. In liturgy, Eucharist, Baptism, proclamation of the Gospel, counseling, Bible study, individual and corporate works of mercy, it is the breaking-down by the Law and the building-up by the Gospel that lies at the heart of the faithful community.

And those who have grasped the truth of the Gospel have the freedom to be for the world. Faith alone is also the core of the faithful community's ministries for justice, its efforts to be present in the midst of this world's suffering and waiting, to invite others to full participation in the faithful community, to be as Christ to all the Victorias of the wider community. We are free for servanthood and evangelism because in living faith we have been grasped by a gracious God. These ministries are not conditions for salvation, nor our works of supererogation. The freedom to give ourselves up before God through the dying and rising Christ becomes the freedom to be given up for the life of the world. By faith alone the faithful community becomes the world's Asphalt Leah.

Martin Luther caught the dynamic of faith alone: "A Christian is a perfectly free lord of all, subject to none ... A Christian is a perfectly dutiful servant of all, subject to all" (LW, vol. 31, p. 344).

To Confess the Faith

There is always the waiting. He is a large, well dressed man with a friendly smile and a kind of formal dignity. His voice was warm and his handshake firm when I met him for the first time. "I am her father," he said in a deep voice, holding my hand. "She asked to see you, but I don't know if she will recognize you now. I can't get her to eat or to open her eyes. I'm afraid my baby's dying, pastor."

I looked down at the bed, at the familiar face of a pretty brown woman of about thirty, her frame now so thin from her long battle with AIDS, transmitted through her husband's intravenous drug use. Her breathing was ragged, her eyes closed.

We had first met when I was her teacher in a Diakonia class. She was a leader of her Lutheran church. She was one of those few people who hold struggling faithful communities together. She sang in the choir, led the Sunday School, taught Bible classes, visited the sick, chaired the Church Council. She was an earthy, fun-loving person and her piety was natural. Her love of her Lord was infectious and touched all those around her. Her struggle with her illness was also a struggle of faith, and she had shared much of it with me.

Her father and I tried to wake her but we could not. So I recited some Bible passages and he, in his deep, strong voice, recited them with me. It is good to know pieces of the *Paradosis* by heart. Then he cried, walked over to a chair and sat down. And then she woke up. She was too weak to speak, but she smiled up at both of us. She kept nodding her head toward something behind me and then I noticed that she was gesturing toward my Communion set. I communed her with the tiniest bit of the wafer, in which sacrament she was again embraced by her gracious God. I gave her a blessing, then a kiss, telling her that her Savior loved her and was waiting. I whispered my own love, then sat down and held her hand.

"I would like to give you a gift," her father said from his chair in the corner. He told me that he memorized inspirational poems and certain parts of the Bible, and then gave dramatic renditions of them. He said he would share a poem with me if I liked. His daughter tried to sit up to listen. He rose to his full height and in a deep voice he gave an emotional rendition of a poem entitled "Heaven's Grocery Store." He gestured, his voice rising and falling dramatically, consumed by his poem, and oblivious to the curious ones in the hall who stopped by the door to listen. The poem described in a simple way the spiritual gifts of faith, prayer, grace, and salvation. When he was finished he wiped his brow, sat down, and smiled at us.

It was certainly a gift he had given me, an unforgettable gift from the heart, a thank-you for caring about his daughter. It was also a father's way of telling his daughter that death was not the end, that heaven awaited her. With a nod of her head toward a box holding bread and wine a dying child of God confessed her faith. With the rendition of a poem, a heartsick father confessed his faith. Both of them, in a room of imminent death, echoed the Apostolic faith of the ages. In a hospital room in Bayonne, New Jersey, two children of God made the church's confession their own. They had nothing in this world except Christ and trust in His promises. Asphalt Leah.

Together each week the faithful community speaks its *Credo* and confesses the faith in the Triune God. Thus anchored in the faith of the ages we are prepared to confess the Faith in many ways large and small in this waiting world. Faith Alone. Until we finally see what we have believed.

(*Lutheran Forum*, Pentecost, 1989)

Chapter 16
The Disciplined Community: Law, Gospel and the *Solus Christus*

> "I'm Father Finn—from Purrgatory," he said in a hearty voice. He had a large red face, a stiff brush of gray hair and was blind in one eye, but the good eye, blue and clear, was focused sharply on Asbury. There was a grease spot on his vest. "So you want to talk to a priest?" he said. "Very wise. None of us knows the hour Our Blessed Lord may call us." Then he cocked his good eye up at Asbury's mother and said, "Thank you, you may leave us now."
> (from "The Enduring Chill," by Flannery O'Connor, in a short-story anthology entitled *The Substance of Things Hoped For*, edited by John B. Breslin [Doubleday, Garden City, N.Y., 1987], p.77.)

Pinned Beneath the Terrible Eye

Flannery O'Connor's Asbury Porter Fox lives in a world of aesthetic delusions, anxious self-absorption and self-scrutiny. He is a latter-day Romantic who, having failed Art, yearns for Death and the final comfort of an intellectual conversation with a priest-of-the-world who is certainly not the numismatic retired Methodist minister suggested by his mother. As he lies on his fevered deathbed he conjures up the figure of an intellectual and worldly Jesuit in his funeral procession. His mother summons the local Catholic priest.

Asbury Porter Fox is the perfect parabolic figure of anthropocentric religion, today's fascination with subjective "spirituality," faith as part of a regimen of growth and human potential. In O'Connor's story, even death is manipulated to serve Asbury's narcissistic delusions. His is a religion without Law and therefore without Gospel. What Asbury Porter Fox gets is Father Finn-from-Purrgatory, the Law incarnate. He appears as a stubborn, anachronistic intruder who demolishes Asbury's illusions and carefully constructed détente with religion.

> "This place is incredibly dreary. There's no one here an intelligent person can talk to. I wonder what you think of Joyce, Father."
> "I haven't met him. Now. Do you say your morning and night prayers?"

> "The artist prays by creating," Asbury ventured.
> "Not enough!" snapped the priest. "If you do not pray daily, you are neglecting your immortal soul. Do you know your catechism?"
> "Certainly not," Asbury murmured.
> "Who made you?" the priest asked in a martial tone.
> "Different people believe different things about that," Asbury said.
> "God made you," the priest said shortly. "Who is God?"
> "God is an idea created by man," Asbury said, feeling that he was getting into stride, that two could play at this.
> "God is a spirit infinitely perfect," the priest said. "You are a very ignorant boy. Why did God make you?"
> "God didn't...."
> "God made you to know Him, to love Him, to serve Him in this world and to be happy with Him in the next!" the old priest said in a battering voice.
> (pp. 78-79)

The scene continues, the priest an implacable, relentless icon of the Law; the boy steeped in languorous self-deception coming to chilling self-awakening. Their exchange concludes this way:

> "Are you so ignorant you have never heard of the Holy Ghost?" the priest asked.
> "Certainly I have heard of the Holy Ghost," Asbury said furiously, "and the Holy Ghost is the last thing I'm looking for!"
> "And he may be the last thing you get," the priest said, his one fierce eye inflamed. "Do you want to be deprived of God for all eternity? Do you want to suffer the most terrible pain, greater than fire, the pain of loss? Do you want to suffer the pain of loss for all eternity?"
> Asbury moved his arms and legs helplessly as if he were pinned to the bed by a terrible eye. (p.79)

Like Father Finn, the evangelical parish is the "terrible eye" of God in the world, the community which relentlessly, implacably, anachronistically, faithfully, lovingly speaks and acts the Word of God. In the midst of a humanity by nature at enmity with God, the parish speaks and acts Law and Gospel in precise tension.

"For all have sinned, and fall short of the glory of God."
"The soul that sins shall die."
"For God so loved the world...."

CATARACTS IN THE TERRIBLE EYE

Begin with the Law. Whether two uses or three, let's not quibble. The Law is a Curb, a Rule, but especially a Mirror. In my catechumenate in an LC-MS congregation, we learned that the Law and the Gospel are an

SOS from God. The Law Shows us Our Sin. The Gospel Shows us Our Savior. The object of the Law is sinful, dying humanity. The object of the Gospel is the Risen Christ. The effect of the Law is to condemn, ultimately to kill. The effect of the Gospel is to make alive, to save. For the faithful parish these are not just theological propositions, but a way of being in the world, of teaching, counseling, praying, acting, confronting, consoling, disciplining, seeking justice. The parish is a collective incarnation in the world of the Word of God, committed to the truth, committed to the Holy Spirit's work of breaking down and building up so that Christ is present in each believer's heart. In sum, the parish is the community of Law and Gospel when it is the community of Word and Sacraments. Like the despised intruder at Prospero's party in "The Masque of the Red Death," nobody wants to hear or face the truth of human mortality in our death-denying culture. A faithful parish ought to be God's terrible eye on the world, but in the current situation, it is all too often either nearsighted, blind, or closed. The terrible eye of the parish, shining God's truth in a rebellious world, is being covered with cataracts.

When the Church buys into the pervasive contemporary medical model, it becomes another social service agency, treating symptoms, feeding dependency, diagnosing the ills of the other, and applying the approved remedy. Therapy replaces the forgiveness of sins. We serve up a pseudo-Gospel which is no Gospel at all apart from the work of the Law. Consequently, our efforts serve only to help the anxious and hurting Asburys of this world to adjust to their neuroses and come to terms with their anomie. Communally, the medical model—"ghetto dysfunction," in one tawdry example from urban planners' lingo—fosters abject dependence on the programs of strangers. But it is both Law and Gospel that enable the Church to speak the words of Jesus: "Stand up, take your mat and walk."

And no wonder the parishes have shown a growing affinity with the medical model that dominates our world. Seminarians are seduced in the course of their education into participation in the anxious self-scrutiny of the times. Some graduate with the notion that our parishes are steps in "career development;" are instruments of ideological, social and political agendas. These new pastors are equipped with Myers-Briggs and CPE handles to make sense of the reality they confront, ready to "affirm" everything that moves. According to the medical model we are the final agents of the world's salvation and our own, the measure of all things. Is it any wonder that when pastors and parishes take the Word of God seriously, proclaiming God's Law and Gospel with passion and conviction, they often seem like unenlightened, antediluvian Father Finn-from-Purrgatory barging into Asbury's playpen of the self?

Please hear me clearly. I am not bashing CPE, Myers-Briggs, or other insights from the disciplines of psychology and sociology. I am grateful for such insights. I am one hundred percent in favor of the ideals of an "inclusive" church and have spent my entire ministry in such situations. I applaud the social service efforts of the Church and its agencies. The parishes I have served were heavily involved in housing and feeding the homeless, as well as serving developmentally disabled children. I believe that advocacy for and solidarity with the poor are at the heart of the public articulation and demonstration of Law and Gospel. Much of the energy of my ministry goes toward building grassroots power organizations in which people take responsibility for their communities and negotiate and confront the institutions of power in their lives "from the bottom up".

Moreover, I am certainly not advocating that pastors stop counseling their people. My own office overflows with children of God whose lives are being torn apart. What I *am* saying is this: the heart of the parish community gathered around Word and Sacraments is to be the "terrible eye" of God in the world, the agent of Law and Gospel. Seminaries must instruct and form stewards of the mysteries of God, not another species of "helpers." It all depends on how we see Asbury lying in his bed. The ministry of a faithful parish will help him to die so that he might live.

Parish Practice in the Disciplined Community

What difference would it make in the life of a parish if the Law were emphasized at the expense of the Gospel? Religion would deteriorate into a minefield of rules. The Church would become judgmental and unrealistic. Those already laden with guilt, convicted by the Law, would be driven to despair or indifference toward their relationships to Christ and the Church. The religious life would ultimately center on human striving, and notions of salvation would hinge on one's success in Lawful endeavors. Such religion would encourage self-righteousness, monitoring the behavior of its people. A parish under the hegemony of the Law would not take liturgy or sacraments seriously. Preaching would become only paraenesis. No community can endure being pinned under the terrible eye of Father Finn forever.

What difference would it make in the life of a parish if the Gospel were emphasized at the expense of the Law? The Church would ultimately end by blessing the rationalizations of unregenerate life. In my experience people often come to the pastor to give their strivings a passing grade. Without the Law there is no awareness of sin, and ultimately no need of a Savior. A parish under the hegemony of a Gospel without Law would also fail to take liturgy and sacraments seriously. Without the Law the Christian life is about the individual only, about feeling good about the self. I have read too many books on Christian "caregiving" that immerse the reader in techniques of "affirmation" without any mention of prayer, liturgy or the sacraments. There is no necessary pathway between the pastor's office, the hospital bed, the neighborhood, and the community gathered to hear and enact the Law and Gospel in Word and Sacraments. No community can long endure wallowing in its own delusions in the absence of the terrible eye of Father Finn.

By way of illustration, let me give several examples of Law and Gospel tension in parish practice.

1. Marital Problems

Although I often make referrals to other counselors, psychologists, social workers, and pastors, marriage counseling is one pastoral ministry I often find myself doing. But I do not switch vocational identities when I counsel. I am still a pastor, and what I have to offer is not only therapy, but the terrible eye. I am a minister of the Word and Sacraments. So we make this covenant at the beginning of our work together: The couple must be present at the liturgy on Sunday morning. Our work together includes confession and absolution, the proclamation of Law and Gospel, remembrance of Baptism, a place at the table of the church's Family Meal, the communal life of the parish. This is the context in which we listen to one another on Monday night. The actual counseling session may not include much "God talk" at all. But the Holy Spirit, present through the Means of Grace, is at work breaking down and building up. If a couple has not been present at liturgy on Sunday morning then I will not counsel on Monday evening. The breakdown of a marriage is a devastating time in people's lives. It deserves the full witness of the Church. Whether by God's grace the marriage can be saved, or whether the heartbreak of divorce occurs, the ministry of Word and Sacrament provides the framework for forgiveness and new beginnings in the God of unconditional grace.

2. Absence from Worship

One of the most difficult areas of pastoral care for me is how to respond to members who are frequently absent from the liturgy. I recently wrote the following in our parish newsletter:

> ...do you dread a call from me because you have to make up excuses about why you haven't been around at church? Well, it may surprise you to know that I don't enjoy making those calls anymore than you enjoy receiving them. In fact, I can't stand it. I have such an aversion to them that I don't do them very often. If you haven't been around the church much, you may have realized that I have not been around to bug you very much either.
>
> I am not interested in getting excuses like some attendance officer... we don't want to put the obligation of being the Church on anybody. The Church is a group of people who love the Lord and want to serve and worship God. If people don't want to be a part of the Church why should we go around trying to make them feel guilty about it? People are free to opt out of the community whenever they choose.
>
> Yet we are also aware that without the Church it is impossible to maintain a faith in and relationship to Jesus Christ... So, how should we respond to your absence? Shall we love you and nag you so that you get sick of us and mad at us? Or shall we love you and leave you alone so that you feel abandoned by us and think that we don't care?...

There is no new pastoral wisdom in the above, except to illustrate that the faithful discernment of Law and Gospel is about real people in real congregations. A parish faithful to God's Law will make some response to the spiritual problems of its members. The alternative, under the guise of acceptance and avoidance of legalism, is to say "The hell with you, it does not matter to us or to God whether or not you have a relationship with your Savior."

3. Substance Abuse and Addiction Issues

The Church is the place where people go when there is nowhere else. But the response of the Church to overwhelming human need, its social service and justice ministries, must include the full Law and Gospel witness of the Church's revelation from God. This witness must be more than occasional charity, deeper than cursory empathy. Consider the following encounter, one with which any pastor would be familiar:

> Oh no, I thought, when I saw him standing outside the church. I was just checking the mail after a ten-hour drive with my wife and three small, very tired children— including over an hour stranded on the George Washington Bridge within three miles of our home.
>
> He said, "I just need a little of your time. I'm an alcoholic and I am killing myself."
>
> And then he started crying. He told me he had been a cop for ten years, and sober for maybe two of them. "And then I saw my son again, and I'm drinking worse than ever. I don't want to die."

"That's a start," I mumbled. He wanted a handout. I was tempted to give the Law a rest, give him something and let him go. I told him to get in my car, and I took him to a hospital where he could dry out. Thinking about the pizza I was supposed to pick up for my road-weary family, I asked him to tell me his story as we drove.

A familiar tale. His drinking had cost him his family, his job, and then his apartment. He had been sleeping in the weeds along the Jersey Turnpike for the past five nights. He looked, sounded, and smelled like death.

I said: "God's grace and resources are boundless. Mine are not. Get into an AA program and stick with it. I'll come visit you in the hospital, and I'll hang in there with you when it gets tough. But if you don't mean it, then pass out by someone else's church. I won't watch you kill yourself."

I got him admitted. He cried some more, hugged me and apologized repeatedly. I prayed with him and said I would see him on the other side of the DT's. When I went back to the hospital he had checked himself out, and I never saw him again. His name is Jim.

There is an insight into the Law of God that Jim taught me. Through the Law God gives us not what we want, but what we need. Jimmy wanted: a bottle, a handout, some sympathy, a place to flop, maybe even the assurance that God thought well of him. Jimmy needed: to get sober and stay sober, to "bottom out," to see and understand the deathward downward spiral of his addiction, to come to terms with the First Commandment.

Social ministry must be a part of the handout to those in need. Food for the hungry, shelter for the homeless, are at the heart of the Church's Gospel outreach in the Name of Jesus. But the Law empowers the Church to give a full response, to get at the source of individual or systemic pain and suffering, to confront causes of oppression and pathology in the Name of Jesus. Too often the Church in society blandly blesses the status quo, offering invocations at flag poles but never daring to pin the individual and communal principalities and powers beneath the terrible eye of Law and Gospel.

4. Support Groups

There is enormous power and wisdom in the experiences and insights of our people. I believe that the parish is holy space for people to hear and help one another, to bear one another's burdens. A recent event has given me insight into the power which the context provided by Law and Gospel, Word and Sacrament can offer such gatherings.

A workshop was sponsored by our parish social ministry committee on the issue of bereavement. The invitation to meet for group discussion and support was accepted by about twenty-five grieving people, about half from the congregation and half from the neighborhood. Much pain was shared, from a recent suicide to the death of children. Strategies for coping, grief experiences, funeral customs were all shared. The conversation was animated and touching. We were far from "grief management" or the monitoring of prescriptive "grief stages."

Grief and mourning, however, are not the same process. Certainly some help was being given in the grief process, which is the mourner's internal response to loss. But a ministry of Law and Gospel is especially helpful in the process of mourning— the shared social response to loss, the meaning of such things to people of faith. Those grieving are pinned beneath the terrible eye. Confrontation with death is the incarnation of the Law. One feels Isaiah's truth in the bone: "All people are grass.... The grass withers, the flower fades, when the breath of the Lord blows upon it." The most vital and compelling moments in our bereavement workshop were moments of prayer; spiritual expressions of doubt, anger and faith; a recalling of the promises of God embedded in the funeral liturgy. The invitation to worship on Sunday morning was gratefully received as a part of the mourning process, as a movement toward the meaning of death and through it to the God who raised Jesus from the dead.

A final word to pastors, each in our own way fitted by ordination with the terrible eye of Father Finn, as we strive to image in our ministry the striving of our respective parishes to see and be as Christ. In these latter days it has been given to us to preach; to baptize; to forgive; to teach; to make Eucharist; to be stewards of the dynamic tension between Law and Gospel. The ordained ministry is not a profession, a job, a function. It is a vocation: to be an *eikon Christi*. Through us and the likes of Father Finn, sinful men and women though we be, it is Christ himself who pins Asbury and all dying humanity beneath the terrible eye, inviting them home.

(*Lutheran Forum*, Lent, 1991)

Chapter 17
Confraternities of Grace: Small Group Ministry

> I myself am hell
> nobody's here-
> only skunks, that search
> in the moonlight for a bite to eat.
> They march on their soles up Main Street:
> white stripes, moonstruck eyes' red fire
> under the chalk-dry and spar spire
> of the Trinitarian Church....
>
> Robert Lowell, from "Skunk Hour" in *Selected Poems*
> (Farrar, Strauss and Giroux, 1976)

Skunk Hour

Skunk hour. I remember the morning after one of the worst of the many snowstorms that besieged New York City in 1994 I was scheduled to lead worship at one of our congregations in the Bronx. I was able to make my way to the church but I did not think many members would show up. I was right. But those who did were no surprise. I had to literally haul several elderly widows over the urban stalagmites deposited by the snow in order for them to enter the church. But in my experience it has always been the widows who were utterly dependable, who never missed a Sunday. Their dogged determination is mirrored in Lowell's poem. In the hour when no one else is around, the skunk determined to survive forages for food by the Trinitarian Church and will not scare!

The evangelist Luke brings the widows into view. Jesus looks with compassion on the grieving widow at Nain. Anna, widowed and attending to the temple for many years, is given a visitation of the Messiah. The dignity and spiritual wisdom of the elderly living alone—single or widowed—is a strong and insistent scriptural theme.

Someone asked a priest who had been around a long time in urban New Jersey what the difference was between churchgoing twenty years ago and today. He answered with two words: "Air conditioning." What he was trying to talk about was what he perceived as a loss of community. When the bells rang before Mass twenty years ago he could imagine the neighborhood on its way to worship. He could see people walking, greeting one another on porch and stoop, combining in a flow toward the church. Today, he says, not totally facetiously, people leave their air-conditioned homes, enter air-conditioned cars, enter an air-conditioned church and return home again without having to come into contact with anyone.

Our atomized world is bereft of community. In the words of the Robert Lowell poem, "I myself am hell—nobody's here." There is much talk these days about small-group ministry as one way to help people encounter one another and the Church around their interests, needs, and hunger for mutual support. It is remembered that the new communities of the Risen Lord met initially in homes, forming human-sized fellowships around the teaching of the Apostles, prayer, mutual burden-bearing, and the Meal. In these communities walls of separation were sundered and people encountered one another in the light of Christ. The Church does not have to look far for models of such confraternities of grace, nor invent them from scratch. The Church has only to gaze down Main Street, "under the chalk-dry spar spire of the Trinitarian Church" at Skunk Hour, the hour of worship when the community of widows faithfully and stolidly are nourished in mutual encounter with the Risen Christ and the hope embodied in such encounters, "and will not scare."

SOME MARKS OF COMMUNAL FRIENDSHIP

> But I have called you friends, because I have made known to you everything that I have heard from my Father....I am giving you these commands so that you may love one another. (John 15:15b & 17)

Support groups in the church must go beyond self-help faddishness. These are some of the marks of Christian communal friendship we can see in the families of Annas and Simeons who form the backbone of our churches.

The community of the widows, widowers, and single elderly folks is centered in Word and Sacraments.

One sometimes hears the joke that the overwhelming presence of the elderly in churches has made those institutions into "God's waiting room."

If it is true that too many of our congregations are graying at an alarming rate as younger people opt out in this secular age, it is also true that the faithful presence at the Church's liturgy of the communities of the widows and older single people is the backbone of the Church's multi-generational life. Their lifelong fidelity to the Third Commandment points the way for all support group ministries. It is the presence of Jesus that shapes the life of single older adults in the Church. In every parish I have served it has been the presence of the widows and widowers who have filled the ongoing Bible studies with their presence, wisdom, and curious seeking. They have agitated for new opportunities to enter and explore Scripture together. Such gatherings around the Word have been opportunities to invite and include those newly grieving. This searching of the Scriptures to provide meaning over a lifetime points to lifelong adult catechesis as another mark of support group ministry.

There was a telling moment in a recent ABC special with Peter Jennings that examined the various Church Growth movements in our country. In an interview with the pastor (or CEO) of Willow Creek, a huge and much celebrated megachurch outside Chicago, the reporter asked why there were no crosses or any other traditional church symbols displayed. The pastor replied something like this: "We're very serious about what Christ did on the cross but to capture the essence of Christianity in a single symbol is a little dangerous, we feel." By contrast, the community of the widowed and never-married elderly that I have served understand that all of life is cruciform; that the holy God is present in the midst of the liturgy; that to welcome the stranger does not mean to cover the beauty of the church with linoleum of unregenerate "felt needs;" that the cross is God's way of coming near to save.

The community of the widowed and single elderly practices communal pastoral care.

Every morning around 7:30 the phones would begin to ring in the neighborhoods of the churches I served. It was the community of widows making the fundamental decision not to begin the day alone. They would check on one another, assure one another: "You are not alone." When someone is sick cards, visits, and prayers flow, the shopping gets done, the medicine delivered, the bills paid, and because someone waits there is also the will toward wholeness and health. There are trips together to "the city" for shopping, theater, music. There is the relentless ethos of inclusion, and when another experiences fresh grief, one more phone rings in the early morning neighborhood.

The community of the widowed and single elderly is a network of compassion reaching out beyond itself.

It has included mobilizing the homebound. In this confraternity of grace no one's gifts are overlooked. These homebound folks organized a prayer chain and undergirded the life of the church's *diakonia* with daily prayer for specific people and situations. Out of their prayers emerged clothing and food for the children of God for whom they prayed. I remember Helen Miller in Richmond, Virginia, who would make the stew each Friday for the Friday night dinner for the homeless in the church basement. When I would pick up the stew on Friday afternoon Helen and I would also share in the Family Meal of the Church, thereby linking all of our eating and drinking and ministry of service to the Eucharistic presence of Jesus.

The community of the widowed and single elderly serves as the communal memory of the parish.

There are those astounding moments of grace when one of the widows tells a story of the early days of the congregation. It may be at coffee hour, in conversation with the homebound, during a Sunday School lesson, or a Bible class. We find ourselves hearing about how, in a former day, the parish worshiped in the local funeral parlor, or how the few members went door to door to recruit the first Sunday School class, or how an immigrant family found in the church a place to make a stand in the new world. The first job, the first apartment, the first friends, the first community was given them in the company of the Church. The community of widows knows not only the stories of Jesus, but also the stories of their corner of the Body of Christ. We learn once again that in a hard time our forebears wanted beauty, a touch of transcendence in their hardscrabble world, sacred space consecrated in the midst of the teeming daily struggle.

Skunk Hour. In our mission to this secular culture, in attempts to share the community of Christ in an atomized and alienated world, we can learn much from the community of the widowed and single elderly. Their focal point, their frame of reference is the Church, built with their sweat and that of their kin, whose pews and windows bear their family names, and in which they sat wide-eyed as children beholding the shapes and forms in which their congregation conveyed the Mystery; in which, now, at the altar, they share their weekly Family Meal, remembering together the death and resurrection of another Loved One.

(*Lutheran Forum*, Pentecost, 1995)

Chapter 18
Family Values

Stephanie

Stephanie, the homeless evangelist of Bainbridge Avenue in the Bronx, died alone in a subway car. During the first week of Advent my wife, Janet, and I sat in the quiet sanctuary of Epiphany Lutheran Church for Stephanie's memorial service, watching the flickering first candle on the traditional wreath. Around us were many of Stephanie's companions in her life's sometimes tortured journey.

She was a regular participant of St. Stephen's Meals at Epiphany Lutheran Church in the Bronx and worshipped there often. Like many of the homeless and poor in the neighborhood Stephanie was not just a recipient of the church's ministry of compassion, but also a church member with her own ministry. Epiphany offers community along with compassion, the Bread of Life along with daily bread. My wife's ministry through Lutheran Social Services has allowed her to share in the ministry of Epiphany. Stephanie was close to Janet's heart.

Pastor Elise Brown greeted the gathered flock, a mixture of congregation members and neighbors, many of them homeless, most of them poor, many of them addicted, others afflicted with a variety of illnesses of body and mind. She gathered us together in the name of Jesus and lifted up Stephanie as one who had shared Jesus with everyone who touched her life. It was Stephanie who took the new Bibles meant for the Sunday School children and passed them out to the homeless and poor along Bainbridge Avenue. Pastor Brown invited other remembrances from the gathered children of God. It was in the midst of this testimony that I was filled with Advent longing and gratitude for the presence of Jesus in churches like Epiphany.

In the testimony that followed I understood that Epiphany was not only a congregation for the poor, but also a congregation of the poor. Here was public sanctuary for the laments and consolations of the community. People spoke about times that Stephanie had prayed for them, encouraged them in trouble and tragedy, and always testified to the power and love of Jesus. One young lady, so strung out and angry she could hardly stand still, read the prayer from the *Lutheran Book of Worship* for those who are addicted. A man sitting in the front row, who had at times been cruel to Stephanie, cried out his feelings of loss and regret. A woman who had recently been homeless testified to the death and resurrection of Jesus and sang a beautiful spiritual. The refrain in each of the remembrances was the same: Stephanie had been a friend of the poor and lonely, and a lover and evangelist of Jesus.

We gave her up to Jesus in the commendation, prayerfully sending this homeless person to her room in God's house of many rooms, where a place had been prepared for her from the moment of her Baptism.

Stephanie's memorial service was not some seasonal made-for-TV "feel-good" holiday story. The cadence of the liturgy was touched by the chaos of broken lives, by anger and rambling incoherence. Many who remembered Stephanie would themselves leave the church remembered by no one, with no place to go, at the edge of survival.

But this is yet a story told in the presence of Jesus, who entered into human existence as one "who did not regard equality with God as something to be exploited, but emptied himself and became obedient to the point of death—even death on a cross." We are all characters in the story of human lives awaiting transformation by the coming of Jesus, the Word made flesh. In the incarnate presence of Jesus ours is also a family story. The parish is a place that creates for everyone space to belong, to be part of a family in Christ. Unfortunately, so often the "family" rhetoric which the church uses leaves out many people like Stephanie: people who have chosen singleness and celibacy; the homeless; the widowed and divorced; single parents; gays and lesbians.

Stephanie's funeral, attended by so many children of God whose only experience of family was in this remarkable parish, was a perfect example of family values as seen through the eyes of Jesus.

AUNT LUCIA AND UNCLE GILBERT

I am the oldest of five children. Every time another sibling was born, I would be sent to stay with Aunt Lou and Uncle Gilbert, my mother's aunt and uncle respectively. They were a part of our family, present at every Christmas and Easter get-together, at graduations and birthdays, summer vacations and other occasions for gatherings of the clan. Aunt Lou helped put me through seminary. Uncle Gilbert struggled all his life with schizophrenia. He had an unusually gifted mind, but things worked out in a way that meant he had to perform labor that was more manual than mental for his daily bread. He was an utterly faithful, loyal man. For decades he arose before dawn, traveled miles to work at U.S. Steel on the south side of Chicago, performed his duties, and returned home to his sister Lou. He never missed church on Sunday. He loved us children, was loyal to us, took an interest in us, looked out for us, was proud of us. He did not have to put his faithful commitment to us in many words: it was there in his eyes and face, in his manner and actions.

Aunt Lou was one of the first women to be promoted to executive level, as a vice-president of a department store chain in Chicago. She traveled and enjoyed the company of close friends in many places. She also never missed a Sunday in church, and supported the parish's ministry as a volunteer in many ways. Her most precious ministry, her family values were lifted up at the funeral for Uncle Gilbert. Pastor Dean Lueking said this: "I have in my mind some words that Gilbert will be speaking. That time will be in the Day of the Resurrection, when God will call us all from our graves and we shall stand before him. Gilbert will not have a long speech to make. But when it comes to the time when we shall thank and praise God for the particular gifts He has given us in our time in this life, Gilbert will have something unique to say. I hear him saying: 'I bless God for my sister. More than I could tell you, she has been a ministering angel to me. I have needed order, security, continuity, and quiet love for my life to hold together. My sister has been the channel through which the Creator has answered this need in my life. Many of you thank God for your spouse, for your children and grandchildren, for noteworthy accomplishments, for well-recognized good deeds done. But my special song of thanksgiving is for a sister, Lucia. Together we have enjoyed the vast silences of the northern forests, the interest of new places in the land to which we have traveled, and the peace of a Christian household. With her, I look forward now to the resurrection life forever, with minds free from every impediment, for bodies made new and glorious in Christ.'"

As for Aunt Lou, she is still with us; she has just celebrated her 100th birthday in a Lutheran nursing home, still nourished by her extended family which includes her church.

SINGLE AND UNATTACHED

How many Gilberts and Lous and Stephanies are there in our pews? How are we equipping them for ministry in their daily lives? Did the trajectories of Gilbert's and Lucia's and Stephanie's lives—not to marry, or to have children—ever render them extraneous to the church's relentless rhetoric idealizing "traditional" families? Can they hear themselves included when the church talks about being a "family?" Do we ever explicitly single out the singles— the formerly married as well as the never-married— for inclusion in Jesus' family? The holy grail of the typical congregation's evangelism efforts is often reaching "boomers with kids." When Martin Marty wrote his book *Health and Medicine in the Lutheran Tradition* in 1987 he interviewed Bishop James Crumley, who said that one of the populations that he saw as unaddressed in the contemporary church is the 35% of Lutheran adults who are single. These folks include not only the homeless, the widowed, and the divorced men and women on the economic margins of society, but also the middle-class "respectable outcasts" who are neither parents nor married.

I have often used "family" rhetoric, as parish pastor, as bishop, and as the writer of the pages of this book. I especially treasure the image of the Eucharist as the "Family Meal" of the church. I have in mind the inclusiveness of the new community in Christ in which all people are welcome and valued at the table. But I am not certain I have always understood the limitations of this metaphor, nor the thoughtless ways it has been used or heard. There are judgmental attitudes that single people hear subtly or overtly in the church's informal messages as well as its official preaching. Single people tell me that among them are:

- The assumption that single people are by definition defective—either gay, socially incompetent (if male), or unattractive/unlovable (if female);
- The myth that singles are swinging hedonists with very busy sex lives;
- The belief that singles are irresponsible, immature, and selfish (because of all that disposable income that is presumably spent on the self);
- The notion that all singles pine to be married and couldn't possibly be happy without a spouse or kids (this attitude is also applied to the married but childless);
- The recognition that the unmarried elderly are left out of the church's calculus. My wife was asked by a single elderly person, very poor and vulnerable, if there is any text in the Bible that enjoins the church to care for her. The only biblical admonitions and parish teaching of which she was aware concerned widows and orphans.

Stephanie had a vocation—on the streets of the Bronx and within the household of faith of her congregation. Aunt Lucia had a vocation of care for her brother. Uncle Gilbert had a vocation at U.S. Steel and in his parish and extended family. Do we ever lift up the dignity of these vocations in the life of the "family" of the church?

Family Values

I tried to address the issue of the Church's family values in a 1992 news letter article to the membership of the congregation in New Jersey that I was serving at the time. It was a time when single parenting on the "Murphy

Brown" television show was attacked by Vice President Dan Quayle. "Family Values" became a buzzword for the religious right. Here is what I wrote:

> Since everyone from the presidential and vice-presidential candidates and their wives to Murphy Brown is talking about "family values" these days I thought I would add my two cents' worth. First, I don't know exactly what that phrase means. If it means that in the best of all possible worlds it would be a good thing for a child to grow up in a home where he or she is loved and nurtured by two strong and loving parents I can't think of any rational person who would disagree, including Murphy Brown. But if "family values" becomes political and moral code words for a very restricted and judgmental view of the world, then I have a problem with "family values."
>
> By that narrow definition there are many in our family at Trinity Church who would not be included among those who have so-called family values. And I believe that is nonsense. Some of our members are divorced, widowed, living alone, with friends or extended family, celibate, single by choice or circumstance, childless by choice or circumstance, as well as others who live in the "traditional" family of two parents, 1.5 children, and a canary. Some of our "non-traditional" families cope with hard circumstances not of their own choosing and live courageous and responsible lives. All within the family of Trinity know about forgiveness and new beginnings, and the fundamental dignity of each human vocation. Instead of talking about "family values" I would rather talk about "valuing families" of whatever circumstance and/or choice (including those who are single), supporting them, cherishing them, and helping to share with them the spiritual resources for loving and caring for those with whom they share their lives. When I refer to Trinity as a Family of Jesus, and the Eucharist as our Family Meal, I do so in the broadest possible sense, including in our love and companionship all humanity of whatever background or particular living.
>
> We are all together a family, not by our choice and doing, but through the washing of Baptism and the call of the Holy Spirit to be joined to the Body of Christ. In Baptism and the Family Meal of the Eucharist, in the love of Christ, we belong to one another at Trinity. And each of us, in our own way, reaches out to one another in Christ's family here at Trinity. Together, through our ministries of love and compassion, we reach out beyond ourselves, continually inviting our neighbors into the intimacy of our church family.
>
> Love one another, as Christ has first loved you.
>
> Bear one another's burdens, and so fulfill the law of Christ.

These are our family values!

PART FOUR
"TO HEAR HIS WORD AND SHARE IN HIS SUPPER...."

Chapter 19
Eating and Drinking among the Tombstones

Chang Lee survived two brutal wars in his mother country, Korea. He lived through the dangers posed by Japanese bombs, Chinese howitzers, North Korean minefields, and American carbines. But he did not survive an encounter with a mugger in the hallway of his own apartment in his adopted country. He was brutally stabbed and ended his earthly journey at the age of 80.

Chang Lee's family are members of Atonement Lutheran Church in Jackson Heights, Queens. His son is one of the leaders of the large Korean group that participates fully in the life of the multi-ethnic parish. Almost 200 people came to the funeral, including many members from Atonement. Lessons and prayers were offered in English and Korean. The casket was set up like a Shinto shrine, with pictures of the deceased, flowers, and two posters with Korean ideograms. One poster gave biographical details; the other held the 23rd Psalm.

Chang Lee died a Christian. He died a Korean. The service was circumscribed by Oriental ancestral devotion, politeness, form, respect. Within this cultural morphology was freedom to cry; to lift up the cross; to sing with emotion and verve "How Great Thou Art" and "Rock of Ages"; to nod and mutter "Amen," and even smile at me as I spoke of the love of Christ that enfolds all creation and holds it before the Father. The prayers, presence, singing, and touching of the community bolstered the Lee family in their deep grief.

A motorcade of 40 cars wended its way down the crowded Long Island Expressway to the cemetery. After the graveside committal each family member bowed low before the casket in respect and deference to another ancestor. Then something remarkable happened— something I had never seen in a decade of ministry. The entire funeral party began walking from the grave, but not to their cars. They filed over to a nearby grove of trees, spread out blankets, food and drink, and had a picnic. One of the family came over to me and smiled, handing me a sandwich and a soft drink. "Eat and drink, pastor, enjoy! Life goes on!" And so it did, as we ate and drank among the tombstones of the Pine Lawn Cemetery, celebrating life in a place of the dead transformed.

The elementary act of eating and drinking in the graveyard was sacramental, communion with the God of creation. A recent study produced by the Lutheran\Roman Catholic Joint Commission places the celebration of the Eucharist in the midst of God's created world, and places that creation in the midst of the Eucharist. In profound simplicity this document affirms that the Eucharist as a movement in Christ toward the Father is for "the life of the world;" that the world is present at the Eucharist; that in the Eucharist the way is open for the transformation of the world; that in the Eucharistic solidarity of God's people the new unity of all humanity begins to emerge; that in the Eucharist God's people are called to service in solidarity with the world; that this ministry in Eucharistic solidarity with the world is one of reconciliation and "fellowship in suffering and hope with all people."

To celebrate the Eucharist in the midst of the world is to give the lie to false divisions of life. There is no "sacred" as opposed to "secular." The Eucharist cannot be trivialized to a "cultic rite," "a practice of right religion," or a "spiritual exercise," as if there were some human domain in which Christ is not present. If the most important tabernacle of Christ's presence is not the world, then no other tabernacle has any meaning. To place the Eucharist in the midst of the world is not to baptize life with extraneous dousings of God. It rather recognizes the presence of the incarnate Lord in everything. The carnal vessels of water, bread and wine, eating and drinking, root the grace of God in the things of this world. We cannot spiritualize away the concrete context of God's love for the world any more than we can spiritualize out of existence a casket lowered into the hard earth or a sandwich eaten among the marble slabs of a cemetery.

CREATION IN THE EUCHARIST

The world is present at the Eucharist, present in the gifts of bread and wine, present as the fruits of our labors, symbolized by our offerings of money. In the village of Solentiname, Nicaragua, the peasants bring to the altar their hoes, plows, fishing nets, and other implements of livelihood. The world is present in the intercessions of God's people, in their yearning for peace, their anguish at the pain of life. The world is present as time, as God's people break free from slavery to *chronos* by getting out of their beds and coming to the altar. Thus they offer their own time, a slice of their history. The world is present in the diversity of the people. One of the joys of ministry among the 16 million people of the New York metropolitan area is that in the incredible ethnic diversity of its neighborhoods the churches are literally in the midst of all the peoples of the world. Even in the most homogeneous of parishes there is still a diversity of age, class, gender, values, aspirations, political positions, economic levels. And each of our people brings their world to the altar in the celebration of the Eucharist, expecting in this eating and drinking a solidarity that includes them, is relevant to them.

The Sunday after Chang Lee's funeral his family was present at the Eucharist. The world was present with them, a world of tombstones and grief, dread and hope, joy and faith, and ancestors who live among "angels and archangels and all the company of heaven." In the midst of this creation present at the altar stands the priest, standing where the first ancestors Adam and Eve stood so long ago.

Eating and drinking is primal communion with God. The hunger of our first parents, which is still our own, is a hunger for God. God filled the hunger with all of creation. In the beginning Adam and Eve were made to be priests, called to bless all creation by acknowledging the Creator, by partaking of it as life from God. Each animal, plant, seed, is shot through with the presence of God. The life between the man and the woman, the end of loneliness, was also the gift of God and communion with the Creator. Life was sacramental, with every moment, every morsel of food, every surprise of beauty leading directly to the Creator, the giver of all good gifts. The world was Eucharist, with the human being as the one who receives it all as life from God and offers it all to God in the act of naming and having dominion over it. To bless, to name, to take responsibility in obedience to the Creator, to eat and drink and partake with reverence and thanksgiving— that was the Eucharistic life of humanity in the midst of God's creation.

The Hall of Mirrors

When a former mayor of New York walked through the neighborhoods he used to ask the folks, "How am I doing?" That is our question posed to the things of this world. Rather than the priest in the Garden offering the creation to God and receiving life from God through the creation, we look to creation to reflect and fill us. We are spiritual hypochondriacs, consumers of privatized religion, seekers of the salvation of our own souls and bodies. We have come so far from Adam's dominion over creation that we have given up control of much of our own lives to experts. Common activities—nursing a baby, disciplining children, making love, participating in public life, even play—are given over to guilds of experts who obfuscate with facts until even the truth itself is just another mirror before which we cringe in uneasy self-scrutiny.

The human condition after the Fall takes on specific context in the urban locus of metropolitan New York—a context repeated throughout the country and the world. People are objects, not subjects of their histories. They feel helpless and lacking control over decisions that affect the life of their world. They lack created solidarity, the collective power for dominion in the world. We are in a values war over who will nurture our children, give them their communal stories, shape their public life. Churches have great difficulty figuring out how to help their people defend themselves and their values in the public arena against those who despise and reject them. Our conditions after the Fall include "redlining" neighborhoods; unemployment; struggles between races and classes; inflation; crime; housing problems; unaccountable changes producing profits for the few;, drugs; inadequate health care. There is a widespread sense of dislocation, of bewilderment and xenophobia among the people of our churches and neighborhoods. These conditions are exacerbated by a huge influx of immigrants and refugees, each with their own needs and their own respective feelings of dislocation.

God called Adam and Eve to participate in the ordering of the life of the world. Our people, on the other hand, retreat from participation in decisions that shape their world into a narcissistic hall of mirrors. They do not change our common world, but tinker with their private surroundings. Escapist vacations and advertising slogans that remind us to "cover the grey," "you only go around once in life," and "getting my head together" are signposts in the retreat from collective action and responsibility, the God-given mandate to participate in the life of the world as worship of the Creator.

Too often the sacramental life of the Church participates in the hall of mirrors. Following the medical model, which is currently used to explain all of life, the priest is only too eager to define ministry as one of the "helping professions." Religion in the hall of mirrors becomes a form of psychotherapy helping people to tolerate anxiety, to be comfortable with their neuroses, and to accommodate themselves to humanity's fallen condition. In the beginning all of life was sacramental, an ongoing Eucharist. Now the grace of God is dispensed in moments, like medicine, to make the person "better," in a thimbleful of water, a dash of oil, a "christening." Even the Sunday eating and drinking is so often a private affair, a picnic in the hall of mirrors, a catered escape from the world.

In the Eucharist all creation is transformed and joins Christ on his journey to the Father. The forces of chaos are ordered in God's new creation.

Jesus, our brother and forerunner, is the Christ who in his Ascension heads up all creation, is the fullness of all things. At the Eucharist the priest, in the ministry of Christ, stands in the midst of creation and offers it to the Father as Eucharistic praise. The world is again in communion with God. Eating and drinking is once more holy, for its object is no longer the food itself but the presence of God. In the Eucharist our faith becomes concrete, carnal, when in the eating and drinking we participate in the death and resurrection of the firstborn of all creation, Jesus the Christ.

THE EUCHARIST IN CREATION

In the Eucharist is the *leitourgia* of God's people in the world. In the eating and drinking the Church becomes the eucharistic presence of Christ in the world. The only true life of the world is life in Christ, life moving to the Father in the power of the Holy Spirit. God's people are called to sacramental living in the world. Their mission is to live eucharistically, as signs of the presence of God in everything. Those who have been filled with the presence of Christ in the eating and drinking at the altar also see the presence of Christ in a picnic in the cemetery. The Church in the world understands that the Kingdom of God, like an early shoot from a hidden seed, is breaking out in all the dark, anonymous corners of creation.

On a cold February night two thousand Christians meet with the mayor of New York City and gain important objectives for their neighborhoods. Their collective attempt to create human community will not in itself bring in the Kingdom. Rather, the multiracial ecumenical efforts of God's people to participate in the unfolding of their piece of God's creation can be seen as Eucharistic signs of the Kingdom, sacramental living.

Nehemiah Housing in the burned-out section of Brownsville, Brooklyn, is another sign of the Eucharist in the midst of creation. This grassroots effort of Christians from many communions to literally rebuild their part of the city with new housing accessible to poor and middle-class folks is a sign in the midst of creation of the new emerging solidarity in Christ which will name and bless the world as communion with God. These houses will be not only shelter from the elements but also dignified life from God.

Even as all creation is transformed at the altar in its journey with Christ to the Father, so also God's people at the altar of the world see all that lies before them with new eyes. The Kingdom, though "not yet," is also "even now." Long ago it was the fervent desire of the faithful to be buried near the graves of the martyrs. When people of means died they provided copious amounts of food to be placed on their graves. It was expected that the poor would visit the graves and eat and drink in the presence of the departed. It was also expected that the poor who dined among the tombstones would offer prayers to the God of creation on behalf of the departed. And in the eating and drinking and praying in the midst of the tombstones life would go on, on this side of eternity and on the other.

One day I will sit down at the table, at the great feast with Chang Lee, with my own ancestors from Adam and Eve to Grandpa Bartling and Tante Lene, with those with whom I struggle now to keep hoping, believing and fighting for human community in the midst of the world. And I will behold face to face the God whose presence is never far from me: in the ministry of God's people at the bedside and nursing home; in the mayor's office; in the diverse journeys of God's pilgrim people who speak every language on earth; in a steak at Bill Luger's and kimchi in a church basement; in the sight of Manhattan from the Palisades, glistening in the first lights of a moonfilled evening; in the sealing of abandoned buildings; in a quiet conversation with my wife Janet; and in the eating and drinking of my life. At the altar, in the cemetery, until the final banquet—all of life is Eucharist, life from God.

(*Lutheran Forum*, Reformation, 1982)

CHAPTER 20
FULL COMMUNION ON THE WAY HOME

"I only cared about the 'man,'" Smiley announced.... "And the ideologies trailed after these impossible events like condemned prisoners, as ideologies do when they've had their day. Because they have no heart of their own. They're the whores and angels of our striving selves." (*The Secret Pilgrim*, by John LeCarré, New York: Alfred A. Knopf, 1991, p. 321)

OF WHORES AND ANGELS

Can Smiley's words be said about ecumenical dialogues? About the proposed Lutheran/Episcopal *Concordat* and the doctrines that it mentions, with names like "evangelical episcopate," "apostolic succession," or "full communion?" Are the dialogues the nostalgic repristination of shopworn ideologies and hierarchies trailing after impossible postmodern events, whores and angels of our striving selves? What is at the core of these and similar proposals? Do they have a heart of their own to care about people for whom Christ died?

When you walk into her room to accompany her in the continuation of her dying, the practice of parish ministry is reduced to its most elemental context. The dying has been hard and her *Kyrie* rips you apart. "Help me, help me, please help me." She just cries and cries and grasps you tenaciously. She wants to go home to Jesus, and she wants desperately to believe that there is a Jesus who will accompany her on her homeward way. She needs the assurance that her sins are forgiven. And here is where the ecumenical term being batted around, "full communion," is given its most intimate and primal meaning. A dying saint of God cries out for full communion through the Communion of Saints gathered around the throne of the Lamb.

You lean down and place your free hand around her head. You speak into her ear, patterning your words spoken by heart to her labored breathing. You open up the treasure of Scripture and speak for her, with her, the Apostolic faith: "In my Father's house there are many dwelling places... no one shall snatch them out of my hand... I am the resurrection and the life... nothing can separate us from the love of Christ." You speak the Lord's Prayer and the Creed. You place a bit of bread tinged with wine through parched lips. Through Word and Sacrament she is gathered into the arms of her waiting Lord. She will not stop crying. You sit and sing several familiar hymns. You are finally silent as she continues to grasp your hand. She will not let go.

Notions of "apostolic succession" and "evangelical episcopate" are reduced to the hand of a dying saint of God grasping the hand of her pastor. The faith of the ages, the vocation of the Church, receives its most sublime purpose. It is about the life and death and new life of sinners justified in the unconditional grace of the dying and rising Christ.

At the deathbed of a forgiven sinner the magisterial and pastoral foci of the ministry converge, not the "whores and angels" of our striving selves but the Abiding Presence of the heart of God. What else does "evangelical episcopate" mean but that my dear friend can trust that the comfort of the Gospel to which she clings as she holds the hand of the pastor— her parish bishop— is the faith true to the teachings of the Apostles, mediated through Word and Sacraments? What else does "apostolic succession" mean but that the treasure of the Gospel is trustworthy and true? And this is my question about the direction and intent of the Lutheran/Episcopal *Concordat* before us, indeed about all ecumenical dialogues: Will they help my friend to know, through the Church, the blessed assurance that Jesus is mine? Through these proposals will the Church be strengthened so that the Law and Gospel will have free course to kill and make alive in the name of Jesus?

DIALOGUE FROM THE BOTTOM UP

I must confess that I want very much to embrace the *Concordat* in its revised form, *Called to Common Mission*. I desire with all my heart to receive with open arms whatever unity is given to the Church by the power of the Holy Spirit in a given phase of its history. And I confess the desire to make an end run past all the troubling theological issues within and between our various communions and dance in the sunshine of what unity and agreement is already apparent. My *satis est* is not to be trusted by serious theologians. I believe that in evangelical freedom we might reap great pastoral and ecumenical blessings by considering a communion of bishops in a recognized apostolic succession. But if what the dialogues have in mind is somehow delousing our ministries and keeping bureaucratic track of them then you have lost me. I am not certain if these bilaterals and their proposals are in living dialogue with actual parish communities striving to believe, teach, confess, and live the faith of the Apostles. I would like to drag these dialogues across the turf of local parish life, where the faithful are gathered by the Gospel through the Word and Sacraments. Before I give my unqualified support to the proposals of the *Concordat* I would like to consider what local ecumenical responsibility would require of us.

In a parish that I once served in New York City, it made sense in 1976 to begin a ministry to Koreans and Hispanics in our neighborhood. Initially we had liturgy in the Korean and Spanish languages. I learned Spanish. Our Korean members taught me phonetically to say the Words of Institution, the Absolution, and the Benediction in Korean. We began a school for Korean language and culture on Saturday mornings for the children. After a time, at the urging of our members, we worshipped together in English. We were the only liturgical church in our immediate neighborhood. Our new members were either unchurched people or those who, after exposure to Lutheran sacramental practice and liturgical life, remained attracted to them. Our worship and church life was culturally rich and diverse, yet retained its Lutheran integrity.

In the parish that I was serving in 1982, we had the opportunity and the invitation to begin another intentional Korean outreach through our parish ministry. A Lutheran Korean pastor had been lined up to participate in this work, and Korean Lutheran laypeople were ready to support it. But this time we declined and helped this fledgling ministry relocate in another Lutheran parish nearby. It would have been ecumenically irresponsible for us to accept this particular multicultural opportunity. Directly across the street from us at St. Peter's, six months earlier, the Episcopal Diocese of Newark had begun a Korean parish.

Instead of beginning a Korean outreach of our own, we at Trinity explored interim Eucharistic sharing with the Korean Episcopalians that was our gift from the bilateral dialogues. We were soon crossing the street back and forth often. The Korean pastor at St. Peter's helped some of our Korean members with immigration matters. Their people supported joint summer church school programs. We worked together with other churches in town (Roman Catholic and Reformed) on joint events for prayer, worship and growth, as well as on housing the homeless and other justice issues. We shared the Eucharist in each other's churches. Korean deacons were trained in our New Jersey Synod's two-year Diakonia training program located at our church. Korean children participated in our Sunday School and youth programs. Over kimchi in the church basement and bread and wine in the sanctuary over a period of years, the Holy Spirit gave us to one another in Christ. We came to trust our common purposes and our common confession of faith.

What does the *Concordat* have to say about churches like ours, and thousands of others at the grassroots level who are living out their faith not just in special ecumenical events but in the flow and rhythm of joint life together in the Spirit? And how do those who oppose the proposal of full communion between Anglicans and Lutherans take these local relationships into account? Put differently, at what point has the life of the Church as it is actually lived by people gathered by the Gospel around Word and Sacraments entered the dialogue of those who propose or oppose the *Concordat?* What difference will it all make to a pastor and a child of God in a room of death and wounded hope?

LEGS ON OUR PRAYERS

Each year the Octave of Prayer for Christian Unity is not simply an event in our town isolated from the fabric of the activities of our individual churches. It is a celebration and public commissioning for our continued work together.

After the liturgy for prayer one year we gathered in the undercroft of St. Joseph's, a neighboring Carmelite parish. That past year a teen in town had committed suicide, and another child had been abused, almost beaten to death. We formed a committee to reach out to the young people in town, and to provide care and comfort in future events. Later that year two little children and their mother were shot to death by the enraged father, who then killed himself. One of the girls had attended our nursery school, the other a local primary school. The deaths hit hard, especially among the young people in Bogota. The ecumenical committee arranged for several opportunities for communal grieving and care. County crisis teams, the police, local clergy, school guidance counselors and others hosted a town gathering. Clergy were available after the meeting to speak with anyone wishing their presence. Into the night we sat with hundreds of our neighbors, crying, listening, praying, the Body of Christ present to the pain of this world in the Name of Jesus. By putting legs on our prayers for unity we acted on the faith we share in the middle of the world for which Christ died, turning the unified face of Jesus to those wounded children of God seeking hope and comfort. In one of his letters to his brother Theo, Vincent Van Gogh said that maybe it was his job to keep the fires of his heart burning, in case one day someone might want to sit down and be warmed by that heart. Burning hearts, prayers that walk, the ecumenical tasks of Christ's Body.

A SMALL, MODEST SIGN?

I appreciate and support the hard work of the participants in our various dialogues with other communions within the Body of Christ. A word fitly spoken with theological precision is absolutely crucial to real and faithful ecumenical progress. Responsible encounter cannot be simply reduced to how it affects the local parish or whether it will "fly" in this or that specific situation. Nor can it be trivialized to "making nice" with the other folks, or romanticized by reduction to vignettes like the one that opened this article. But local parishes *will* be affected; separated Christians *are* trying to figure out how to "make nice" with one another in the Spirit of the unity we already share in Christ; and notions of ministry are ultimately nonsense apart from such vignettes. There ought to be a burden laid on the consciences of ecclesiastical leaders to listen from the top down and take the church in its parish concreteness with utmost seriousness.

There is also a grassroots ecumenical burden. We must find ways to express and live out the relationships which are already ours in the Spirit of Christ in such a way that we are continually asking of ourselves, "Why not?" The annual Thanksgiving prayer service is no longer enough.

If we really think about the nature of the church as it actually unfolds on the local level we realize there is already full communion, in countless encounters, across the width of the Body of Christ. The priests at the Roman Catholic church near the parish that I served in New Jersey routinely referred spouses in troubled marriages to me for counseling. We quietly visited one another's members and prayed for them when we were in the hospital. And sometimes, if the truth be told, when requested we fed folks not of our communions with the Body and Blood of Christ. When I married divorced Catholics referred to me by their priest, he stood with me at the altar. The priest knew that I performed those weddings under one condition: that the couple be fed at his altar. And they were, because every priest of the Roman communion has a pastoral "internal forum" that allows him to speak and enact sacramentally the Gospel on behalf of his people. When my son had Sunday morning baseball games he would go to Saturday night Mass. The priest knew him and fed him. Ecumenical responsibility these days requires something of a tightrope act. Quietly, with pastoral sensitivity, the internal forum must support and nourish the great hunger of God's people for communion with one another and with God. Publicly we must make explicit the present facts of our separation, so that the great longing of our people may be heard and so that the converging paths toward mutual recognition of Baptism, Eucharist and ministry may have theological integrity.

Such was the ecumenical tension in the neighborhood in which I ministered for over a decade. We worked together. We struggled for justice together. We prayed together. We studied the Holy Scriptures together. We came to respect and cherish one another during our time of extended Octave of Christian unity and social action. But we still eat by ourselves. Even our Anglican and Lutheran churches across the street from one another do not share a rhythm of Eucharistic hospitality, only occasional celebrations. And that is a pain that must not only be noted, but exacerbated. The tension between the unity we do share and the separation we yet endure must be heightened. Have the experts involved in the bilateral dialogues listened to expressions of this tension?

And here is why I support, with many grave reservations, the proposal for full communion between the Lutheran and Episcopal communions. What if local Lutheran and Episcopal parishes really acted on what they believe, teach and confess? What if the believers of Trinity Lutheran and St. Peter's Korean Episcopal decide that the width of a street is too big a gulf between reconciled sisters and brothers in Christ? What if, in the confidence of the Apostolic faith we confess and share we decided that responsible ecumenism would not allow for two separate churches where there is one faith, one altar, one font, one reconciled ministry in recognized continuity with the ministry of the Apostles? Maybe then the *Concordat* could make a concrete difference in encouraging the reunion of a family of believers created by the presence of Jesus in the Word and Sacraments among them.

One small, modest sign to help a dying world see Jesus more clearly.

(*Lutheran Forum*, Easter\Pentecost, 1991)

CHAPTER 21
EMBODIED ECUMENISM: THE UNITY OF CHRIST'S BODY AT THE LOCAL LEVEL

THE SOUL OF THE CITY

I was sitting on a chair at the Battery Park in lower Manhattan, in the "ecumenical section," waiting for Pope John Paul II to arrive. Wind was gusting and rain pelting. People were wet, uncomfortable, impatient. Around me, in a communal drenching, sat the president of Union Theological Seminary, Protestant judicatory representatives, Orthodox priests, parish pastors, and other notables and anonymities, all with some claim to membership in the Church of Jesus Christ. One wag leaned into me, pointed to the grey inferno of New York Harbor and remarked, "I guess God is telling us he really is Jewish."

Soon we heard the noise of the crowds, and we knew that the papal retinue had arrived in the park. As the Pope came into view the cheers intensified. He was regally garbed, and accompanied by other princes of the Church. The Pope ascended the platform in front of us. He looked right at us, extended his hands in blessing, and said, "I greet you as brothers and sisters in Christ."

Soon new cheers erupted for a tall, smiling man dressed in an orange "Parks Department of New York" windbreaker. He shot his thumbs up in the air and hollered out his favorite line, a line repeated in every neighborhood in the city, "How am I doing?" The cheers told him that he was doing just fine. He was Edward I. Koch, the then newly elected and wildly popular mayor of New York City. For many he epitomized the Big Apple: brash, a little offensive, tough, feisty, spirited, intimidating, streetwise.

The two leaders symbolized for me the arena of grassroots ecumenism: the Prince of the Church and the Prince of the City. For it is in the realm of local prayer and Bible study, as well as local engagement in efforts of corporal mercy and social justice, that ecumenical engagement takes on reality. Later, the Pope addressed a crowd of sixty thousand in Yankee Stadium, in the shadow of some of the deepest poverty in the world, but also of some of its most vibrant neighborhoods. John Paul said: "The city needs a soul. And the people must give it." As people find one another in the Body of Christ, they become a part of the ecumenical vocation of doing the soul work of the city.

LOCAL CONNECTIONS

As of 1994, the ELCA finds itself at a time of impending decisions concerning its public ecumenical posture as it studies proposals for more explicit fellowship with the Anglican and Reformed communions. Perhaps as significant are proposals which are not yet on the table, the larger looming presence of the Western Catholic and Orthodox traditions, and how current ELCA proposals would affect the unity of Christ's Church at its deepest and most primal levels.

I would like to return to the Pope's encouragement concerning the "soul work of the city" to speak of the Church's ecumenical task from the perspective of the local parish. Such areas of ecumenical soul work in my experience have included: lively encounter with Scripture; worship that witnesses to the unity of Christ's Church; mutual engagement in corporal works of mercy; and community organizing that seeks to help people live out their faith in the public arena.

Some of the liveliest Bible study in which I have ever participated has grown out of the community organizing process. Leaders from local churches evaluating a stormy meeting with the mayor and city officials about housing and jobs study the account of the Exodus and its public drama of faith in God. Neighborhood church leaders on retreat, planning for outreach to inner-city young people study the account of the paralytic in Mark 2, seeking ways to create holes in the roofs of our religious assemblies for the needs of the community to come down before the healing presence of Jesus. As lay people receive training to interview their fellow members and neighbors in the community as good listeners, they study the story of Jesus and the Samaritan woman at the well in John 4 and the story of Mary and Martha in Luke 10. The study of Scripture takes on power and urgency in the ecumenical soul work of the city as people act on their beliefs in the public arena. Stories of Creation, not Machiavelli's history lessons, inform their understanding of politics; the Eucharist and the Cross, not ideology, stand at the center of their grassroots understanding of community.

The Body of Christ works together as one through groups involved in corporal works of mercy offered in Jesus' name. Networks for sheltering the homeless, interim housing for mothers and children living on the street, soup kitchens, direct-help programs like FISH, and many other mutual ministries of Christ's Body place Christian people in company with one another. The activity of the Church in the world becomes evangelical, as turned-off and forgetful or lapsed people come into contact with these ministries of mercy. There have been enough studies and forums and workshops and lectures and position papers put out by Council of Churches organizations. Community organizing and groups of people committed to the corporal works of mercy put legs on these prayers and positions, embodying the mission of God's people in real-life situations. The prayer and Bible study I have experienced in training for caregivers who work in the city's shelters has been profound and renewing. Nehemiah housing springing up in Brooklyn, the South Bronx and elsewhere; PASS plan programs that give inner-city kids in Paterson and Passaic a job and a scholarship and a mentor for staying in school; AIDS hospice care; these and many other programs giving shape to the "soul work" of the city are built on the prayers, Scriptural insights and *koinonia* of the grassroots ecumenical church.

Along the way we learn a certain modesty about the ecumenical enterprise of our wider church bodies. Working together in the inner city with AME, Baptist, and Hispanic Catholic expressions of Christ's Church, we begin to respect the work the Holy Spirit is doing among them. We do not need to reproduce their styles of worship and devotion and label them Lutheran if we are truly ecumenical. Yet our corporate lives as denominations do change, grow, become renewed from the "soul work" we share with brothers and sisters in Christ. Such renewal comes from respect and reverence for the Spirit's power to produce faith in the dying and rising Christ in so many ways. At the grassroots level, the priests from St. Joseph's, the neighboring Carmelite parish in Bogota, New Jersey, would pray with members of Trinity Lutheran; the priests, together with the Lutheran and Reformed pastors, would meet with their neighbors in the wake of the slaying of three children in the neighborhood; their people would fill church basements and pin down local officials on affordable housing for seniors. And on Holy Saturday, outside St. Joseph's on Palisade Avenue, hundreds of believers would gather to hear the story of the women at the tomb told in the languages of the neighborhood (Spanish, Korean, Polish, Illong), and pray together as a public witness to the impending and continuing resurrection presence of Jesus.

This rich (and sometimes banal) life of Christ's Body lived in the day-to-day, must be on our hearts as we struggle for formal mutual understanding about the Apostolic faith, formally articulated and continually enacted.

Grassroots ecumenism of this kind involves a spiritual decision. We believe that any notion of salvation is historical, worked out not in some other world but in this one. We believe that such soul work of the city—building coalitions that bridge the differences among us (and the listening, compromise, prayer and study of Scripture that undergird it) is a step toward the human solidarity that animates our beliefs. Participation in the give-and-take of community building is not apocalyptic. In itself it will not bring in the Kingdom of God. It is proximate, fluid, a part of how we live out our most deeply held beliefs. If there is any enduring quality to ecumenical soul work—of people finding their voice and a new sense of respect in public life, it is that the process is a sign of hope, an affirmation that the Kingdom of God, like a rash, breaks out in the rhythm of human life in the forms of justice, respect, dignity, and love. Ecumenical soul work is an affirmation that history is not turning in on itself, but headed toward redemption under the guidance of our common Lord.

Coda: Of Mayors and Babies

I add a coda to these remarks about ecumenism "from the parish." This is the description of one example of grassroots ecumenism, some of which was initially published in *The Cresset.* We go back to Mayor Koch and the soul work of the city. The night was February 27, 1978. From all over the borough of Queens over a thousand people came to St. Francis Prep auditorium. It was the coming-out party of a fledgling ecumenical citizens' organization, the Queens Citizens' Organization (QCO), based in churches across the borough and schooled by organizers of the Industrial Areas Foundation (founded by the late Saul Alinsky).

QCO had shown from the beginning a willingness to hold public officials accountable, and a disciplined persistence in pursuit of its goals. Queens Borough President Manes, stung after a grueling accountability session with QCO, had predicted it would be gone from the scene in six months. Mayor Koch had agreed to the meeting because he had signed a written agreement at a "candidates' night" in the heat of the mayoral campaign. His staff was wary of QCO. The meeting was shrouded by tension, possible controversy, and much interest. The presence of TV cameras and media personalities gave the meeting the aura of a "happening." The spectacle of the mighty Mayor meeting feisty church folk on their own turf provided a public tableau of irresistible interest.

I had just left my wife, who was in the hospital to give birth in the morning by Caesarean section, and arrived late to a scene of electric excitement. As I walked through the cordon of police, the sight took my breath away. The delegates were all gathered around large vertical signs that identified church and neighborhood. I saw St. Catherine of Siena from Cambria Heights, a black Roman Catholic church in a section of Queens slowly being abandoned by city services and available credit. Over on the right was St. Rose of Lima from a poor section of Far Rockaway. Gathered close by was a cluster of three churches—Lutheran, UCC, and Roman Catholic—from middle-class Woodhaven. And then I saw the familiar faces of my own people, gathered around the Atonement Lutheran, Jackson Heights sign.

We had voted on local issues to bring before the mayor. We had recruited fifty members to attend this meeting. Some of us had been involved in the planning, role-playing, and prep sessions that went into the meeting. Among us were a public school teacher, a fire fighter, a welfare mother, a laborer, a shop owner, a high school student, a pastor waiting for a baby. We were of most races and many backgrounds. Some could have passed for Archie Bunker.

The mayor arrived a few minutes after I did. We were both about forty minutes late. He came in surrounded by his retinue, like a heavyweight champ entering the ring, and immediately began hobnobbing with the media folks. Soon Father Eugene Lynch, chair of QCO, introduced the mayor to polite applause. I will never forget my feelings of pride and hope at that moment. I felt history. We were dealing with those who make decisions that affect the life of my family, church, neighborhood. The drama was on.

The meeting was stormy. The mayor tried to take over the meeting and evade the issues. He ended up walking out. The political fallout and protracted publicity were intense. Church folks were news for days (including front-page *New York Times* coverage). But the grassroots Church had achieved what no one will ever give us—respect. Quietly over the next several months, and after further, less tense meetings, the mayor delivered the commissioners of sanitation, police, transportation and others to negotiating sessions in Queens. A host of community issues were solved at these meetings. The issues raised at the initial bristling confrontation with the mayor were also addressed responsibly. A wary, but respectful and dignified relationship between the mayor and the churches of QCO had been forged. We were engaged ecumenically in a task as old as creation: to exercise dominion and stewardship in God's world.

Grassroots ecumenism of this kind involves a spiritual decision. We believe that any biblical notion of salvation is historical, worked out not in some other world but in this one. We believe that such soul work of the city—building coalitions that bridge the differences among us (and the listening, compromise, prayer and study of Scripture that undergird them) is a step toward the human solidarity that animates our beliefs. This participation with a mayor in the give-and-take of community building is not apocalyptic. In itself it will not bring in the Kingdom of God. It is proximate, fluid, a part of how we live out our most deeply held beliefs. If there is any enduring quality to ecumenical soul work of people finding their voice and respect in public life, it is that the process is a sign of hope, an affirmation that the Kingdom of God, like a rash, breaks out in the rhythm of human life based on justice, respect, dignity, and love. It is an affirmation that history is not turning in on itself, but headed toward redemption.

The morning after that meeting in February of 1978 our daughter Rachel was born. Three Sundays later the grassroots ecumenical Church continued the soul work of the city with an act as public and earthy as a meeting with the mayor. I baptized Rachel in the name of the Father and the Son and the Holy Spirit. The grassroots ecumenical church does not leave its children at the font after we baptize them. The act of Baptism is an act of responsibility for the child. We extend the font to meetings with the mayor. The issues of drugs, education, jobs, are baptismal issues. Baptism is the wellspring of the soul work of the city, the source of the company we keep with one another in our journey to being one with Jesus forever.

(Lutheran Forum, Advent, 1994)

Chapter 22
Assisting Ministers: Identity and Function

An Open Letter to all Assisting Ministers at the Liturgy

Let me tell you about John Brady, an Assisting Minister of the parish that I served for over a decade. He has never administered the chalice or read a lesson. He does not lead in the prayers or chant the deacon's litany. He does not serve as an usher or sing in the choir. He has never vested, carried a cross, or lit a candle. But John is one of the most effective Assisting Ministers of the family in Christ at Trinity Church in Bogota, New Jersey.

John runs a factory in Paterson. One day he asked me to meet him there to talk about Baptism with one of his employees, an 18-year-old father. The new baby's mother was 16. They were new to this country, not members of any parish, and the baby's arrival had rekindled their curiosity about the church and its sacraments. We met in a corner of the factory; and between my broken Spanish and their broken English we had a conversation about the Gospel, Baptism, the Body of Christ and Christian nurture. Our weekly sessions of baptismal preparation, a catechesis into the faith of the church, were attended by many of the workers during lunch hour. The couple asked John Brady and another employee of the factory to be sponsors. In a factory in the depressed town of Paterson, John Brady was an Assisting Minister, sharing the Gospel, linking people to the weekly liturgy and the power of the Sacraments.

Gabriella Maria became a child of God through Holy Baptism because of the ministry of John, who stood with the family at the font and still brings them to the liturgy. Thinking of John brings me to the first point I would like to make concerning the ministry of Assisting Ministers:

Everyone present at liturgy is an Assisting Minister.
Liturgy is the work of all the People of God. It is something we all do. Your willingness to assist in the liturgy makes you a living reminder to all

that we are in this work of worship together. The point of our worship is this: to offer praise, thanksgiving and adoration to God through Christ in the power of the Spirit. As we worship, by God's grace, we experience God's presence among us. All that we do, say, sing, sign, enact— even our times of silence—must move relentlessly, with single-minded purpose, to enable this to happen. Any goal other than attention and responsiveness to God's presence is not worth the effort and is something other than worship.

Albert Schweitzer recounts his memories as a child, attending long and ponderous liturgies with his parents. He received little at the cognitive level. Yet watching his reverent and awe-filled parents going through the weekly motions of the liturgy filled him with a life-long understanding of the mystery of God, an awareness of the Holy.

You remember, don't you? I do. My parents were the first Assisting Ministers in my memory, teachers of the Eucharist, stewards of the mysteries of faith. My father, a church musician, began his Sunday morning "work" of liturgy before he left home, running through passages on the piano, arranging sheet music, leaving early for sacristy, rehearsal room and choir loft to make all things ready within his area of responsibility. In the pew my mother paid attention to me and my four brothers and sisters. She put up with my restlessness, was always available for questions, pointed out page and hymn, slipped me M&Ms, put a hand on my shoulder. When my siblings and I got really hard to handle other Assisting Ministers around us would help us worship. I still remember the "gum lady"—that's what we called her; I never knew her name was Mrs. Ladwig until later—who would slip us some Chiclets at just the right time. But my mother stared straight ahead when the pastor took the bread and wine and she left me to my own devices when she went to kneel at the altar. The look she gave me when she returned to the pew ushered me more surely than any sermon or confirmation class into intimations of transcendence, the Real Presence.

POWER OF PRESENCE

So I say it again: Everyone present at worship is an Assisting Minister. The squalling baby assists us to remember the Babe of Bethlehem and the intrusive nature of Word made flesh. The old ones who need to be helped to the altar, or the infirm who wait for the bread and wine to be brought to them remind us how precious it is to belong, and to make the effort to "do this in remembrance of Me." Even those who are now saints in heaven hover around us as Assisting Ministers, reminding us that this liturgical community includes "angels and archangels and all the company of heaven." And your formal presence in the chancel as an Assisting Minister puts us in midst of all this.

Which leads to my next point:
Service as an Assisting Minister in the formal liturgy is part of a renewal in the Church's understanding of worship.

Our "Green Book" says it clearly. Through Baptism all of life is worship that includes all of the washed and regenerated people of God. Liturgy and the Sacraments are not things, but actions. Christ makes the Sacraments happen. The Church makes liturgy happen. This liturgy, centered on the Word and Sacraments, and thus on Christ, is a joint enterprise with Jesus and the worshipping community. We are all in this together— with the dying and rising Christ.

For example, in the Eucharist we do not dispense a commodity as much as we participate—with Jesus—in a journey to God. All give. All receive. All celebrate. All remember. And all the baptized are forgiven. You help bring this to mind. The congregation is not a collection of passive "receivers" in this understanding. The clergy are not the only "doers." That dualistic understanding mirrors the view that ministry is "service," doing something for someone. Rather than service we must think of Presence. Presence means we do things *with* rather than *for* them. Presence mirrors the solidarity of God in Christ with all creation.

So we are present with one another in the liturgy. Together we remember God's mighty acts, celebrate God's grace, seek God's mercy, proclaim God's Word, share at the altar, pray for all God's people and for all creation, sing praise to God's Name, and become equipped to share in Christ's mission. You have specific responsibilities as we do these things on behalf of all. While a called and ordained pastor presides over the preaching of the Word, the ministry of Absolution, and the administration of the Sacraments, the liturgy has always been the responsibility of all of us. Indeed as we listen and pray, eat and drink, and pay attention to one another as the baptized community of God we share a variety of tasks: preparation of the altar, reading lessons, leading prayers, offering money and bread and wine, ushering, singing, distributing the Eucharist, presiding over M&Ms and Chiclets, listening for the still, small voice...

SPIRIT OF HOSPITALITY

Let me now say a word about the spirit in which the worshiping community shares in these tasks:

I like the increased use of the idea of "hospitality" to speak about the climate we try to create when we seek in our liturgy together the Presence of God.

Hospitality is a word with a sturdy history in the Christian tradition, from the welcome offered to strangers by medieval monastic communities to modern notions of sanctuary in our troubled world. It echoes the greeting of the Risen Lord to His friends: "Shalom." If, in our assisting ministry of pew or chancel, we are truly hospitable to others, then we might find ourselves becoming channels for the hospitality of the Christ who promises his presence where two or three are gathered together in his name.

I should add that this welcome is not a hospitality that draws attention to itself. Too many chatty and chummy pastors and assisting ministers have introduced "Good morning" as a new rubric and their leadership is more like Phil Donahue than a representative pointing to Christ. Ritual hospitality is not self-indulgence in drag, but a modest and dignified sign of the hospitality of Christ.

The best way I can describe hospitality is something like this: *Paying attention, with care.* When people are asked to pay attention they know exactly what we mean. Attention takes time, energy and trouble. It doesn't just happen. It is work to stop our normal preoccupation with ourselves and attend to something or someone else. Paying attention is a deliberate and conscious act— dare we say our liturgical "work?"

In liturgical hospitality:
We pay attention to one another.

There ought to be no such thing as worshiping with strangers. Help the stranger find her place in the liturgy, even if you must open your own hymnal to the correct rubric and give it to her. Help the parent with the three squirming children—and let them know with a smile or gesture that you understand that God wants these children present. When you pass the peace, look the other in the eye with kindness. Spend a moment in the touch of the handshake. Watch the Assisting Minister and pastor in the chancel so that we may rise, kneel, respond, sign the cross together.

In small and human ways let us say to all present, "We are glad you are with us." We smile at one another. We go out of our way to greet those in our midst whose lives are being torn apart by heartache. We understand together in our Eucharistic hospitality that liturgy is evangelism and pastoral care and fellowship in Christ at the deepest level.

When you administer the chalice do not scan the crowd, hurry the action, or behave as if you were a Eucharistic vending machine. Pause before each person. Let them take the chalice and lovingly guide it to their lips. Say distinctly, "The Blood of Christ, shed for you." In your hospitality you will help enable their "Amen," the affirmation of faith in the Presence. Pay attention to each person who approaches. Look her or him in the eye. Remember what it is you are offering them. Everyone who receives the chalice from your hand has a right to the full hospitable dimension of this holy moment. And always remember that you are a part of this dear Family in Christ.

In our liturgical hospitality:
We pay attention to the world.

Like John Brady, we bring with us our life situations and their attending questions. The tabernacle of Christ's Presence is the world in which he was born, served, suffered, prayed, died and rose again. If we pay attention to Jesus at the liturgy we can expect his presence also in our real worldly concerns and existence. Our monetary offerings go not only for our own maintenance but also to places of hurt and hope in the world. Our prayers are led by the Assisting Minister. When the Assisting Minister leads the prayers there is solidarity between the liturgical community and God's creation. To pay attention to the world is the business, the liturgy and "work" of all the baptized people of God. In our prayers, and in our lives of ministry motivated by our liturgical encounter with our loving God and one another, we pay attention to those in bondage in South Africa, the victims of environmental disaster, the homeless and the homebound, the AIDS patients, the dying, those without the Church.

Those Assisting Ministers who serve in the formal liturgical functions should be a little like John Brady. They ought to be those who visit the sick, commune the homebound, invite to the liturgy, encourage those who have fallen away, organize response to human need, search the Scriptures, pray daily for the Church and the world, and provide leadership in the parish. And some should be deacons, to order and make explicit and illumine for all of us the congruence between the Presence of Christ in the celebrating community and that same Presence in the world.

INNER RENEWAL

Finally, in our liturgical hospitality:
We pay attention to what is happening inside us.

When we pay attention to the Word, our neighbors, the world, what pastors and Assisting Ministers are doing in the prayers, bread, wine, water, hymn and proclamation, something stirs within us. It has been said that contemplation is a long and loving look at what is real. In the "work" of hospitality, of paying attention and responding, we begin to feel the Real

Presence of God in Christ, the Way, the Truth and the Life. It is the single-minded purpose of every liturgy to help make this response of faith possible. And then we can say, "I was glad when they said to me, 'Let us go to the house of the Lord!'" (Psalm 122:1)

If you have really paid attention as Assisting Minister in chancel or pew, you will know that you have been at work. Your vocal cords will be strained. Your back and maybe your knees will ache. Your mind will be reeling with the concerns of each person with whom you have been present. You will be full of questions and challenges about the next actions in your life of ministry. In short, you will be remembering your Baptism. These are all a part of the light burdens and easy yokes of the Lord Jesus.

In one parish that I served, on the second Sunday of every month, as the gifts of bread and wine and money are brought forward during the Offertory, several Assisting Ministers come forward and place their Communion sets on the altar. Their ministry is part of the gifts offered by the People of God. After the Family Meal has been distributed the Communion sets are filled with what remains of the bread and wine. The benediction is spoken by the Presiding Minister. Some among all the Assisting Ministers present (all the baptized!) again come forward. They are given the Communion sets and the flowers from the altar. The work of the liturgy is not ended, is never ended.

The hospitality continues as those bearing the Eucharist prepare to go forth to pay attention to and "re-member" the Body of Christ who are ill, hospitalized, imprisoned, homebound. The organist strikes up the hymn. The choir leads the singing. The little ones sigh with relief. The acolyte and crucifer—perhaps wearing the latest in "church Reeboks"—begin the journey from chancel to narthex and beyond. In the procession are the Assisting Ministers, those who have served liturgically, and those who bear the Eucharistic elements. They follow the cross, bearing the presence of Jesus into the corners and margins of the world. The Assisting Ministers remind us that our work of liturgy is not now finished, but has only begun.

(*Lutheran Forum*, Advent, 1987)

Chapter 23
To Carry God in the Mouth: Singing the Faith

"Wie selig sind doch die, die Gott im Munde tragen." ("How blessed are they who carry God in their mouths"). From Cantata BWV 80, "Ein' Feste Burg," by J. S. Bach

"The Church's effectiveness in evangelism is in direct relationship to the integrity of its liturgy." (Aidan Kavanaugh)

Papal Seekers' Service

Songs can become icons. Like the "Windows" icon, you click on it and a whole world of binary connections unfolds. The song playing in the background of your first kiss; the song you danced to the night you proposed; the song that evokes a broken heart, a new baby, a particular place or time or person ... you hear the tune and a whole world comes flooding into consciousness. So on a trip to my home town of Chicago recently, I found while jogging through the old neighborhood that music became linked with place; tunes came unbidden and flushed through me: "Runaround Sue," the second movement of Haydn's "Clock Symphony" (my first record), "Runaway," "Surfer Girl," "Sheep May Safely Graze"... the music carried my story and my memories.

I grew up in the home of a church musician, yet my experience is not unique. Before the faith was told to me it was sung to me. With bedtime prayers, in Advent and Lenten devotions around the table, in Sunday School and children's choir, in formal liturgy and driving in the car, I learned to know Jesus through the songs of faith. In such a way, through the centuries, liturgy and music together have served the Church as an icon of Christ's presence, an *eikon Christi*. In the marriage of music and liturgy the people of God, through the generations, have "carried God in their mouths."

Lutherans have always been a singing people. Word and Sacrament surrounded by fine music has characterized our heritage. Luther was able to hear and adapt the melodic and speech patterns from the world around him and live into them, holding folk music together with the highest-quality texts of theological integrity. In his 1520 *Treatise on the New Testament,*

That is the Holy Mass Martin Luther proposes that the ability to distinguish what is central and constitutive in the Eucharist—and in the music and all other forms that accompany it—from what is additional and secondary is "the greatest and most useful art." At the center is Christ, present in Word and Sacraments. The test is always: What enhances the proclamation of Christ, the *solus Christus?* When forms of any kind are presented as if required by God, as if necessary for grace, the Church itself is threatened. It is not that one does without music or ceremony. Luther himself said, "I neither wish nor am able to displace or discard such additions." No, what is essential is to distinguish these formal and ceremonial matters from the center, which is Christ, and to require them to serve the center.

Milan Kundera once defined kitsch as "shallow emotions, deeply felt." Kitsch is the perfect accompaniment to the "Song of Myself" in this present age. The postmodern assumption holds that nothing can be communally verified. We cannot trust texts, traditions, creeds. There is only the I, no reality beyond me, nothing carried in the mouths of the generations. This is why I am uneasy with the proliferation of so-called "seeker services." They cater to the hegemony of the subjective in today's world. I am much in sympathy with the Church's need to share Christ's claims in today's world in ways that can be heard and received. Alternative and indigenous liturgies can be very helpful here. Diaconal service by the baptized in the world, the study of Scripture, spiritual mentoring, weddings and funerals, credible invitations into the Church's life, striving for justice and presence with the poor are all ways in which the Church connects with spiritual seekers in the Spirit's power. But we cannot lose the sense that in the liturgy and music of the Church it is Christ's claims that are lifted up; it is Christ who addresses us and will not be forced into our epistemological molds. My feelings and strivings and felt needs are subordinate; in the music and liturgy the Gospel must be conveyed: *Christ for me, through the Church.*

Yes, there is something odd and incomprehensible about the *magnum mysterium* of God's grace and sovereignty. And the liturgy and music of the Church illuminate the center of the mystery, the *solus Christus.* The recent papal masses in the New York City metropolitan area were wonderful examples of "seeker services" of integrity and iconic power. The masses were public, like all liturgy. The world was able to listen in on the activity of the faithful. The music was indigenous, combining the sounds of the diverse world around us with performative excellence. The flow of the Mass was illumined by comment and interpretation. Yes, it was certainly odd to those with little experience of Christian worship, but no less odd than a man's rising from the dead. The Gospel was proclaimed. The Church's solidarity with the poor was boldly asserted. The liturgy was also pastoral care of the faithful. Questions could be asked—why are there just these old guys up there?—because the Church was being itself, with all its earthly warts. The people there were fed.

Mouth-to-Mouth Resuscitation

In the stories of two women one can trace the musical connections of the evangelical and apostolic faith. Frauke Hasemann was a musician and teacher. Her work at the Westphaelische Kirchenmusikschule in Hereford, Germany, and at the Westminster Choir School in Princeton, New Jersey, was a ministry to many. Her special gift was to teach a generation of musicians how to help children sing with all their God-given ability. She helped teach the church to respect the children for their Baptisms' sake, to refuse to objectify them into terminal cuteness in kids' ghettos cut off from the liturgy of the people of God. Children can sing the Mass and adorn it with beauty.

In a former time the children's elders and society encouraged their participation in the life of the Church. Released-time religious education, blue laws, the examples of previous generations all supported the communal spiritual life of children. Times have changed. It is now the children who are the best hope of bringing their elders back into the life of the Church. If we teach them to sing well, to carry in their mouths the *solus Christus* in their music, they will teach the music of the Church to a generation of adults who have abandoned the Church's life. In the center of such evangelical and liturgical love of children stood Frauke Hasemann.

I became acquainted with this minister of music near the end of her life when she was dying of cancer in a hospital bed. My father had asked me to visit her. I came with bread and wine. We talked of many things. When she reached out for the comfort of faith, feeling bereft of spiritual resources, I reminded her of the texts she had sung all her life and taught others to sing. She remembered and smiled. "Oh how amiable...How lovely is thy dwelling place.... How lovely shines the Morning Star..." We shared the bread and wine. All of it was sacrament and icon of Christ's presence. "Wie selig sind doch die, die Gott im Munde tragen." At her funeral it was the music of faith which carried Frauke—and us—to the throne of the Lamb.

The Lutheran connection between music and liturgy is transcultural. Pastor Heidi Neumark of Transfiguration Church in the South Bronx writes about the time Maria showed up at the Mass bearing God in her mouth. Maria and her three children had come to the South Bronx from Honduras. Her youngest had Downs' syndrome. After a journey in which they were robbed of all their money and her ten-year-old daughter was threatened with rape they arrived poor and homeless in the Bronx. And showed up one day at the public liturgy of Transfiguration.

Pastor Neumark tells how the music of the Gospel was conveyed that day. "I would like to think that their coming was the result of a successful evangelism strategy, but Maria remembers better. 'We came because the Holy Spirit pointed out this church to us.' At the time of the offering, Maria came forward. 'We don't have any money yet,' she said, 'but we can sing.' And so Maria and her three children stood up before a sea of unknown faces, like those who in John's vision had conquered the beast to stand beside the sea of glass with harps of God in their hands, and Maria and her children sang the song of the Lamb. They sang a song of Zion in a new land. We are all learning to sing the song of the Lamb in an alien land. For many, Maria bears the label 'illegal' or 'undocumented.' But Maria will never be undocumented in the body of Christ. She has a document that she carried safely across the border to the Bronx— her Baptismal certificate."

COMPANIONS OF CHRIST IN SONG

The coffin carrying the body of a 47-year-old woman was brought up the steps, as six family members and friends walked into St. Barbara's Roman Catholic Church in Bushwick, Brooklyn. The doors then closed against the morning sunlight, and from inside the vast emptiness of the ornate old church, voices rose in song. Most of the singers were elderly Hispanic men and women. Their thirty-four voices were strong, easily carrying the hymn, "Juntos con hermanos" back to the coffin near the doorway. One longtime member says, "We can't stop the killing. We can only cope. Our singing may not be beautiful. But we sing with love."

The old are burying the dead in this neighborhood. The daily Mass and its elderly faithful have rerooted their worship into the life of the hard streets around St. Barbara's. There were 181 funerals in 1994 for young people who had died of AIDS or violence. In a *New York Times* article Father John Powis says, "For years we have been having funerals for the young people of this parish. Typically they will have been away from the church since childhood, but the families come and ask for a Mass. At the Masses there was never anyone there beyond the family, sometimes not even them."

Here is a modern parable of the confluence between liturgy, music, and the life of the world. The faithful elderly gave up their 8 A.M. Mass to accompany the grieving, bearing God in their mouths at the 9:30 A.M. Requiem Masses. St. Barbara's is a sanctuary full of pain, but not of silence. The church sings its song of the dying and rising Christ, and those whose lives are being torn apart hear it. That is mission, to make public the mystery of faith.

"We are not a choir, we are voices, and we try our best," says Lydia Aquino, a grandmother. "We sing, and the family feels the strength. I think our singing gives them more faith." It is the ministry of the Church to help the people of God to find their voices and sing the great *Kyrie, Gloria, Nunc Dimittis, Agnus Dei, Dona Nobis Pacem*, in word and deed, where the paralysis of this world can hear it and take heart. The Church carries in its mouth the restless passion of Jesus for the lost and the poor of this world.

I first met Father John Powis in a church basement in Brooklyn almost twenty years ago, in the early stages of the formation of East Brooklyn Churches, a church-based community organization. I remember when the music of faith and hope sounded to Father Powis and neighborhood residents like the cough of a bulldozer revving up to clear ground for the thousands of Nehemiah homes that transformed a blasted, abandoned landscape. The rhythm of mission is always thus: from the chancel to the streets and back to the chancel again.

Ricardo Echevaria, who accompanies his mother every morning to the Requiem Masses says, "It is hard to see how much suffering the young are having. That's why changing the Mass to have us come and sing was good. It is not always easy to come, but we do. It gives a sense of companionship."

Companion. *Con pan.* With bread. Companions of Christ, companions in Christ. Some of the singers come from a nearby home for the aged. Others arrive after sending their grandchildren to school. Luis Gonzalez has taken to going to the funeral home the night before the Mass to reassure the family that there will be company the next day. "I go tell them they can call for us anytime." Often the bereaved families will join in the singing, and many families have found their way back into the life of the parish. Milagros Vega remembers the funeral for her 32-year-old brother. "My brother had a beautiful funeral. We talk about it to this day." The older members have learned how to give comfort, how to talk to the families. The *cantus firmus* of this renewal of mission in Brooklyn is the music of the liturgy.

The companions of Christ, bearing God in their mouths, turned to meet the tiny procession coming up the center aisle. They sang the responses as well as the hymns and held hands. The doors remained open after the coffin and family were gone, and the sunlight streamed back into the old city church.

"It fills us with joy to sing, not just to speak," said Maria Melendez.

"It is more praising of God," 78-year-old Placida Tejeda added. "To sing is to pray twice."

It is the vocation of the Church to practice the song we will all sing when we are homeward bound. In Christ all of life and mission is doxology.

(*Lutheran Forum*, Advent, 1996)

PART FIVE
"TO PROCLAIM THE GOOD NEWS
OF GOD IN CHRIST...."

Chapter 24
Bishop and Parish

> Love is a many-splintered thing.
> (Langston Hughes, *Simple's Uncle Sam*)

> The divine power, though it is exalted far above our nature and inaccessible to all approach, like a tender mother who joins in the inarticulate utterances of her babe, gives to our human nature what it is capable of receiving; and thus in the various manifestations of God to humanity, God both adapts to humanity and speaks in human language. (St. Gregory of Nyssa)

The heart of the Church's life is worship of the living God. We are shaped in faith and mission by liturgy, the presence of Jesus in Word and Sacraments. If, as Kierkegaard said, "Purity of heart is to will one thing," then the one thing about liturgy is that it is an encounter with the living God, lived out into the world. But that one thing takes many forms in our part of the world. My installation as Bishop of the Metropolitan New York Synod of the ELCA included prayers in the eight languages of Lutheran worship in Brooklyn. In our synod, on the Lord's day, one can worship with a traditional setting of Holy Communion from the *Lutheran Book of Worship*; a mariachi Mass; or a jazz or Gospel music liturgy. In the variety of cultural contexts, pieties, languages and settings of our synod the "one thing" of our liturgical life can look like many things. This variety is an issue for the whole Church that seeks to translate the high Christology of our Lutheran expression of the Gospel into our different cultural settings. Are we divided or united as we assemble for liturgy across the Church?

I believe that the great tradition of the Church is like a phone book that can have many entries, but still be about one thing. It unites our transcultural elements and their various liturgical expressions. Come with me to a storefront mission congregation near Yankee Stadium and see how elements of the life at New Hope reflect our unity as Lutheran Christians. In the small building clusters of children and adults are studying the lessons for the day with leaders being trained in the Diakonia program. The groups of people gather for the liturgy, feeding into the worship their conversations and insights about the day's pericopes. Acolytes and crucifer lead the procession the fifteen feet from the entrance to the altar. The songs have a Gospel beat. The music from the cultures and rhythms of the neighborhood are attached to the structure of the Western Roman Catholic liturgical tradition. The Prayer of the Day, lessons, Gospel, sermon (including many testimonies of God's power in people's lives), Creed, Prayer of the Church (more testimonies, extended intercessions), anointing for healing, Eucharist, Benediction. Offerings of money for the Church's ministry are received together with food and clothing for neighbors burned out in a fire. Many of those worshiping are in various stages of recovery from a variety of addictions. There is a lively sense that the liturgy is public, set in the midst of the community and its concerns. The *Didache*, if you will, set to a salsa beat....

I asked one of the leaders of the service why he attends New Hope. In his answer, culturally conditioned, see the "one thing" of Lutheran identity being etched anew:

- First, he spoke about the opportunities for deeper encounters with his ethnic traditions and piety in nearby churches. But then he pointed to his jeans and said, "They accept me here the way I am. I feel welcome. Nobody judges me." He was speaking, of course, of justification by grace alone. God comes to us as we are.
- Second, he talked about how New Hope seems serious about study of the Bible, and is an ally for him in sharing the Faith with his children. "You are serious about the Story here." This Lutheran theologian was describing the power of "Scripture Alone" as it illumines the "one thing" of our life together.
- Finally, he said that he appreciated coming to a worship in which he knew what to expect each week, at least in some of the liturgy: the Story, the Meal, the Bath. The life of the community gathered by this *ordo* of our liturgy is all a part of the "Christ Alone" of our identity. Each Lord's day Christ meets us, in a faith that stretches across the centuries in our liturgy.

Christ comes to us to unite us, in all of our many-splendored diversity. May the "one thing" of the Gospel in liturgy and Word and Sacrament-shaped service always be the heartbeat of our synods and congregations.

In the light of this understanding of worship, and the proposals of the *Concordat*, what are bishops good for? Among many things, these two:

To cultivate and remind the Church of the "one thing" that is its heart and life—the presence of Jesus in Word and Sacraments.

To signify the unity of the many and diverse communities who cohere in their continual worship of the living God, in word and deed.

(*Lutheran Forum*, Pentecost, 1997)

CHAPTER 25
THE TRIUNE SHAPE OF THE CHURCH: *EPISCOPE* AND THE TRINITY

LOOSE HIM AND LET HIM GO

> Jesus said, "Loose him, and let him go." "Loose him" means "forgive him." We've got some forgivin' to do. Take away the fetters from his hands; let him work one more time. Take the chains off his feet; let him walk one more time. Take the napkins off his face; let him see and speak one more time.
> The reason we're here this morning is not just because a resurrection happened, but because there's one goin' on. Every time I see a brother come to Christ, there's a resurrection goin' on. Every time I see a man put down his bottle, there's a resurrection goin' on. Every time I see a man hug his son, there's a resurrection goin' on. Come forth Lazarus, break those chains. Throw off those fetters. Remove that napkin. Son of man, stand up on your feet. (Rev. Johnny Ray Youngblood, from a sermon preached at St. Paul Community Baptist Church, Brooklyn, New York. Quoted in Samuel G. Freedman, *Upon This Rock: The Miracles of a Black Church* [New York: Harper, Collins, 1993])

> Then there came a suggestion, seemingly friendly, to my reason. It was said to me: Look up to heaven to his Father. Then I saw clearly by the faith which I felt that there was nothing between the cross and heaven which could have grieved me, and that I must either look up or answer. I answered and said: "No, I cannot, for you are my heaven." I said this because I did not want to look up, for I would rather have remained in that pain until Judgment Day than have come to heaven any other way than by him. For I knew well that he who had bought me so dearly would unbind me when it was his will. (Julian of Norwich, "Showings," in *Classics in Western Spirituality* [trans. James Walsh, S. J.; New York: Paulist, 1978])

It is the work and will of the Triune God through the Cross of Jesus to unbind humanity, all creation from sin, death, and the power of the devil. Yet this work of the holy God also becomes the work of the Body of Christ. At the tomb of Lazarus we have the Holy Trinity teaching the shape of the church. It is Jesus who stands at the tomb, offering prayer to the Father who sent him. In that power he commands Lazarus to arise. The Holy Spirit binds together the Godhead in the miracle of resurrection and creates faith in those who witness it. But what follows is more than metaphor. "Unloose him and set him free," Jesus commands the witnesses.

Such is the very rhythm of ministry in the Name of God the Father, Son and Holy Spirit. The dying and rising Christ becomes present among us in Word and Sacraments. Jesus stands before our tombs, giving Eucharist to the One who sent him. In the power of the Holy Spirit we believe in him. With the Word proclaimed and enacted we, like Lazarus, have already passed from death to life. What remains is the ministry Jesus gave to the witnesses: "Unbind him and set him free." Proclaim the Word. Administer the Sacraments. Live out their implications in the world by touching body, soul, and spirit with triune love. Call it what you will: mission, evangelism, social ministry, small-group ministry, stewardship, catechesis, spirituality, whatever. If it is disincarnate, detached from the Triune God's promised presence in Word and Sacraments, it is just whistling in the graveyard, sitting shivah over the corpse of Lazarus.

The *cantus firmus* of the healing of Lazarus is the impending passion, death and resurrection of Jesus. In fact it is this life-giving event which precipitates the events that lead to the Cross. It is only at the Cross that the Holy Trinity can be known to us. At the Cross the holy God touches us in triune love and unconditional grace. The Cross looms over all ministry in memory of Jesus, just as it loomed before Jesus at the tomb of Lazarus. The shape of the command to unbind and let go is cruciform.

I have always believed that it is the particular ministry of ordained leadership in the Church to tend those connections between the Church's mission and the dying and rising Christ made present in Word and Sacraments. Such Word and Sacrament focus—enabling the Church's "unloosing" ministry to cling to the crucified and risen Christ—is a charism as important in my ministry now as a bishop as it was when I was a parish pastor.

> And Jesus looked upward and said, "Father, I thank you for having heard me. I knew that you always hear me, but I have said this for the sake of the crowd standing here, so that they may believe that you sent me." When he had said this, he cried with a loud voice, "Lazarus, come out!" The dead man came out, his hands and feet bound with strips of cloth, and his face wrapped in a cloth. Jesus said to them, "Unbind him, and let him go." (John 11: 41-44)

DEAD END FOR THE MAINLINE?

So read the cover headline of *Newsweek* on August 9, 1993. The article title continued the theme. "Religion: The Mightiest Protestants Are Running Out of Money, Members and Meaning." A 1998 article in *Newsday*, a daily newspaper distributed in New York City and Long Island, gave Protestant congregations in Long island, Brooklyn, and Queens a similar gloomy forecast. The fiscal, theological, and morale problems of our Lutheran communion are well-documented, public, and pervasive. We are often divided, discouraged and distracted. What a time to become a bishop!

We are being told that denominations are dying. Maybe, maybe not. What is not an option for Lutherans, however, is a drift into congregationalism. In the way of Jesus nobody goes it alone. As synodical and churchwide leaders try to plan for the future in the midst of diminishing resources, I fear the tendency these days to collapse wider church connections into nothing more than a kind of ecclesial United Way, providing goods and services to individual congregations. That the wider church see and cherish once again the local congregation gathered around Word and Sacraments as the primary grassroots mission outpost is essential. But to organize parishes as consumers, or to pander to a parochial sense of the church, is neither wise nor faithful. In the first centuries, the church in Macedonia was hooked up to the church in Jerusalem by prayer and money. The unity of the church was tangible in the living out of its mission. The teaching of the Apostles was continually lifted up. It should be no different among the parishes of Poughkeepsie, Montauk, and the Lower East Side of Manhattan. We are running in fright from questions raised at benevolence time. "What has the Synod done for us lately?" We need to begin to answer, "That is a faithless question." The question is rather, "What is God doing among us, and how can we faithfully participate in the command of Jesus to those resurrection witnesses: 'Unbind him and let him go'?"

So let me suggest a modest role for leadership in the wider Church, centered in faithful bishops and the ministry of oversight they exercise with their staffs. It is that ministry of tending the connections between the Son of God standing at the tomb of Lazarus, calling out to his Father in the power of the Holy Spirit, giving life to Lazarus; and the mission of the Church to unbind and let go. It is a ministry of lifting up the perspective of the Cross over all that we do together.

These are a few of the "teachable moments" which seem to call forth such ministry:

Pastoral visitation: As the congregation is built up through encounters between pastor and people, so also is the wider Church. Regular, ardent visitation of a synod's pastors, teachers, deacons, and other public ministers helps to tend the connections between the ministry of Word and Sacrament and the activity of the Church. Visitation includes prayer, walking or driving the neighborhood, Confession and Absolution, agitation for spiritual and vocational maturity. The conversation helps strengthen the pastor's vocation to baptize, to teach, to make Eucharist, to hear confessions and pronounce absolution, to preach, to pray, and to lead communities of Jesus. Also important here are visitations of social ministry agencies, seeking their rootedness in congregational life shaped by Jesus in the Word and Sacraments.

Vacancies, candidacy processes, orientation of new ministers: These are all opportunities for increasing the coherence between the font, the pulpit and the altar, and the "unbinding" ministry that flows from them. The bishop and staff know their flock. They can lift up examples of faithful ministry centered on the presence of the Triune God in Christ. I think of the liturgy at St. John's in the South Bronx. The rhythms and tunes of the liturgy are African-American, in a Gospel and Spiritual idiom. The historic form of the liturgy is respected. The people who come forward to the Eucharistic presence of Jesus in bread and wine can also, if they wish, walk over to one of the waiting deacons for personal prayer. In some congregations anointing for healing is also available. The "unbinding" is physically and visually linked to the presence of the dying and rising Christ at the altar. Other ministries which flow from that parish: interim housing for the homeless; shelter ministry; church-based community organizing—all have their focus in the Cross and the explicit weekly connection to Jesus.

Public assemblies of the Church: Synod assemblies, "worship days," milestones in the lives of parish or pastor, stewardship and benevolence events, meetings of the ministerium, conference events and the like are all opportunities for faithful worship and teaching of the connections between life and Lord.

Pastoral ministry: Pastoral ministry is my highest priority and joy. It is a ministry shared by the entire staff of the Metropolitan New York Synod. I see the Synod's two hundred and thirty-five congregations (speaking sixteen different languages every Lord's day), over one hundred schools and early childhood centers, twelve large social ministry organizations, and hundreds of rostered leaders as a large parish. My first major effort, shortly after election as bishop, was to meet individually out in the synod with every parish pastor. There was only one item on the agenda: "How's your soul?" Episcopal visitation is a regular part of my ministry. During the summer I have led worship at every outdoor ministry and many parish summer programs. I regularly meet for prayer and mission strategy with the Chief Operating Officers of all of our social ministry organizations. I regularly visit the schools and classrooms of our synod. I have met with most of the church councils. The visits and meetings are pastoral, intended to encourage in the faith and arouse people to missional faithfulness. The pastoral dimension of episcopacy takes shape in the baptisms of pastors' babies, spiritual conversations about faith, hearing confessions, celebrating the Eucharist and preaching often, teaching the faith at synod and conference and parish levels, conducting a 'chrism' Mass each year during Holy Week. I have kept vigil with our pastors in their dying, baptized their babies, and joined them at the altar to witness their marriage vows. The "unbinding" ministry is at the heart of the pastoral ministry of the bishop's office.

STANDING AGAIN BEFORE THE TOMB

He was paying much more attention to the sermon than any five-year-old has an obligation to. He should have been enduring the rantings of the visiting preacher while being bribed with Froot Loops and coloring books. But he was right there, sitting with his grandmother, staring in rapt attention.

He followed me around during the Sunday School hour; when I would turn around I would almost knock him over, he was so close. He was touching, lurking, striving for attention with the kind of skin hunger those of you who work with children will understand. We are abandoning a generation of children, and their hunger for safe touching, carnal reassurance is palpable.

He was back again at the second liturgy, sitting with Grandma, boring into me with singular concentration as I preached. In the narthex I asked his grandmother, "What gives with the little buster?"

"Your grandmother," she said.

My grandmother had died in Christ the night before the liturgy, my grandmother whom I had communed the last time I was with her as she fought through the fog to remember me. During the sermon I had pointed to the altar and told the assembled congregation that my grandmother would be there at the Eucharist. We say it, don't we? "At all times and in all places... with angels and archangels and all the company of heaven...." I had invited those present to think of their own loved ones joining Grandma at the crowded altar with the communion of saints.

And this boy had blurted out, "Mom's here!" His mother had died in Christ a short time before. And then he had wanted to stay in touch with the one who had announced to him the startling news about her presence at the altar. And then he had told his Grandma, "I want to hear again about Mother being here."

We have a faith a five-year-old can understand. That is the point of the unbinding ministry we share in the Name of the Father, Son and Holy Spirit.

We are connected together in, with and under the presence of the dying and rising Christ in all that we do. I think of all the unbinding ministry which came together in this moment of faith. The boy had been baptized into the Triune God; the mother had attended a Lutheran high school; the school and church communities had sustained this single mother, her son and his grandmother, and accompanied her in her dying. It was bereavement ministry, support for the grandmother, nursery school and Sunday School, ministry of pastor and deacon and teacher and all the baptized, support across the generations for these two children of God, support which had nurtured the hope and expectation that blossomed at a simple announcement of the resurrection.

We who are privileged to be called to ministry across many places carry these stories with us and share them with the church. The encounter of Jesus with Lazarus, of the witnesses who unbind and set free the new life of Christ, is repeated over and over, all these centuries over, until Christ stands at our tomb, unbinding us and bidding us home to the Father.

(*Lutheran Forum*, Pentecost, 1994)

Chapter 26
Lost and Found: Growth and Evangelism

> The presentation of the Gospel message is not an optional contribution for the church. It is the duty incumbent on her by the command of the Lord Jesus, so that people can believe and be saved. This message is indeed necessary. It is unique. It cannot be replaced. It does not permit either indifference, syncretism or accommodation. It is a question of people's salvation...it merits having the apostle consecrate to it all his time and energies, to sacrifice for it, if necessary, his own life. (Pope Paul VI, *On Evangelization*)

> But while he was still far off, his father saw him and was filled with compassion; he ran and put his arms around him and kissed him...the father said to his slaves, 'Quickly, bring out a robe— the best one— and put it on him; put a ring on his finger and sandals on his feet. And get the fatted calf and kill it, and let us eat and celebrate; for this son of mine was dead and is alive again; he was lost and is found!' (Luke 15:20, 22-24)

The Prodigal Father

It begins with God. There is a sense of urgency and passion about evangelism that has its genesis in the profligate, prodigal Father who goes flying down the dusty road, arms outstretched to the son who had shown him up for a fool. The prodigal son, in effect telling Daddie dearest to drop dead, walks away from his father, clutching his inheritance, treading in footpaths made by Adam and Eve, you and me. We call it sin. It leads away from God. It ends in death.

This wastrel Father lavishes all his extravagant, inflated love on the son. Make no mistake about it, this is a public humiliation for Dad. No self-respecting Semitic father would lose face by going out to the one who had walked out on him and thus put him to shame. Let Junior come groveling home to get what's coming to him! Let him crawl through a gauntlet of jeering villagers. Let the father's honor be restored! Let the kid beg and eat dust! Let justice be done!

But there goes the prodigal father, arms outflung, now around the boy, lifting up the son! Let that biblical image sear itself into the heart of a Church that would call itself evangelical!

There is more. Another Son is lifted up by the Father. This cruciform lifting-up, this ultimate disgrace, is the very wisdom and love of God. For the love of the Prodigal Father so overflows that he will even squander the life of his own Son.

This gracious Father cannot contain his joy. The lifting up on the dusty road prefigures Easter resurrection. We are all caught up in a wave of joy. No wake this, but a feast. No death in a parentless pigpen but life by drowning. No humiliation but honor. This Father knows full well where we have been, and how far the gulf has widened between him and his beloved children. He has heard the cry of his own lifted-up Son. "My God, My God..." He knows what the pigpens of unregenerate human life are like. "For this son of mine was dead and is alive again; he was lost and is found."

The fatted calf, the raising of Jesus from the dead, the Easter promise of the Church is this Father's answers to the demands of justice. The Church is now the outstretched arms of the prodigal Father in the world.

Any discussion of evangelism must begin with this picture of the urgent passion of the God of Scripture. The Good Shepherd searching for the lost sheep; the woman turning the house upside down for the lost coin; the mother hen brooding and weeping over recalcitrant chicks; the eternal Word seeking flesh; the call of Matthew; the invitation to dinner for Zacchaeus; a conversation at a Samaritan well. The images and stories and events overflow in a picture of such astounding, relentless Divine hunger to be reconciled with all creation, that the evangelical torpor of so much of our church life is indeed occasion for sadness.

Jesus, God incarnate, calls Peter to fish for people. The risen Christ calls the same Peter to feed the children of God. Missionary and pastoral zeal belong together, reaching out and building up, an evangelical church faithful to the prodigal love of God. Building up and nurturing the faith of the people of God through Word and Sacraments, and reaching out with the Gospel of Christ crucified and risen into the midst of the world are inexorably linked to the reconciling passion that springs from the heart of God.

MISSION AND CULTUS

John Cochran, in a presentation on "Eucharist and Evangelism," identifies the wholeness of the evangelical vision:

> We must recognize the elasticity of these two gospel mandates- to make Eucharist and make disciples— in relation to the whole of the Christ-event and the whole of the world. It is in the nature of a sacrament that simple elements and simple words reflect or bear microcosmically on everything

the Lord says and does for the people. From common bread and cup to simple words of remembrance and giving thanks to the cosmic proclamation of *life, light* and *resurrection*, the movement and interplay are dramatic, elastic, life-giving for believers. Not only is the meal the sign of cultic identity, but the images of grains of wheat and grapes gathered mirror the universality of the church's mission, signal the objective of unity in Christ and witness the diversity of the elect. Similarly the making of disciples provides amply for careful teaching and universal scope...the mandates/the facets of the face of Christ do not oppose each other but overlap, share common soil and seek common ends. So we hold one to the exclusion of the other only at our great peril. We have come to such a time of great peril in the evangelical outreach, both pastoral and missionary, of our Lutheran communion. We have separated out from their dynamic tension these missionary and cultic facets of evangelical ministry. Evangelism, and evangelical catholic confessional and liturgical substance, presently exist in their mutually exclusive guild worlds, each with its own vocabulary, its own approved techniques.

Our Lutheran communion shares with mainstream Protestantism a steady decline in membership and evangelical initiative. Many pastors are demoralized by the lack of perceived results in their evangelism, or uninterested in the whole enterprise. Some, claiming faithfulness to catholic substance, hide behind their splendid or "aesthetically correct" liturgies, thereby excusing their failure and laziness. There are pastors who never walk their parish, seldom visit people, remain aloof from the communal and social issues of neighborhood life, and make no attempt to find ways to credibly invite strangers into the "faithful" cultic life of the congregation. Some let their own members slip away with minimal concern. Yes, it is true that each gathering of the people of God around Word and Sacraments on each Lord's Day is a sign of transcendent hope, whether in the most vibrant or the most desultory parish. Yet such gatherings apart from the urgent evangelistic passion of the profligately graceful God toward the lost and the prodigal children of this world are disobedient evasions of evangelical responsibility. Before Peter was commanded to feed, he was commanded to fish!

When Lutherans committed to confessional faithfulness and rich sacramental life retreat from the Great Commission, they leave the field of evangelism wide open to those who identify with the so-called Church Growth Movement. Their claim, too often borne out by evangelically disobedient Lutheran parishes, is that sticking to "old-fashioned" liturgical form and theological substance is a recipe for dead and dying churches with passive and inarticulate layfolks.

Within the arid landscape of much of Lutheran evangelical outreach the Church Growth Movement makes a compelling appeal. It incorporates an unvarnished, timeless zeal for "souls." In a small periodical published by the Lutheran Church-Missouri Synod and entitled *Evangelism*, I read a heartening story of a small Lutheran parish in Florida that has shared its life with the growing number of Haitian, Hispanic, and Arab neighbors in its surrounding community. The account put the reader in mind of Roosevelt's hundred days, with one idea after another being used or discarded, every possibility explored to reach and embrace strangers with the Gospel and build up the membership of the church. In its appeal to Scripture, and in its joyful pursuit, this parish's ministry is a winsome testimony to obedience to the Great Commission: "God has commissioned us at Our Savior to make disciples. This is an ongoing task until the second coming of Christ. Amazingly, we have never received any formal training for cross-cultural ministry. It's all been God's work of grace, as He has led us. We pray that He will continue. God hasn't failed us yet!" (*Evangelism*, Spring 1990, p. 54). To the extent that this account sounds naïve or a throwback to a less enlightened era, to that extent is our catholic substance evangelically impoverished. Yet, sadly, the Church Growth Movement has formed a closed guild of its own that would substitute missionary methods for the Means of Grace. As the pastor of Our Saviour's exciting ministry listed the "cross-cultural church growth factors," the following comments betray a passion for fishing at the exclusion of feeding: "We seek receptive people. We do not spend time and energy on resistant people....Periodically we seek to build bridges by connecting all four congregations (each developed separately according to "the homogeneous unit principle"). We emphasize our oneness in Jesus Christ through quarterly potluck dinners, fifth-Sunday choral exchanges, and holiday parties" (p. 54). Sadly, the Eucharist, together with mutual cultic life and communal discipline, appears to be no longer useful for growing churches who would express their unity in Christ. The cleavage between mission and pastoral nurture- fishing and feeding— leading to the atomization of the Church's evangelical outreach is tragic.

In an excellent document entitled "Evangelism and Church Growth," the Commission on Theology and Church Relations of the Lutheran Church-Missouri Synod highlights much of what is truly troubling about the Church Growth Movement for confessional Lutherans. The Missouri study touched on the many ways in which a theology of glory pervades this movement. It examined the new jargon, such as "soil testing" and "homogeneous unit principle," which would seek to guarantee the numerical success of Church

Growth enterprises. It cautioned against marketing a palatable Jesus, rather than faithfully articulating Law and Gospel. It makes this trenchant summary:

> The church faces the challenges of the future in a "world-come-of age" in the confidence that God has given it the resources necessary to carry out the mission...we are chiefly mindful of the means of grace, the Gospel and the sacraments. Strictly speaking, the means of grace are the only "resources" through which God calls, gathers, enlightens, sanctifies and keeps the church in the one true faith and therefore through which He builds His church. In this sense the means of grace are not simply one item among many others. They are the most crucial dimension of the church's life and work. Where the means of grace are taken seriously, the whole life of the church will be shaped by them. "The real adornment of the churches," our Lutheran Confessions can therefore state, "is godly, practical, and clear teaching, the godly use of the sacraments, ardent prayer, and the like." (P. 12)

The Means of Grace—Word and Sacraments and the people of God gathered around them—are the waiting arms of the Prodigal Father, outstretched in passionate embrace of the child returning home. It is the Church, the Body of Christ, which in the power of the Holy Spirit grasps prodigal creation in the grip of a gracious God. The retreat from the Means of Grace, of which the recent plea by one "successful" pastor for "entertainment evangelism" in *The Lutheran* is but the most egregious example, is the great danger of the Church Growth Movement.

But there are others. This movement, under the rubric of "soil testing," encourages a congregation to be very pragmatic. Strategies must be employed that are compatible with the local situation and that will work. When a strategy is not effective, it should be abandoned and a new one developed. If the parish that I served in New Jersey between 1982 and 1992 had "tested the soil" before it began housing homeless families in its parish house next door, it never would have attempted such folly. The move engendered hostility and controversy in our community. Yet this modest attempt to live our catholic substance evangelically ("given and shed for you and for all") has been both a demonstration of the seriousness of our evangelical outreach, and an opportunity to incarnate a conversation about Law and Gospel in our community. Nor have we neglected to invite the family living in our midst to partake in our eucharistic life. Feeding and fishing. In fair weather and foul.

EVANGELICAL PASSION AND PARISH RENEWAL

Let us work to renew the Church in the urgent passion of the waiting, prodigal God of all creation, not apart from, but precisely through the evangelical catholic substance of confessional and liturgical integrity. What is needed is not new persuasive evangelism techniques, new multicultural strategies, new denominational programs, new judicatory enlistment of the faithful in this or that current activist cause. What is needed is not a theology of glory, nor allegiance to sound marketing and sociological principles. What is needed is a renewed passion for the lost and prodigal of this world, a passion that includes the physical and social needs of those who suffer, a passion for justice, but primally a passion for the reconciliation of each sinner with the waiting God of grace. The love of the wastrel Father must become our own by the inspiration of the Holy Spirit.

This understanding means that we will see the parish with renewed eyes. Evangelism will not be just one of the many programs of the church but its one ministry. Sunday Schools, projects for social service and social change, parish schools, youth groups, choirs, all the activities of faithful parishes will be pointed toward extending an invitation to the neighbor to join those who gather around Word and Sacraments, the waiting arms of God. This understanding means that our national and regional church bodies will also once again regard the parish as the primary locus of missionary activity of the church. In Newark, New Jersey's largest city, there is only one Lutheran congregation, a fragile yet vibrant planting of God's new creation. In one area of Newark's central ward, we discovered there are no mainline churches— in fact there are no social institutions of any kind. I conducted and supervised over five hundred one-on-one interviews in a community organizing effort. Judicatories will have to wrestle with this challenge: What is more important than planting and maintaining parish communities of Word and Sacraments that fish and feed in memory of Jesus? More than means to membership recruitment or implements of top-down strategies, we need to cherish and nourish renewed parish life which would extend its life into the life of the world for which Christ died.

Where parishes are intimately involved in the issues and suffering of their communities, where invitations to new life in Christ are routinely and effectively made, by God's grace and in God's time evangelism happens. I remember from past ministry what happened in the wake of a tragic death in Teaneck in which an African American youth was shot by a Caucasian police officer. It was to our parishes that an anguished community turned for comfort, space for dialogue, and hope for the future. Our Lutheran parishes had combined a rich sacramental life with fervent commitment to their neighbors for many years, and the Holy Spirit enabled them to be incarnations of God's waiting arms within their beleaguered community. Let us pray for the

Holy Spirit's rekindling power, so that we may renew our evangelical outreach in the vision of the foolish Father, the prodigal lover of his children.

Some years ago I was asked to reflect in an editorial in *Lutheran Partners* on the homogeneous unit principle of the Church Growth Movement and its relationship to evangelism in multicultural settings. Some of the reflections I set down then still seem relevant to our present opportunities for evangelical renewal:

"There was a time when a parish I served in New York City spoke a mix of English, Spanish, and Korean on Sunday morning. The small church's response to a rapidly changing neighborhood had been touching and effective. The parish then decided to integrate completely, to worship all together in English. The Korean language and culture were taught to children so that they would remember their identity. Cultural expressions in worship and our common life together were rich and varied and sometimes vexing. After an absence of five years I returned to worship and preach. The church is still well integrated; its leaders in outreach and liturgy are inclusive of the many diverse people who call that parish home, and they remain a parable of the power of the Gospel to break down barriers and create a Christ-centered community. The Meal, Baptism, catechesis, the story of Jesus and Israel, these were the things we held in common.

The homogeneous unit principle of evangelism makes sociological sense—birds of a feather do flock together. But a strategy derived from the findings of the social sciences cannot be allowed to replace the Gospel mediated through Word and Sacraments as the organizing principle of creating communities of believers as a sign and invitation of the Kingdom of God. The heartbeat of the parish and the neighborhood is the Eucharist and the Great Commission. The Eucharistic community of the parish is the center of all evangelistic efforts. It carves out a neighborhood around the congregation for which it claims responsibility and uses every means at its disposal to invite all who live within the shadow of the steeple to a place at the Table and the weekly Family Meal. Is it not through the Means of Grace of Word and Sacraments that the Holy Spirit creates faith, Jesus is present, and disciples are made? When that center holds firm, all other forms of ethnic diversity and missionary methods become not only possible but salutary.

Including the stranger is always risky, sometimes impossible (or so it seems), sometimes foolish to a world that is all too aware of the subtle nuances of racism, paternalism, and the flocking habits of birds. Original sin is real. Yet I will never forget the most stunning Easter celebration of my life. After baptizing five Korean families in the multilingual parish that I mentioned earlier, I was asked by the Korean members to accompany them to a clothing store in the South Bronx. One of our members had had to work on that day and his fellow Christians wanted to be sure he participated in the Easter Eucharist of our community. What a parable of evangelism it was to be led into the world with the Body and Blood of Christ by newcomers to our parish who were moved by resurrection faith. In Christ, without forgetting our own unique ethnic journeys, we all become 'birds of a feather,' children of the one God who waits and seeks and embraces in everlasting love and grace."

(*Lutheran Forum*, Reformation, 1990)

Chapter 27
Evangelism, Church Growth and the Swinging Door

The Doorman

I remember Ernie the doorman. He was a German immigrant who lived alone with his developmentally disabled son in the nearby warren of five-story apartments near the subway in Jackson Heights, Queens. For many years Ernie had been the doorman of the Park Lane Hotel in Manhattan, a grand hotel in the old style from a time of hospitality and graciousness. In the Park Lane's salad days, when the Kennedys, Fritz Kreisler, ladies of the evening, and other greater and lesser notables availed themselves of its hospitality, more often than not the sentinel and greeter was Ernest. He was born to be a doorman, and to create with the tip of his hat the illusion that you had come home.

When he retired from being the doorman of the Park Lane Hotel, Ernest became the doorman of his beloved Atonement Lutheran Church in Queens. He would arrive early, pick up the debris of Saturday night in our neighborhood that had been deposited around the entrance, replace pencils and Communion cards, light the candles, get out the bulletins, and open windows or make sure the boiler was running. When I arrived he always had a cup of coffee ready for the two of us, and in the early morning before the first arrivals he would tell me of the history of the church, the neighborhood, details of the struggles of its members, concerns about present challenges. He moved about the church as if he were moving about his own home, and he made me feel as if he were sharing his home with me. He made everybody feel that way. He was a link between the old guard in a dying parish, and the newcomers in the neighborhood who spoke different languages and whose skin color was different from ours. I think in those early morning hours when the gentle doorman and the young pastor bent over cups of coffee the seeds were planted about what kind of a church Atonement would be in its changing, challenging neighborhood.

As the people began to arrive the doorman would greet each one personally. Newcomers would be brought to the sacristy and introduced to the pastor with the same pride and hospitality with which Ernest would introduce his own son. He remembered birthdays and anniversaries; he knew who had been sick and who was looking for a job; he found out whose brother or aunt in the neighborhood was unbaptized or in need of a pastoral visit; he agonized over those who had fallen away and made sure that the church never cut them loose. He brokered needs with those who had the ability to meet them. And he helped create for all of us disparate characters, from over twenty different ethnic groups, the impression that when you entered the doors of the church you had come home.

THE DOOR

> So Jesus again said to them, "Very truly, I tell you, I am the door for the sheep. All who came before me are thieves and bandits; but the sheep did not listen to them. I am the door. Whoever enters by me will be saved, and will come in and go out and find pasture." (John 10:7-9)

The lesson of the doorman is that evangelism is not some closed guild but the ongoing passion behind every activity of the Church. And the lesson of the One who is the Door is that at the center of an evangelical Church stands the Good Shepherd, present in Word and Sacraments and the community that that Presence brings into being. With Jesus at the Door, the ministry of the Church is public, extending its font and altar and life into the midst of the world. With Jesus at the Door we remember that Word and Sacraments are enacted in the midst of creation because Jesus is stationed at the gate of the sheepfold, leading in and out to pasture. Ernest making the sanctuary and its altar and font ready; Ernest greeting the arrivals from the neighborhood as they entered; Ernest connecting them and this pastor with the needs of people in the community; Ernest a parable of the twin mandates of the Church: attending to the presence of Jesus in Word and Sacraments, and welcoming the stranger to that presence.

WHICH DOOR?

There is so much for our instruction in what has become known as the Church Growth Movement. There is a passion to bring the unchurched to Jesus that puts to shame the evangelical torpor of too many of our churches and pastors who separate in their practice the mission and cultic factors of the Church's life. I am as inspired by the hunger for evangelical outreach of so many pastors and parish leaders as I am astounded by the disinterest or hostility I encounter in so many others. Yes, it is true that each gathering of the people of God around Word and Sacraments is an eschatological sign of transcendent hope, whether in the most vibrant or lackadaisical parish. Yet apart from the urgent passion of the Door of the sheepfold toward the lost and prodigal of this world, such gatherings can also be evasions of evangelical responsibility.

What is also instructive about the Church Growth Movement is its refreshing practicality. This movement has enriched the Church with many ideas worth trying in order for the Church to share its life with the world. The analysis brought to bear on why churches grow, on how the conflict which inevitably accompanies change can be addressed, is pragmatic and helpful. In my present ministry I have been exposed to many good ideas and happily passed them along, as well as some incredibly bad ideas I have equally happily ignored.

Yet there are some aspects of this movement which trouble me greatly. A theology of the Cross is supplanted by a theology of glory. It is as likely that God could be calling the Church to a time of countercultural exile as to a time of Constantinian growth. Marketing language, the hegemony of the "felt needs" of unregenerate humanity, the retreat from confessional language and integrity and from sacramental ardor, are in danger of replacing the Door of Jesus with the playpen of the self. Confessional and liturgical faithfulness is not cultural imperialism and repristination. Confessional and liturgical faithfulness is the source of the Church's identity and evangelical mission, the shape taken by Jesus the Door in the Church and in the world.

To point out the distortion of the Church without evangelism, or evangelism without the Church is nothing new. What God has joined together let no one put asunder! And powerful expressions of Eucharistic evangelism are happening. In Black and Latino neighborhoods the form of the Mass vibrates with songs and rhythms of cultural integrity and relevance, as well as with evangelical passion and effectiveness. In one pastoral vacancy in the Bronx the outreach to Spanish-speaking people is being led by a Latina deacon. Through Bible study, music, vibrant liturgy from within the culture God is leading many new people to the life of the Church. They are now asking the Church to instruct them in the history and meaning of the liturgy. I have seen "seeker services" offering the Word of God and the Meal that were not puerile, nor did they cover the beauty of the Church with linoleum. They drew people into the Church through the Door of Jesus. I have also, sadly, seen Church Growth activity that so badly distorted the message of the Church that although it initially packed them in it became, in Shakespeare's words, "full of sound and fury, signifying nothing." The Church exists to signify nothing except Christ crucified and risen.

OPENING THE DOOR

In the early morning activity of an urban doorman we can perhaps latch onto an image to help us think about centering every activity of the Church in the evangelical passion of Jesus the Door. Let me share these church growth principles from Ernie the doorman:

- The Church's primary evangelical activity must be to prepare itself to welcome the unbaptized and the unchurched. How can we make the font, the altar, the Word public and accessible? Renewed attention to the rite of Christian Initiation of Adults and continuing catechesis ought to be carefully explored.
- Attending to the needs of people—remembering the poor—must be a pervasive sign of the Church's evangelical seriousness.
- An evangelical Church must continually nurture the baptismal vocations of its people so that their discipleship in the midst of the world can point to the Door of the Church.
- Pastoral acts (Baptism, Communion instruction, marriages, funerals etc.) and teachable moments (hospital visitation, crises or times of joy) should be seen not as isolated acts but as processes of extended ministry. Keeping in touch with those touched by the Door can lead to support groups for the bereaved or single parents, to early childhood centers or latch-key programs, to church-based community organizing or annual baptismal reunions.
- In remembering Ernie's placement at the door between the old guard of a dying church and the diverse neighborhood outside I am convinced by our experience that cultural relevance and catholic substance can powerfully anchor new communities of Jesus.
- Finally, Jesus the Door stands in the midst of communities suffering great spiritual hunger. Ernie was greeter not only for a local parish, but also for a vision of spiritual rest and embodied eternal hope.

I was with Ernie when he died at St. Clare's hospital on the West Side. I saw the many strangers he had welcomed into our church begin to circle around his frightened son, claiming him as their own. I fed Ernie with bread and wine as he began his final homecoming. As his ragged breathing gentled and ceased he was already standing before the Door, being welcomed by the Great Shepherd—creating not the impression, but the reality of home.

(*Lutheran Forum*, Lent, 1995)

CHAPTER 28
HIRTABREV – FOLLOWING JESUS TO THE BREACH

ONE PURE THING

> "You shall be called the repairer of the breach, the restorer of streets to live in." (Isaiah 58:12b).

> "Blessed are the pure in heart, for they will see God." (Matt. 5:8)

> Purity of heart is to will one thing. (Kierkegaard)—in conversation with Jim Wind of the Alban Institute.

The one pure thing in our life as a synod, willed by the Holy Spirit, is to follow Jesus together.
Follow. Jesus. Together. Three words, each with power and direction for us.

Follow ... an active verb; to get up, get out of our undercrofts, to leave behind our fear of the future, to be on the move... "Where are you going?" they asked him. "Come and see," he said. Our collective heart longs for, wills, the kinetic energy of faithful following.

Jesus ... We follow, and are shaped by the One we encounter in Word and Sacraments. This is the center of our life, this is our heartbeat. Jesus, precious Savior, is the destination of the pure in heart.

Together ... When I was standing before my grandmother for the final time I saw her gaze at me, squinting and trying to remember; then a huge smile and joyous exclamation, with open arms..."I don't remember your name, but I know you belong to me!" We follow Jesus together because we belong to

---

Author's Note: Hirtabrev, literally "shepherd's letter," is the term for a Swedish bishop's pastoral letter. In a *Hirtabrev* the bishop addresses pastors and church leaders, exhorting them to faithfulness in the spiritual journey and to maturity in leadership. The bishop also teaches a common vision and ecclesiology for the parishes of the diocese. At each of our annual synod assemblies I try to make my report more of a *hirtabrev* and less of a report to the stockholders. This chapter is based on my first annual report after being elected bishop, a *hirtabrev* calling the synod I serve to communal life and mission in the "breach" in the walls of the city (Isaiah 58).

one another in the Spirit's tether. Our text provides a compelling example, and wonderful images for reflection today on our life as a synod following Jesus together.

> Is not this the fast that I choose: to loose the bonds of injustice, to undo the thongs of the yoke, and to break every yoke? Is it not to share your bread with the hungry, and bring the homeless poor into your house; when you see the naked, to cover them, and not to hide yourself from your own kin? Then your light shall break forth like the dawn, and your healing shall spring up quickly; your vindicator shall go before you, the glory of the Lord shall be your rear guard. Then you shall call, and the Lord will answer; you shall cry for help, and he will say, 'Here I am.' If you remove the yoke from among you, the pointing of the finger, the speaking of evil, if you offer your food to the hungry and satisfy the needs of the afflicted, then your light shall rise in the darkness and your gloom be like the noonday. The Lord will guide you continually, and satisfy your needs in parched places, and make your bones strong; and you shall be like a watered garden, like a spring of water, whose waters never fail. Your ancient ruins shall be rebuilt; you shall raise up the foundations of many generations; you shall be called the repairer of the breach, the restorer of streets to live in. (Isaiah 58:6-12)

Many scholars see chapters 56-66 of Isaiah as a single unit addressed to the members of the community of Israel who had returned from exile in Babylon. The message joins the community in their concern to rebuild the walls and ruined streets of a ravaged Jerusalem and surrounding neighborhoods. They are also concerned with rebuilding faithful commitment to the cultic life of the covenant: 'You shall raise up the foundations of many generations.' The burning question for the writer of our text is whether the community and the nations that join them are worthy to stand in unity and justice when God appears and Zion is restored. Can Israel's people, standing before the breach of their ruined city and broken communal life, the breach of the hungry, the ruined streets, the naked, the homeless poor, the oppressed, the afflicted, while pointing angry fingers at one another, be fully servants of the holy God?

Our synod, like Israel, longs to be faithful to the faith of the 'foundations of many generations.' We too are in a situation of change and turmoil. Are we in our synod a community before God capable of willing one resolute thing?

I will arrange my report to you around some of the images from our text:
Kin: "Not to hide yourself from your own *kin*..."
- We follow Jesus *together.*

Kin. We are a family who belong to one another in Christ. We will spend some time talking about what it means for us to be together. Who are we as a synod, a community before God? What does it look like when we hide ourselves from one another? What causes us to 'point the finger?' What would it look like if we were to renew our kinship in Christ the kin, our brother? We will speak about the following of Jesus... together.

> When you see the naked to cover them, and not to hide yourself from your own kin?

Breach: "You shall be called the repairer of the *breach*, the restorer of streets to live in..."
- We follow Jesus together *to the breach.*

The breach is a way of talking about our brokenness, but also a way of talking about healing encounters with the Risen Christ. Where do we follow Jesus together? To the breach, the place of our brokenness and healing. The post-exilic Israel of our passage was intent on rebuilding the Temple and restoring the purity of their cultic life. The God of Israel told them, 'Look around you!' *God called them to the breach.* 'Announce to my people their rebellion, to the house of Jacob their sins' ... the oppressed workers ... the bonds of injustice ... the thongs of the yoke ... the oppressed ... the hungry ... the homeless poor ... the naked ... your own kin ... the afflicted ... your needs in parched places ... ancient ruins ... the breach ... the ruined uninhabitable streets....

When we follow Jesus to the breach, what do we see? What does that look like around here? We will talk about the breach as we talk about our life as the ELCA, our synod, our congregations and institutions, our communal life in our society, our ecumenical and interfaith relationships.

> Your ancient ruins shall be rebuilt; you shall raise up the foundations of many generations; you shall be called the repairer of the breach, the restorer of streets to live in....

Watered Garden: "You shall be like *a watered garden...*"
- We follow Jesus together to the breach *abundantly gifted by the Holy Spirit.*

Our giftedness as a synod, our garden, gifted and baptismally watered by the Holy Spirit, is so pervasive and diverse it almost defies description. But it springs from the one thing of our life together: Jesus. We are a people shaped by the presence of Jesus. That is why every community gathered around and by Word and Sacraments—whether fifty or five hundred are gathered, whether in sanctuaries of splendid architecture or Bronx shelter or nursing home or country chapel, whether in English or one of sixteen other languages spoken in our synod— is a miracle. God is with us! Jesus is present! From that heartbeat and to it flows all of our giftedness. Sometimes, although we don't mean to, we act as if God has held out on us, as if we must hoard our meager resources or we certainly will not survive. Gifted people, we are not called to survival, but bold following of Jesus together!

> The Lord will guide you continually, and satisfy your needs in parched places, and make your bones strong; and you shall be like a watered garden, like a spring of water....

We are called again today by the dying and rising Christ, in the inspiration of the Holy Spirit, to follow Jesus together. That is the one thing which animates and shapes the many and diverse things of our corporate life.

- We are kin in Christ,
- Led by Jesus to the breach,
- Gifted as a watered garden.

This whole day will flow toward the altar, the healing at the breach, where we will again encounter our heart's desire in Word and Bread and Wine, carnal and earthy presence drawing us together and leading us onward.

Our Gifted Kinship Together in God's Watered Garden

Testimony from the watered garden

Let's lift up some of the wondrous giftedness of this synod. I recently spent two and a half weeks in one-on-one conversations with most of the clergy serving in congregations. This kind of relational visitation of lay and rostered leadership will be an ongoing priority for me. These conversations were held at various parish locations around the synod. These were powerful experiences for me and I came away from them with some strong impressions:

1. Vocation: Our pastors are still in touch with the call to ministry around which their lives have been shaped. They spoke of their faith and of their vocation with conviction.

2. Isolation: Many of our parish pastors, for many reasons, have felt alone in their ministries, or wish that the relational structures of our synod could be strengthened. The breach is very much a part of our synod and parish life. There are issues which vex us and divide us.

3. Consecration: There is much heroic ministry happening. I hear story after story of faithful efforts to follow Jesus like that of St. John by the Sea in Long Beach. They are reaching out to the Long Beach in the breach: the homeless, the undocumented, the de-institutionalized who are addicted or mentally ill. These children of God are members of this congregation. There

are many examples which we don't read about in the *Lutheran New Yorker*, anonymous faithfulness in all the settings of our synod, places where through the efforts of our kin in ministry you and I are there.

- When a parish in Long Beach baptizes a refugee family you and I are there.
- When parish leaders and pastor in New Paltz hold meetings with the mayor and other leaders in the community around local needs and issues as part of a 'rerooting' mission strategy process you and I join these conversations in the breach.
- When parish leaders in Rocky Point, Long Island risk a bold building program to prepare to meet and serve the next generation of spiritual seekers we build together.
- When Carmelo Maldonado teaches and mentors the faith for junior high city kids at Queens Lutheran School, you and I join him and all rostered teachers.
- When students gathered by the campus ministry of the state university at New Paltz build housing through Habitat for Humanity, you and I wield a hammer with them.
- When hundreds of hungry and homeless eat a meal in Woodstock or Saugerties you and I are their companions.
- When someone celebrating recovery 'one day at a time' leads the prayers at New Hope in the Bronx, you and I pray and lead with them.
- When a chaplain prays with someone with AIDS at Lutheran Medical Center or a rostered deacon leads worship in a New Rochelle nursing home, you and I are with them.
- When two parish leaders leave their Nehemiah homes in Brooklyn and the South Bronx—homes we built together through church-based community organizing—and when they plan and lead a meeting with the mayor around providing the community jobs at a living wage, you and I are there.
- When the saints of Danish ancestry in Brooklyn make a gift of their beloved Salem Church and its assets to the founding of Salaam Church and the sharing of the Gospel to our Arab brothers and sisters, we are all present at this Gospel transaction of grace.
- When I give young men and women their first communion tomorrow at the Bishop's Church in Hauppauge, Long Island, you all will be joining me in presence with a congregation discerning its mission in the coming "suburban century."
- When Bishop Mushemba lifts up the bread and cup in our companion synod in Tanzania, and when churches in Staten Island participate in the welcome of hundreds of Liberian refugees, we are together forging a global mission field right in our synod.

As my grandmother said to me: "I'm not sure I know your name, but I know you belong to me."

Our kinship as God's people stretches backward to the post-exilic community of Israel contemplating the breach of their covenant life together, shattered by exile, wondering what to do next. They proposed business as usual, a fast as they hade always known it. God said, "Look around you.... *this* is the fast I choose." We, too, look on the "ancient ruins," remembering better days. We, too are tempted to choose the fast as we have always known it: holding on to ethnic identity, familiar cultural worship forms and organizational structures, and sometimes creating a haven in the midst of changing neighborhoods and times, a refuge from the breach. God also says to us, "Look around you... this is the fast *I* choose."

God called them and us to 'rerooting'... into the covenant lived out into the breach... into the shaping power of Jesus... into the welcome of the stranger which built our parishes and received our ancestors... into the breach today in the world around us... into our own giftedness and kinship as a community in Christ.

Our giftedness includes our staff, our ELCA and ecumenical partners, our lay and rostered leaders, all of us together living in the watered garden of the Giver of all good gifts.

> The Lord will guide you continually, and satisfy your needs in parched places, and make your bones strong; and you shall be like a watered garden, like a spring of water, whose waters never fail.

Some proposals to nurture the kinship of our watered garden

When the family sits down to share a meal it is important that everyone eats. If one person's plate is heaped with food and another across the table has no food at all it is a family matter of deepest import. When one of the family is missing from the table it matters deeply to everyone sitting down to eat. When the household of Jesus in Jerusalem sat at table together with the Greek and Hebrew widows the mutual accountability of the table was a matter of family justice. When the family of Israel sat down together they were asked by God, who's missing? You can't eat your own meal or declare your own fast apart from the breach. What does it mean to be kin in Christ? What does it mean to be a synod?

There are hopeful signs that our kinship in Christ is being strengthened in the Spirit's power. Our level of mission support has been increasing. It's about the relationships, not the money. We belong to one another because we belong to Jesus Christ. Your generous response to the dollar campaign of our AIDS task force demonstrated our resolve to stand with those suffering in the breach.

Our public liturgies dedicating new facilities we built together at Trinity, Lower East Side and Transfiguration, Bronx demonstrated our resolve to follow Jesus together as repairers of the breach, and restorer of streets to live in. Our gifted watered garden flowers in these and many other places. Can our sense of the Church sustain these and other kin? Will we stay at the table together, or each build our own table and eat our own meal?

> Is it not to share your bread with the hungry, and bring the homeless poor into your house; when you see the naked to cover them, and not to hide yourself from your own kin?

We have spent a lot of time in our synod using the 'rerooting in the community' mission strategy process to bring forward bold proposals to connect again with the neighborhoods of our parishes. We will not "reroot" anywhere if we do not "reroot" (or reform) our life into the core of our Word and Sacrament tradition.

- I call on the lay and clergy leadership of every congregation to visit the household of every one they have nurtured to baptism in the past five years.
- I ask every congregation to study the first eleven chapters of the book of Acts in the coming year, as we together lift up the sources of a mission which is accountable, bold, carried across boundaries, and Spirit-driven. I will ask staff to prepare a study guide which lifts up our own context for mission. Let us return to the Word together.
- I am asking the communications committee to work with Pastor Fred Schumacher, editor of *For All the Saints: A Prayer Book For and By the Church*, to prepare a devotional book for use in our synod based on this wonderful resource (published by the American Lutheran Publicity Bureau, Delhi, NY). I want our kin to be in daily reflection in the Scriptures and in prayer.
- Can Lutherans nourish a public reputation as a communion serious about teaching the faith for discipleship in the world? What a renewal in faith and mission it would signal among us if every congregation invited the community (and its membership) to an annual course on the basics of the Christian faith.
- It is Jesus we follow together. Whatever the frequency, let us lift up the eucharistic heartbeat of our kinship in Christ.

INTO THE BREACH

Recently I stood with Bishop McGann of the Roman Catholic Diocese of Rockville Center as we addressed the founding assembly of Long Island Congregations and Neighborhoods. Lay and pastoral leadership and resources from our synod have been critical components in the birthing of this organization. We faced a multi-racial, interfaith gathering of over a thousand people from all over Long Island who brought forward issues in the breach of their communal life to the healing power of God. This public resolve to stand in the breath with power and conviction is one of the most heartening signs of public faith I have witnessed. That prayerful moment of collective faith visible in the public arena is a powerful witness to the call of God to be 'repairers of the breach.' We are called in our congregations to disciple people in the faith who are capable of participating in the decisions which shape our public life.

Where will we stand as a synod, and where will your bishop stand publicly as a witness to the Gospel in the breach? Where we must first stand, as the highest priority, is with those who are without the Gospel, leaving the 99 in the pen and relentlessly seeking the lost sheep. They are religious seekers, those who hunger for a noble vision, those in the breach who have been left behind by everybody. There are so many issues touching people in the breach: addiction, education issues, women and children in poverty, bias crimes and violence. Running through them all (and in the breaches of our own life together) is the fault line of racism.

Let me outline a few issues where I believe that our faith compels us to follow Jesus together into the breach. In each of these areas we can and ought to debate the best way to respond. We have no special expertise for this or that public policy. But as to where we shall stand in the breach, I believe that with some of these issues it is almost as simple as "the Bible tells me so."

Work: The fastest way to kill a family is to defund it. When there is not meaningful work with a living wage all the other social heartbreak will follow. The social covenant around work has collapsed. In every congregation you have members who will tell you what it is like to have your benefits taken away, your job "downsized," and then to be "temped" at half your previous salary. Look at the effects of IBM, Grumman, Brookhaven Labs, and others on the economy and availability of jobs in our region. And this isn't just a city issue. The highest unemployment rate in the state of New York is in Sullivan County, where our synod has four congregations. And when so-called welfare reform leaves people at minimum wage and unable to afford child care or training for better jobs at liveable wages, I believe it is an offence to God. Workers are called to the vineyard. Lutherans have placed a very high value on a sense of vocation. Where do we stand if we believe God owns the vineyard?

Food: If I told you there is a place where one in seven children go to bed hungry you would think I was talking about some Third World country. I'm not. We live in that country. The Long Island Congregations community organization I mentioned above is responding to serious cuts in availability of food. The federal Food and Nutrition program (FAN) has told a local program, "You're feeding too many people" (mostly frail and impoverished elderly). They are defunding food for five thousand hungry people in Long Island. Where do we stand who pray "Give us this day our daily bread"?

Health Care: The world of health care is changing rapidly, moving from a fee-for-service to a managed healthcare environment. What will this mean for people who are poor? Or not poor enough? The underinsured have no chance at all here. In this environment those with AIDS in prison are being deprived of the new medicines that prolong life. In an environment that basically says "I'll cover this group of people for the ceiling of this amount of money," I believe we are losing the fundamental value of accessible healing for all people. Recently Long Island Congregations gathered the testimony of over a thousand children of God to head off the closing of three community health centers across Long Island. Where do people stand who worship the One who said, "Come to me, all you that are weary and are carrying heavy burdens, and I will give you rest"?

The Stranger and Sojourner Among Us: My grandparents came to this country from another place. Most of our congregations were built by welcoming the stranger. My grandfather got his first job, his first help with filling out forms, his first place to live, his first welcoming community through his church. Today the stranger among us, along with the poor, is the scapegoat. Far from seeking out the stranger in the breach, as Scripture and the example of Jesus and the Early Church consistently urge us, we attack and blame the immigrant. Even legal immigrants, here for over thirty years were attacked in the "welfare reform" bills recently passed. In our shrinking world where do those stand who believe "He's got the whole world in his hands"?

It's pretty basic. Where do you stand when a large part of society stands somewhere else? I hear no outcry from the public or those who make policy in this country about a safety net, or bottom line values. Here's where I will stand, God willing, with you. We follow Jesus together into the breach to stand with those who ask: Do I get to work? Do I get to eat? Do I get medical care? Can I come in? Will someone help me to see Jesus?

Some proposals to follow Jesus together *into the breach*.
- I call on each of our congregations to have fifty conversations with people in the breach in the coming year. These conversations can

include those who do not have a church home, those who are hungry, homeless, immigrant, unemployed, poor, or in many other situations in the breach. We have several resources for the building of these relationships:
- + the schools and early childhood programs of our synod
- + the social ministry organizations related to our synod
- + the church-based community organizations to which the congregations of our synod relate (such as Long Island Congregations, South Bronx Churches, East Brooklyn Churches and others), which teach parish leaders the art of one-on-one relational meetings.
- + the "rerooting" mission strategy process of our synod

- Let there be a 'summit' of pastors and lay leaders of our synod involved or interested in involvement in church-based community organizing to develop a strategy in our synod for use of this discipline, as we move out into the breach.
- I call on five conferences in our synod to organize an introduction to our synod's 'rerooting' mission strategy process, and I call on the use of this process in five pastoral vacancies.
- I call on the cadre of synodically authorized deacons and graduates of the Diakonia program to consider forming a "church planting" missionary team (catechists, organizers of Sunday School, after school programs, social ministry, evangelists) to begin one new outreach ministry in the Hunts Point section of the Bronx. I also ask them to corporately fund a synodical ministry "in the breach."
- Let the theme of the next church days be "Repairers of the Breach," with congregations reporting on their conversations in the breach and workshops be presented that nurture these conversations.
- I will develop, with Rev. David Benke of the Atlantic District of the Lutheran Church-Missouri Synod, a proposal to Wheatridge to fund a staff person who will help organize congregational social ministry with the efforts of our social ministry organizations to stand in the breach.

Last Sunday I baptized Zackry Barrett at the 155th anniversary liturgy of Trinity, Kingston. I am reminded that our primal centering in Word and Sacraments is public and the source of our following Jesus to the breach. When we baptize our babies (of any age) we do not leave them at the font. It is baptismal ministry to follow them into the world, into the breach. Whether they will learn in school, have a good job, live in a society of just opportunity is ministry of baptism. When we eat at the table of the Lord's Supper and someone in the breach eats alone, or has no food, it is the very body and blood of Christ that lead us to be repairers of the breach.

CHAPTER 29
HIRTABREV — COME TO THE TABLE: KOINONIA AS MISSIONARY ACCOUNTABILITY

> In those days Mary set out and went with haste to a Judean town in the hill country, where she entered the house of Zechariah and greeted Elizabeth. (Luke 1:39-40)

THE VISITATION OF EXPECTANT COUSINS

The first visitation is from God. The angel appeared to Zechariah and Mary announcing their place in God's plans, a visitation of babies. Gabriel announces to Mary, "I have been sent to you to bring you good news." Mary does what the shepherds did. She goes with haste to share the news. She visits kin across the kitchen table, as we do when our hearts are filled with God's blessings. But this visitation by God transforms this visit of kin. Even their greetings are transformed into doxology. "Blessed are you." Cousin Elizabeth blesses Mary: for the gift in her womb, and then for her faith. Mary in turn blesses God. "My soul magnifies the Lord..." *Magnificat.*

And look who is at the table of the visitation. There is a mute priest, struck dumb by his narrow expectations of God's miraculous visitation, forced to be silent and watch the unfolding gift of new life. How many of us here in these latter days have seen our faith and zeal slowly erode, our expectations diminish as we attempt faithful ministry in a culture which is indifferent to it, in a culture that blames the poor and the sojourner among us? And how often have we been struck dumb with surprise at the many small and large miracles God works among the faithful when we have least expected it? Fellow mute priests of God, Zechariah is with us at the table. Expectant mothers join our own visitations as the Church accompanies us through life's passages. Kicking and vulnerable babies, nascent life is present, even if it cannot be seen. Our own stories of expectant life for ourselves

---

Author's Note: Hirtabrev, literally "shepherd's letter," is the term for a Swedish bishop's pastoral letter. This chapter is based on the 1998 report to the Metropolitan New York Synod Assembly.

and our congregations join Mary and Elizabeth at the table. The "breach" in the walls of the city (Isaiah"s image of those who are poor, broken, vulnerable, strangers, cut off from God) are present at the table through Mary's song: "He has lifted up the lowly; he has filled the hungry with good things...." At the table we are connected across time, our ancestors in the faith join you and me as Mary sings: "His mercy is on those who fear him from generation to generation... according to the promise he made to our ancestors, to Abraham and his descendants forever." Mute, spiritually tired priests, expectant believers, unseen kicking new life in the wombs of our churches, people in the breach, our kin in Christ across time and space.... Come to the Table.

A Twentieth-Century Visitation

Each Friday afternoon during my intern year in Richmond, Virginia, I would visit Helen Miller with consecrated bread and wine. She lived alone below us in a very poor part of the city. During the day many came to her table, for she helped raise the neighborhood's children. Domestics, bus drivers, factory workers, secretaries, waitresses would bring their children to Helen and then go to work. This homebound woman, with the help of one able-bodied young woman, would sit in her chair with a TV table in front of her and interact with the children all day. She prayed, admonished, hugged, read and told stories, sang, and became for them a daily visitation of God's grace and care. She ruled her roost with dignity and joy!

After communing Helen with bread and wine, I would bring the stew that Helen had prepared to the church basement for the Friday night dinners for the homeless in the fan district of Richmond. The Eucharist continued.

At the Table We See the Marks of the Church

These tables have some things in common with our synod table:

- The tables are *powerfully gifted*. There are resources here at tables of poor women and their vulnerable babies. The Holy Spirit is alive around these tables.
- Those gathered around the tables are *companions and partners*. New and transformed relationships are the fruit of the Gospel. We are kin. Helen Miller was related to the homeless in a church basement as their companion (*con* means "with"; *pan* means "bread"in Latin and Spanish; "companions" are literally those with whom we share our bread). I also like the word "partner." In the early Church the partners around the first

church tables had "all things in common" (*koine* in the Greek). Their *koinonia* partnership defined them.
- Those around the table are *growing in faith and discipleship*. Elizabeth blesses Mary for her faith. Mary recalls Scripture in her song. Helen Miller receives the Eucharist. Mute priests learn to trust God. At the table we grow in faith. We follow Jesus more fully. We become cheerful givers; tellers of the old, old story; lovers of the poor; moored in prayer, Scripture and worship. At the table we learn to rest in God's promises.
- Our table is set in the midst of the world. It is public. From the table *we are sent into the world*. I will use the words *apostolate* and *apostolic* a lot in our time together at the table. They are not meant to denote hierarchy, but to remind us that, like Paul and the early Christians, we are sent into the world. Our table is not a catered affair in a place apart from this Mars Hill on which we live our life. We are sent to this table. Mary remembers the breach in the walls of the city, the pain of the world, as she sings her faith into Gospel for the poor. Helen Miller is surrounded by the breach every day, and feeds those in the breach with stew every Friday. "For God so loved... the world."

This is the view from the Table: *We are gifted companions, following Jesus in the Breach.*

A Table in Brooklyn: Salem Begets Salaam

To be a bishop is to be a visitor. My visits last year took me to 88 of our synod's 238 parishes to preach, teach, lead worship or retreats, as well as to most of our conferences. I have joined in worshiping God in the sixteen languages of worship in our synod. One visit was especially memorable. On a gorgeous, sun-drenched Sunday in May, the second-best thing that happened in the New York metropolis was the perfect game pitched by David Wells of the Yankees. I know, because when I turned off the car radio after parking in Brooklyn, he was carrying the perfect game into the seventh inning. The *best* thing that happened in our metropolis that day was the moment when Pastor Harriet Wieber and the leaders of Salem Lutheran Church (of Danish origin) in Bay Ridge handed the registry of the congregation and its 103 years of pastoral acts— one hundred and three years of resting in the promises of God in the passages of the lives of the people of Salem— to Pastor Khader El Yateem and the leaders of newborn Salaam Arabic Lutheran Church. Salem begets Salaam, not a sullen minority being forced out of their church in a changing neighborhood, but free and faithful Lutherans from two very different cultures, sharing immigrant roots, taking the time and supreme effort to fall in love with another set of table companions in all of such love's vulnerability.

There is so much of our giftedness and companionship which has gone into the constructing of this table of Peace: the sweat equity and vision of then-Bishop James Sudbrock and Pastor Grace Olson, our former mission director, who toiled to help set the table; our partners at the seminary in Philadelphia; our churchwide partners in the Division for Outreach. Virtually every congregation in the Southwest Brooklyn Conference was represented, leaders and pastors who have shared in so many ways with Salem's becoming Salaam.

That moment when the folks at Salaam were saying to the folks of Salem, "The church you cared for is in good hands," is so rare and precious that we ought to reflect on it for a moment. This was not a "bumper sticker" moment of surface congeniality, nor a trendy multicultural showpiece. These folks walked through the pain and exhilaration of letting go of the familiar and the comfortable and being grasped by the transforming power of the Gospel. This moment is a reminder that "rerooting" in the community, our apostolate to the world, is nothing less than a call to dying and rising in the power of the Cross and Resurrection of Jesus. It is a reminder that every congregation must accept the invitation to the funeral of the church it remembers. "Behold, I am doing a new thing," says the Lord. Jesus did not survive his crucifixion on Good Friday. Neither did Salem in its former life. But Jesus rose again on Easter. And so did Salem, speaking the Salaam of Jesus to its new neighbors.

I am awed by the many ways this dying and rising occurs in our synod. Resureccion (Spanish) and Epiphany (English), Hempstead have nurtured life together into the organization of Resureccion as our newest (along with Salaam) church. Koreans and Anglos at Messiah, Flushing are living life together, as are folks in many other stories of "rerooting in the community." We are beginning to use this "rerooting" strategy in our vacancy processes, as piloted at Our Savior, Atonement in Manhattan, where relational meetings with over one hundred people in church and community helped this congregation to keep mission to the community as their highest priority as they sought a new pastor. I am also reminded that heroic ministry happens around small tables, like that of Elizabeth and Mary. It is sometimes almost miraculous that congregations hold their own and continue to serve, even as the culture turns further away from church life and resources diminish. We are gifted in so many large and small ways through faithful ministries of dying and rising to new life.

A Table in the Household of Philemon

Take a moment to reflect with me on the nature of the Table of the church through the eyes of the Apostle Paul as he sends an interesting letter to Philemon. This little book gives us a fresh look at Paul— not the Paul seen through the eyes of Melanchthon, as the maker of a compendium of doctrine and theology, nor the Paul put in service to Luke's worldview and theology of history— but Paul the Apostle on the run, constructing a mission theology in the midst of the action, sometimes messy, sometimes with a lot of loose ends. See how he improvises on the authority of the Gospel and his own authority as a servant of the Gospel to strengthen the table; affirm his converts' partnership; nurture the faith, companionship and giftedness around the table; and turn it toward the world.

As in all his letters Paul lifts up various partnerships in his relational salutation. He reminds these partners that wherever they are, they are joined together in the Spirit's tether. Paul is always naming names: "Apphia our sister," "Archippus our fellow soldier;" and Paul is always drawing connections between places, in this case a jail and the household of Philemon. The benediction at the end names more names and places. Paul's apostolic leadership is one of minding and bringing to mind the connections, the *koinonia* in the church.

He centers the partnerships by naming their source: "Grace to you and peace from God our Father and the Lord Jesus Christ." He sends words of encouragement to help strengthen their faith and discipleship. He prays for them, reminds them of their giftedness, and exhorts them in the Christian life: "I pray that the sharing of your faith may become effective when you perceive the good that we may do for Christ."

But this is the Paul of practical theology. This bishop is addressing his synod about their life together. Like the best preachers who claim a pulpit for God, he claims the public reading of his letter in the liturgy for God. There is table business to discuss, and it is public business. He is appealing for Philemon to place a seat at the table for Onesimus, the slave who has left Philemon's house. There is even a play on words here. Formerly Onesimus was *achrestos* (useless to Philemon— without Christ), but now he is *christos*, useful to both Paul and Philemon. Paul calls this slave his own son. "Now Philemon, Onesimus has been caring for me on your behalf. I could command you to let me have Onesimus, but I'm only appealing, and giving you the opportunity to voluntarily witness to the Gospel by sending him back to you." Paul is teaching table manners here. A slave is Philemon's partner in ministry to Paul in jail. Now he must see Onesimus with new eyes. Paul calls Onesimus no longer a slave, but a "beloved brother" to Philemon. They are kin now, tablemates. The Gospel transforms relationships, status, even the economics and politics of the household and community.

What we see in this letter is Paul exercising servant leadership, an iron fist in a velvet glove, reminding us of what Luther would later call our status as both slave and free. This is subtle, carefully stated power, which comes as an invitation to reconsider how things look on the surface. Paul gives Philemon his freedom, but he is not free to do nothing. Paul doesn't say "the hell with it" and leave him alone. He will have to make some response since the nature of the Table has been made clear to him. The letter is read publicly. And Paul says, "Prepare the bishop's suite for me." He is coming. In short, the Church is accountable to the Lord of the Table.

The servant authority of the Way of Jesus is all we have to hold God's Table together. We are accountable to one another. We are gifted and must stop poor-mouthing, as if the Holy Spirit has held out on us. All the gifts we need to do the work of God in this place are already on the ground. We are partners and companions and we will not allow our differences or our indifference to keep us from the Table together. We will not leave each other alone. We were born to serve and follow Jesus, and we will measure our success and growth not through a theology of glory and success, but by the growing number of disciples who are serious about, and continually being formed in their faith in church, home and neighborhood. We are sent into the world. This Mars Hill is the object of our life together. We will not allow ourselves to be preoccupied with the things of the Church at the expense of our witness in the world. When the Table is set in the midst of the world things change. Slaves become brothers and sisters. As I visit with the staff, and as we do many things, we are really only reminders of the strength, authority and accountability of the Table. When Paul said these words, they were a reminder of the continual visitation of Jesus: "One thing more—prepare a guest room for me, for I am hoping through your prayers to be restored to you."

A Table in Tanzania

> Jerusalem, Jerusalem, the city that kills the prophets and stones the those who are sent to it! How often have I desired to gather your children together as a hen gathers her brood under her wings, and you were not willing! (Luke 13:34)

Mary had another heartbreaking visitation at the foot of the cross. Michelangelo immortalized this moment in his sculpture of the

Pietà, Mary's arms receiving her dead son. Pietà. A mother hen brooding over her chicks.

Tanzanian Pietà. There in the corner, on a bed of straw in a hut in the village of Kashura, a mother is holding her child, burning and nauseous with malaria. This pastor standing over them had no intelligible word to hurl into that abyss. Only a pair of arms to encircle the passion of mother and child, a muttered prayer in a foreign language. We then resumed vesting in the small room of suffering. Outside, around the table some twenty homebound elderly wait for the bread and wine, too frail to make the long and arduous journey to the church for Sunday liturgy. After speaking the Words of Institution in Swahili I become an instrument for the mother hen to embrace her children through the Body and Blood of Christ. An eighty-year-old holds out her baptismal card for me to sign, unfolding in tangible evidence a lifetime of reception of the Table meal of the church.

On a hillside of the poor village of Bushasha, near the Uganda and Rwanda borders, we meet under a tree. The congregation has been unable to rebuild their sanctuary, bombed by Idi Amin more than fifteen years ago. With song and testimony the congregation welcomes us. Then we walk down the hill to a small hut. Food is shared, gathered for weeks in advance by the village, a real sacrifice of hospitality. Then those most poor in the village are fed as well. Pietà.

So many Pietàs in this place. Bishop Mushemba had told me about the terrible toll of El Niño, blasting the drought-ravaged land with torrential rains, fetid pools of dirty water breeding carriers of malaria. The bishop and his helpers had recently done an assessment among the district pastors of the diocese; many members of the churches have suffered from malaria recently, and too many of them have died. This recent heartbreak is adding to the pandemic of AIDS and chronic hunger in this part of the world.

Pietà. I saw the church as a mother in the breach, encircling the children with kindness and love. In the hospital at Ndolage (where the love offering from our synod will help build an airstrip to fly in needed medicine and doctors), the orphanage at Ntoma, dispensaries in remote villages, in village congregations, in creative partnerships with governmental and ecumenical partners, the Lutheran Church in Tanzania is cradling the children in its maternal arms.

See the marks of the Table through Tanzanian church life and witness, illumined by Swahili words:

- *Roho Mtakatifu* (Holy Spirit). The Table in the Northwest Diocese is one richly gifted by the Spirit, overflowing with partners and companions in the midst of scarcity. The seminary at Ruhija is situated on the same campus as the training school for evangelists, the music school, and the African arts school. In even the remotest villages there are trained musicians, teachers for home Bible studies, local self-reliance through mills built by women's groups and local artisans. There are powerful institutions for education and health. Worship is lively in this fastest-growing Lutheran communion in the world.

- *Karibu* (Welcome!) *Upendo* (love). Hospitality is bred in the bone in Africa. Everywhere we went we were welcomed with drums, song, food, testimony, prayer. The highest priority of the Church in Tanzania is evangelism and witness, to proclaim the Gospel and welcome new people to the Table of Christ's love. This priority is also for the pastoral care of those already around the Table. In a place with little physical infrastructure of roads, running water, electricity, etc. there is a powerful spiritual infrastructure. This church is built to get out the Gospel, for an apostolate to the world in word and deed.
- *Baba Askofu* (Bishop, Shepherd). I still have an image of Bishop Mushemba waiting on the airstrip in Bukoba, standing in the rain to welcome us as our tin can of a plane arrived. The bishop symbolizes the ministry of the Good Shepherd, and also the unity of One Flock, One Shepherd. The church in Tanzania is connected, the worship is both blatantly African and resoundingly catholic. The drum was not allowed into the sanctuary by the European missionaries until 1940; it had been considered pagan. Now African tunes, rhythms, tribal melodies are being recovered in the service of the Gospel, exactly as Luther returned Scripture and worship to the people of God in their own musical context.

Three views of the Table from which we can think about our life together in our synod: a view from Brooklyn, from the primitive church, from contemporary Africa. In these perspectives we reaffirm that around our Table we are "Gifted Companions Following Jesus as We are Sent into the Breach."

Part Six
"To serve all people, following the example of our Lord Jesus...."

Chapter 30
The Diaconate: Consecrated DPs

Day and night they wander, the nomads of our society. You see them shuffling up and down the streets and alleys, lurking in doorways, sleeping on subways. Shopping bag ladies and homeless men shout out at nameless demons in the city crowd. The displaced persons of the cities, these DPs living at the edges, are caricatures of the restless heart of humanity. The rootless poor are prisms through which we glimpse what the Scriptures mean by the *anawim* (a Hebrew word for people on the margins of life) or "the least of these." There are others: boat people with no home and no place to go; refugees and exiles in grim internment camps; homesick immigrants in an alien culture; sharecroppers and migrant laborers; families without fathers; the sick and the dying; the unemployed and the students who graduate from high school unable to read; the strung-out and the handicapped; the powerless and the prisoners; the hungry and the aged; the poor in spirit, the abused, and the unborn.

"You always have the poor with you." This word from our Lord as John records it is a promise, not a dismissal. In the *anawim*, the "least of these," Christ has promised his hidden presence. In the poor Christ has provided for the possibility that the church may always remain "in situation." The Christian life, and the life of the church, is assigned its place among people who need to be served. Outside the concrete sphere of service there cannot be true sacramental living—that quality of life that continually points to the presence of Christ in the world, living nourished by daily reference to Baptism and frequent participation in the Eucharist. In the ministry among the least of these there is integrity between the real presence in Holy Communion and the Christ who must be fed, clothed, visited and liberated. A Christianity that ignores the Incarnation is simply not possible.

The Bible calls this service of the poor *diakonia*. It is a concept without much glamour; indeed in such early Greek writers as Philo *diakonia* is used disparagingly. It means something like "waiting on tables." Yet this word is at the heart of the Gospel. Everything that was done by Jesus who came from the Father, including his earthly ministry, his self-emptying, his humiliation and death on the cross can be summed up in this word. *Diakonia* and its biblical relative *diakonos*, or deacon, paint a picture of service that is flexible, available, humble; service that involves organizing a response, is useful in a given situation, is freely given and takes many forms. As illustrated by the church's response to the plight of the widows in Acts 6, *diakonia* is also at the heart of the one apostolic ministry. The church laid hands on Stephen and six other deacons because distributive justice on behalf of the widows was so integral to its witness. Perhaps the composite picture of *diakonia* in the New Testament can be summed up in one phrase: creative service of the apostolic church in solidarity with the poor.

Somehow in the development of the diaconate this acute identification with the poor became more symbolic, less literal. The history of the diaconate can be regarded as an oft-repeated attempt to detract from the original practice. Starting in the primitive church, in what has been called the "tunnel period," we see what enters the tunnel and what comes out of it a hundred years later, but what happens in the tunnel remains obscure. The deacon enters the tunnel a waiter, only to emerge on the other side as a near-priest. Indeed the diaconate becomes a quasi-novitiate, a step on the way to the priesthood. The deacon has been removed from the backs of the tables and guests (towel over arm) and is seated somewhere near the head of the table (the towel is now a clerical vestment known as the maniple). That is where the deacon still sits in many Christian churches, a respectable displaced person. Too often the congruence between the depiction of service that a liturgical deacon represents and real down-to-earth service is only accidental. The deacon emerged from the tunnel out of his—or her—element.

Our Present *Kairos*

We are at an important moment in our history as Lutheran Christians. We have, in the recent decisions regarding closer fellowship with the Reformed and the Episcopalians in the United States, the opportunity to do more than just swap pulpits and make nice. In the fullness of our time we have opportunity to gain deeper clarity concerning the nature of our service in the world and the ministerial shape of that service. Can we use this time to rethink the diaconate in the following contexts: as a part of a longed-for catholic consensus in the church; as a part of the efforts as churches of the Augsburg Confession to receive the implications of the remarkable Faith and Order document, *Baptism, Eucharist and Ministry*, as a gift to the one, unitary mission of the Church which seeks, in an ordered ministry, to live in solidarity with the poor and to improvise service among them?

We are encouraged by the BEM document to think ecumenically about the one ordained ministry in terms of the historic threefold office of bishop, presbyter, and deacon. To be sure, the BEM document does not reflect unanimous agreement within these categories; they have varied histories and understandings among and within the various communions. But the document outlines broad areas of agreement for studying the ministry, and situates discussion in the direction of and within Jesus' high-priestly prayer for the unity of God's people.

We have unique resources within our own history, and among the communions around us, to help us consider seriously an expanded diaconate with a unique quality of apostolic service in solidarity with the poor. In the Roman Catholic Church we have seen a dramatic turnaround in the visibility and service of a permanent diaconate. No longer is the diaconate seen solely as an "intern year" on the road to some supposedly higher office. Rather, deacons live in the faith that Jesus becomes present to others through their table service in solidarity with the poor.

There are rich resources for the diaconate in the deaconess movement within several Lutheran communions. These consecrated women have traditionally taken responsibility for programs and services that required either technical expertise—such as nursing or teaching—or huge amounts of Christlike, self-sacrificing love and compassion—such as settlement houses, inner-city parish programs and other ministries on the margins. Further, Lutherans have recently experimented with several attempts to live out the diaconal implications of the Gospel. I think of the diaconate among the African American churches of the LC-MS on the South Side of Chicago, the current Order of St. Stephen in Baltimore, and the Society of St. Lawrence that flourished in the New York metropolitan area in the 1970s and 1980s. The ELCA's recent study on ministry proved mostly inconclusive, nudging the church toward a lay order of Diaconal Ministers.

THE HEART OF THE MATTER

At the heart of all the reasons to consider a vibrant, revived diaconate is this: in the diaconate the church will see imaged, and continually be reminded of, the essential diaconal character of all ministry. Creative service in solidarity with the poor is the heart of all ministry. All Christians have a vocation to serve in memory of Servant Jesus. Yet it must also be admitted that what is the responsibility of all can become the responsibility of none. It is to this question of accountability that *Baptism, Eucharist and Ministry* speaks directly.

Deacons represent to the Church its calling as servant in the world. By struggling in Christ's name with the myriad needs of societies and persons, deacons exemplify the interdependence of worship and service in the Church's life. They exercise responsibility in the worship of the congregation: for example by reading the Scriptures, preaching, and leading the people in prayer. They help in the teaching of the congregation. They exercise a ministry of love within the community. They fulfill certain administrative tasks and may be elected to responsibilities for governance. (BEM, "Ministry," 31)

We do not need an understanding of the diaconate, or the ministry of the laity, that takes the job description of the pastor and parcels it out among clericalized laypeople. We do need to recapture some of the ontological significance of service among the poor. Where the calling—what I feel about my God-given task—and vocation—what the church discerns about me—are congruent, one will perhaps find the deacon. A deacon is who someone is, just as much as what someone does. Can we see the diaconate as God's gift to the church, pointing the way to the true *Sitz im Leben* of its ministry? Concrete solidarity with the "least of these" must not be spiritualized out of existence. A thriving, ordered diaconate will not allow it to happen.

Let there be varieties of service. Let there be educational deacons; "little sisters and brothers of the poor"; evangelistic deacons; administrative deacons; deacons assisting bishops in responding to acute needs in parish neighborhoods or remote rural areas; deacons organizing or filling in the gaps of church programs of nurture and outreach. Let there be leadership and organization for continuing growth, spiritual formation, prayer, and support in ministry. Let there be an initial period of theological training and internship. But let the deacon's frame of reference and context of service always include solidarity with the poor, and thereby sacramentally image for the Church and the world utmost respect for the hidden presence of Deacon Jesus.

Even as I commend the diaconate as an integral part of the one ordered ministry of the church, I know there are some dangers to avoid. We must emphasize that *diakonia* is never this or that agenda of utopian activism. It is not a panacea by which the church joins the "helping professions" in solving every problem of the world through rational means. *Diakonia* is, quite simply, creative service in solidarity with the poor, however defined—possibly you and me on our bad days.

KEEPING THE FOCUS

What will deacons do? It depends on the situation. Sometimes the deacon will be called upon to teach, to lead the prayers of the people, to train others for service in liturgy or world. Some will organize the Church's response to corporate issues affecting the common life. In our own parish one such diaconal person organizes us to respond to specific needs: collecting food and clothing, attending meetings and reporting back concerning causes of hunger in our community, organizing letters to legislators about the homeless. Some will be involved with Bread for the World or other organizations that attempt to elucidate global issues.

Some will organize parish responses to appeals for benevolence: nursing homes, inner-city hospitals, prison ministries, rural presence and the like. Some will be community organizers in the public arena, seeking power and allies in the service of social change. Some will organize powerful responses to budget priorities of state, city and denomination. They will organize the fabric of the parish to serve the needs of its own and its neighbors, including its resources of people, money, values, real estate, influence, prayers, and liturgies.

When someone is suddenly taken ill their children will be cared for; the sick will be visited; support groups for the widowed and single parents and unemployed will be organized; the convalescent will receive hot meals; the elderly will get a ride to church or the doctor's office; the rent and utilities will be paid in an emergency; the families of infants baptized in the parish will be systematically visited; parish schools will be staffed with teachers who are also ministers of Christian nurture; the immigrant will receive help in filling out incomprehensible forms and help in learning English; the refugee will find housing and acceptance; food pantries will be full and shelters will be staffed. The ministry of the deacon, flowing out of communities of Jesus rooted in Word and Sacraments and communal prayer, will be a sign of the Kingdom of God.

St. Lawrence was a deacon of the early church. He was responsible for safeguarding the treasures of the church—funds for distribution to the poor, as well as the priceless chalices, candelabra, and other objects. He was commanded by the Roman prefect to gather together all the treasures of the church for disposal. In three days' time Lawrence summoned the ruler to the church. There were found all manner of unfortunate people, the sick, the leprous, the lame, the blind, the poor, the widows and orphans. Lawrence had sold all the church's earthly treasures and distributed the proceeds to those sufferers, the least of the city of Rome. Lawrence swept his hand over the crowd of unfortunates and is reported to have said: "These are the treasures of the church. Here are the gold coins I promised you, shining jewels too that adorn Christ's temple. These are the church's necklace, these her gems, these her wealth...." Lawrence died a martyr, following in the steps of Jesus, whose ministry was always on behalf of "the least of these."

Peter was a deacon of the modern Church, a middle-aged resident of Astoria, Queens. While on retreat with fellow Christians, praying and studying together to support one another in diaconal living, Peter died suddenly. He left behind a life of diaconal service. He had taught Bethel Bible Series classes, visited the sick and homebound, counseled drug addicts, and shepherded his congregation's youth program. He had preached and led the prayers. At the time of his death he was training a cadre of fellow members for a thorough ministry of presence to the homebound of his parish and neighborhood. At his funeral the church was crowded with the treasures of the Church: elderly in wheel chairs; young people he had helped get off drugs; casualties of the institutional Church who found their way back through his ministry; three pastors with whom he had served and prayed; hundreds of folks from all walks of life who were drawn to the dying and rising Christ through his service. Deacon Peter never let us forget the true treasures of Christ's Church. Such is the power of the diaconate.

All God's people are called to serve. The deacon is called to enter the sphere of service voluntarily, and in primary identification over a lifetime lift up the poor as the context of a ministry of integrity. Deacons remind us that we are all diaconal people—displaced persons—whose life of service and very presence in the Church of Jesus is subversive of the values and myths of success and salvation prevalent in our culture. The deacons' life of service is lived—for the Church and the world—in memory of Deacon Jesus who came not to be served but to give his life as a ransom for many.

No longer will care of the poor be left to social ministry committee busy work, denominational "victim of the month" promotions, the pastor's discretionary fund, sporadic acts of charity, or statements and resolutions passed by assemblies and conventions. In the diaconate as an integral and continuous order of the Church's one ministry, the deacon's life becomes a channel of the Holy Spirit to serve and be served with the "least of these." In this ministry we are helped to see, in a sacramental way, that the nomad in the doorway is us; that the poor and the homeless are mirrored in our own restlessness; and that the presence of Servant Jesus among the poor is also our own salvation.

(*Lutheran Forum,* Lent 1984)

Chapter 31
Diakonia: A Mom-and-Pop Theological Store

This is a brief two-fold tale—of a grassroots dream of the empowerment of the people of God called "Diakonia;" and of the involvement of some of "Diakonia's" people in a renewal of the historic diaconate. It is important that the tale remain two-fold. In the ELCA nationally there is no official recognition of the office of Deacon (except for those "grandparented" into the ELCA from the AELC as part of the constituting agreement). Recently the Metropolitan New York Synod has begun a synodical expression of the diaconate, under the ELCA's rubric of "synodically authorized ministries." The renewal of the diaconate is one part of the tale. The other part of the tale is the spiritual formation and theological training program known as "Diakonia," whose students are a diverse group of laypeople: some are in training as candidates for the synodical diaconate; most are parish leaders seeking to deepen their knowledge, commitment and service to Christ through their parish church and their daily life.

Meet a Deacon

Let me introduce you to one of the rostered deacons grandparented into the ELCA from the AELC. Her name is Carole; she is a middle-aged woman who works in a Manhattan office during the week and was one of the first students in the Diakonia program. Each Saturday Carole helps prepare for the next day's liturgy, in which she will serve as assisting minister. She obtains the names of the sick, elderly, and homebound she will visit on that day and during the week ahead. She confers with her pastor about the calls she will make, about their plans to involve more of the people of her Lower East Side Manhattan parish in service to their fellow members and neighbors. Then she makes her visits, which sometimes include the distribution of the consecrated elements of the Eucharist. On Sunday after church Carole will assist her parish in feeding the homeless of the neighborhood, as this parish does each Lord's day and every day during the week.

Carole's admission into the diaconate, like that of all synodically rostered deacons, followed a rigorous path. There was much conversation about discernment of her call with her pastor and fellow members. Carole completed two years of theological training in the Diakonia program and a year's internship that included twenty hours of service per week. Her vocation as a deacon of the church was confirmed by a call from her parish and by the authorization of her bishop and his committee.

Since her consecration as a Deacon by her bishop, Carole has served as a link between liturgy and service, between clergy and laity, between Sunday and Monday. Her work has encouraged others to find their own baptismal calling to serve, and she has helped to encourage and organize these gifts of the church's ministry among all the people of God. Especially telling is Carole's connection with the Table of the Eucharist and the Table of food for the hungry. The Deacon helps embody the connection, in Word and deed. Carole serves as a living reminder of the diaconal nature of all ministry in memory of Jesus.

Grassroots Theological Education

For the past twenty years on a June afternoon a wide cross-section of the Lutherans in the New York metropolitan area have assembled to worship. The occasion is the annual graduation ceremony of "Diakonia." Graduates have attended classes in one of the several geographical tracks of the program in New Jersey, New York City, Long Island, and upstate New York, as well as a track in the Spanish language. The highlight of the liturgy is the Affirmation of Baptism. Over seven hundred graduates, including Carole have made the spiritual journey known as "Diakonia."

For all their diversity the graduates have had one common focus: for two years they have grounded their vocation to serve Jesus in the history, liturgy, Scriptures, and practical tasks of the church. And they have developed a keen awareness of the intersection of their biblical and theological heritage with the times, events and people of the world around them. The program is parochial in the best sense.

The Diakonia story began over two decades ago. In 1978, Union and Auburn Theological Seminaries in New York City invited three city parishes to join them in a year-long study of the needs in local congregations for theological education and leadership development, and the possible role seminaries might play in meeting these needs. I participated in that venture along with laypeople from the parish I served at the time, Atonement Lutheran Church in Jackson Heights, Queens. We received a grant from Auburn Seminary to work on our congregation's specific needs.

Atonement's basic need was one shared by many urban congregations: we had no serious program of theological education and spiritual formation for parish leaders. It was necessary that a program of this type include leaders from the minority groups of parish and community, that it be economically feasible and geographically accessible to the neighborhood people; and that it be intellectually rigorous and of excellent quality. In sum, we were seeking a project in theological and spiritual formation that would faithfully transmit our Lutheran heritage with an openness and generous catholicity that would empower the ministry and leaders of the parishes it served.

What evolved from this process with Auburn and Union Seminaries was "Diakonia." The present program structure requires students to take courses across the breadth of subjects offered in a typical seminary curriculum. The twelve five-week courses are offered over a two-year period. The classes, which are three hours in length, are taught in each of the Diakonia locations by local pastors and others with special expertise in given areas. But course work does not begin to give the picture of what happens to students in the program. People's lives change. There is a rhythm of worship led by students; there is prayer; there are retreats. Each Diakonia class becomes a community of pilgrims in the faith, a supportive fellowship of people who teach and learn from one another. The intersections between students, neighborhoods, parishes, and the tradition of the church become sources of transforming power. Those who delve deeply into the mysteries of the faith also find themselves more profoundly committed to Christ and to the church. I have seen parishes renewed by theologically informed, expressively confident, and spiritually committed graduates.

Over the years students have entered the Diakonia program for different reasons. Graduates have included a mother of eight from the Bronx who wanted to deepen her ongoing ministries of teaching Sunday School and caring for stray children in the neighborhood. Teachers in Lutheran parochial schools have added a solid theological and Biblical base to their vocation to share the Gospel with children. A student from Queens works with deaf people, is fluent in sign language, and has been invaluable during a pastoral vacancy of two deaf congregations in Queens and Harlem. A woman from New Jersey visits the sick on a regular basis with more confidence and effectiveness.

Other Diakonia students have started hospices for people with AIDS, begun nursing home ministries, conduct prison ministries, organize parish ministries for victims of domestic abuse, help immigrants, serve as community organizers building affordable housing for the poor. Students have included a Hispanic parish worker; a Bishop's Assistant who directs the New Jersey Synod's Office of Governmental Ministry; a retired banker who teaches confirmation classes; and a widow who teaches English as a second language to Korean Lutherans.

And the pilgrimage of faith that is "Diakonia" does not usually end with graduation. Several graduates have become pastors or are presently enrolled in seminary. Bronx graduates met for a time on a regular basis for mutual prayer, support and growth. They have helped staff the ministries of mercy in the borough, and worked with local pastors to lead a summer program of Bible study and evangelism. Graduates of a Long Island location meet weekly for continuing growth. Similar programs of ongoing spiritual formation have been formed within other tracks of the program.

A Revived Diaconate In A Renewed Church?

You won't find a detailed blueprint for the ordering of ministry in the scriptural witness. According to the New Testament there certainly are deacons in the earliest Christian communities, but they don't seem to be constitutive of the life of the church and their function is certainly not spelled out with precision. Yet the idea of service, *diakonia*, is ubiquitous in the apostolic writings, is at the center of the one apostolic ministry (Acts 6), and in one way or another is institutionalized in the life of the apostolic church.

The office of deacon was indissolubly linked to the church's celebration of the Eucharist. The implications of the Eucharist in the early church included practical service to the needy—the corporal works of mercy. The community's offering of gifts at the Eucharist was the source and symbol of the church's provision for its poor and distressed members, the charitable relief that inspired Polycarp to speak of the widows as "God's altar" (Epistle 4:9). Lutherans have the richest possible resource to consider a renewal of the diaconate: regular and frequent celebration of the Eucharist. Deacons who, like Carole, serve at both tables on the Lower East Side embody this possibility. Further, there is a rich history among North American Lutherans of service to the poor; *Hilfswerk*; the deaconess movement; social service agencies; the history of gathering and providing for waves of new immigrants to the cities and rural areas of the United States and Canada.

In 1987 I participated in a Faith and Order consultation on the diaconate and the implications of the "Baptism, Eucharist and Ministry" document. Present at that conference were representatives of over thirty of the communities of the Christian family, from the Orthodox and Roman communions to the AME, the Baptists, and the Brethren. In the sharing of the judicatories' documents and in mutual conversation, it became apparent that there is a renewed interest in the diaconate throughout the church. The interrelationship of Christian service and liturgy, a renewed understanding of *diakonia* as the heart of all Christian ministry, a hunger for a unified sense of ministry among all the people of God (lay and ordained) were on the minds of all members of the convocation.

Could the closing years of the twentieth century be a Spirit-filled time for renewal in the one church of Jesus Christ? And can we Lutherans be bold to rethink the diaconate in the following contexts: as a part of a longed-for catholic consensus about ministry in the church; as a part of the efforts of the churches of the Augsburg Confession to receive the implications of BEM into their life; as a gift to the one, unitary mission of the church that seeks, in an ordered ministry, to live in solidarity with the poor and to improvise service in that situation in memory of Jesus; as a means to multiply service to the poor as "God's altar"; as a means for the church to call forth the variety of gifts bestowed on its people including the gifts of leadership among minority people? The turn of the millennium, in sum, may be the fullness of time for a renewed diaconate, to help keep the church in sustained touch with two passionate concerns of its risen Lord: the oneness of his body and his abiding presence with the poor.

BACK TO *DIAKONIA*

Whether or not there will ever be an officially recognized diaconate among Lutherans nationally, there will continue to be service, concern for the poor, ministry in daily life, and lay vocations devised in evangelical freedom to meet the needs of the day. However the ordered ministry may be eventually reconfigured as a result of the studies of ministry and dialogues with our Anglican and Reformed friends, the renewal of our Lutheran communion will require a biblically literate, theologically knowledgeable, and spiritually vigorous laity. The grassroots model of *diakonia* could serve such training and renewal.

There are now over thirty synodically rostered deacons in the Metropolitan New York Synod serving under call to congregations. There is a synodically authorized deacon serving on my staff as an Assistant to the Bishop. These are non-stipendiary ministries. In both urban and rural areas across the church, leaders are considering training for lay and diaconal vocations to meet some needs occasioned by a paucity of ordained pastors. At the grass roots, at least in my part of the world, there is a hunger on the part of many to live lives of service, focused on "the least of these" in church and neighborhood. They are asking for support, inspiration and encouragement from the wider church. There are a variety of Associates in Ministry offering their service to the church. Where will these persons, and others called to new opportunities for ministry, receive training, encouragement, and grounding in the history, liturgy, theology and traditions of our church?

There is a continual need to identify and equip people called to vocations for service among minorities in our neighborhoods. "Diakonia" grew out of such a need in our own ministry and has been enriched by many students from these communities over the years. Hispanic, Asian and African-American graduates have enhanced the invitation of their parishes to all who live in the shadow of their steeples. The ELCA has a deep commitment to inclusive ministry. That commitment must begin by investment in the growth of its parishes and their leaders. The Latino mission strategy of the Metropolitan New York Synod is undergirded by graduates of the Spanish language track of Diakonia beginning outreach programs in congregations which are starting Hispanic ministries.

A "Diakonia" graduation is one small sign of the Kingdom in the New York metropolitan area. A note in the bulletin of the 1989 graduation read: "At this graduation, three of our fellow class members are deeply on our hearts and minds today ... they were called to their eternal rest by the Lord of the church. They are much beloved by their classmates and their lives shine through with the ideal of love and service in Jesus' Name. Their service and praise of God continues in the presence of Jesus love."

In a time of casual commitments and preoccupation with the self, privatized religion, and desiccated Christian witness, twenty-seven servants of Jesus, including the three whose service continues around the throne of the Lamb, paused on Trinity Sunday to thank God for the privilege of service in, and reflection on, this wondrous love. Earlier in the morning Deacon Carole had assisted in serving the Family Meal of the church, then served at the table of "God's altar" of the poor.

(*Lutheran Forum*, Advent, 1990)

Chapter 32
Priests and Deacons: Earthly and Heavenly Partnership

> This ancient church in modern dress pledges itself to "call forth, equip, certify, set apart, supervise, and support an ordained ministry of Word and Sacrament and such other forms of ministry that will enable this church to fulfill its mission. (William Lazareth, *This Ancient Church in Modern Dress* [Minneapolis: Augsburg Fortress, 1991], p. 8)

Body and Soul

"How's your soul?" our teacher in graduate school at New York Seminary would ask us in greeting. Interestingly, most often people would respond not about some ethereal entity, but about this ache or that pain of the body, this distress or that trauma of the mind, this depression or that confusion of emotion, this need for money or that need for shelter. Bob Washington taught us with his gentle question that concern for the soul always has to do with body, mind, emotion. The whole person is engaged in the concern of the Church. As bishop, when I periodically visit each of our parish pastors I always begin the pastoral conversation with that question: "How's your soul?"

Marcus Miller, one of my classmates at New York Theological Seminary, now Bishop of the Northeastern Ohio Synod of the ELCA, remembered Bob Washington's question as he described the mutual ministry of Word and Sacrament and Word and Service he shared with Deaconess Judith Hosheck during his days as a parish pastor in Brooklyn, Ohio:

> Let me tell you how that worked with Helen Walkley. When I came to Good Shepherd eleven years ago, Helen was already confined to the chair in her living room, a victim of MS. As Helen's pastor, I saw my responsibility to visit her regularly in order to read Scripture, share the Sacrament, and remember her Baptism with Helen. Alongside that ministry of Word and Sacrament, my colleague Judith Hoshek also ministered to Helen. She visited Helen every week, saw to it that Helen was visited by other mem-

bers of the parish and thereby connected to the Body of Christ, oversaw the regular delivery of Sunday liturgy tapes, discussed the sermon and lessons from the liturgy with her. She organized rides for Helen when necessary, made money available when needed, purchased medicine when necessary. Indeed, Judith cared for Helen's soul and organized the parish concern for her soul.

When Helen died, her funeral was a true celebration of the resurrection. When I paged through the eight pages of logged visits that we made with Helen over those years at home and hospital I realized that our ministry to and with Helen was a sign of cross and resurrection.

Pastors and bishops need to understand that their ministry is not threatened by the presence of a ministry of Word and service, but enriched, clarified, and then empowered by the ministry of the diaconate. (from testimony given at an ELCA hearing on the Study of Ministry)

A Look at a Book

In the Epistle to the Ephesians we read the following concerning the multiplicity of the Spirit's gifts for ministry: "The gifts he gave were that some would be apostles, some prophets, some evangelists, some pastors and teachers, to equip the saints for the work of ministry, for building up the body of Christ." (Eph. 4:11-12). What many parishes and pastors do is take this list of spiritual gifts and write them into the pastor's job description. The results are disastrous both in terms of overworked and overwrought clergy, and underutilized and theologically immature laity. For all of the compelling reasons why Bishop Lazareth's proposal for an ordained ministry in two forms, of Word and Sacrament on the one hand and Word and Service on the other, should get a hearing in our Lutheran segment of the Body of Christ, this practical reason seems to me most salient. Pastors need help in the form of colleagues in the parish's ministry. And the laity need all the encouragement, equipping and inspiration they can get as they serve the risen Christ in the world.

William Lazareth wrote a book back in 1991 on the ordering of the Church's public ministry which is still relevant today. Indeed, we have built on his proposals in the Metropolitan New York Synod, which Lazareth served as its first bishop, in shaping a synodically authorized diaconate. Lazareth places this ordering of ministry within an ecumenical and confessional context. "Here [the ordering of ministry] is clearly a critical area of the church's faith and order where the urgency of Christ's will for church unity should prompt us to seek to reconcile and renew more than four hundred years of inconsistent, 'emergency' Lutheran polity traditions. Moreover, this effort should be based strictly on the evangelical catholic basis of what is both confessionally permissible and ecumenically advisable for church unity in mission today" (p. 15).

In proposing two forms of ordained ministry— Word and Sacrament (pastors and bishops), and Word and Service (deacons and teachers)— Lazareth has preserved the ecumenical convergence of BEM (all three orders of Bishop, Pastor and Deacon are present in his two forms) and avoided direct confrontation with the conclusions of the Ministry Study of the ELCA (which did not call for an office of deacon, but left the door open for various offices of Word and Service at the synodical level). We do not have in his proposals a cadre of pastors under a hierarchical bishop, but rather colleagues in the ministry of Word and Sacrament with differing areas of oversight (*episkope*). The form of Word and Service is flexible enough to offer a wide range of ministries and models for supporting the ministry of the baptized in daily life.

Lazareth's identification of three Biblical ways of "ministering" or serving, lifted up by Augustana 28 as ministry "for," "by," and "to" the Gospel, is especially helpful. Ministry "for" the Gospel is the work of Jesus the Christ in the power of the Spirit. Ministry "to" the Gospel is the oversight of the office of Word and Sacraments. Ministry "by" the Gospel is the evangelistic witness of all baptized Christian laypeople to the presence of Christ in God's world. All forms of ministry reflect the *solus Christus*. "The Gospel that alone constitutes the church is the saving promise of God's work in and through Christ for the salvation and service of humankind" (p. 23).

The author emphasizes that the two forms of ordained ministry exist to work together "...to enable and support the priesthood of all baptized saints in carrying out God's mission in the world" (p. 17). They are ministry "to" the Gospel for the sake of ministry "by" the Gospel. Far from co-opting the ministry in daily life that every Christian receives in Baptism—as some fear—a ministry of Word and Service will join a ministry of Word and Sacrament in equipping, signing, and encouraging all of God's ministers in our wounded world.

I especially appreciate Lazareth's confessional appeal to engagement in the life of the world and the church's proper and distinctive Christ-like concern for the poor. These two forms of ministry side-by-side continually lift up for all the church the full depth of caring for the souls for whom Christ died. "[The diaconate's] Word and Service reinforces the Word and Sacraments in daily life. It proclaims the cruciform unity of body and spirit, of service and salvation, in the incarnational Word of God." (p. 86) What Bishop Lazareth is here describing is the mutual ministry of Pastor Miller and Deaconess Hosheck in caring for the soul of Helen Walkley.

A Parish Renewal of Diaconal Love

> "All service ranks the same with God
> With God, whose puppets, best and worst,
> Are we: There is no last or first."
> (from "Pippa Passes," Robert Browning)

Bishop Lazareth concludes his argument for a ministry of Word and service. "For all the outlined reasons of service, unity, and mission, it is high time to unify and regularize at least some of these needed and helpful diaconic ministries into a professionally trained and carefully supervised ordained public office of the church." (p. 86) I agree. That is what we have done in the Metropolitan New York Synod through the establishment of a Synodically Authorized Diaconate. I think that a revived diaconate is relevant to the church at this millennial moment for three main reasons: Such a revival would advance the ecumenical proposals of the Lima document (Baptism, Eucharist and Ministry) in practice as well as spirit. A diaconate would keep the "least of these" always at the heart of the one ordained, Apostolic ministry of the church. A diaconate would, as stated above, offer much-needed help to ministers of Word and Sacraments and much-enhanced support to the ministries of all the baptized Christians in the world. What I would like to offer here are some suggestions for the shape and implementation of these ministries in our parish life.

Candidates for diaconal ministries would require a period of theological education and spiritual formation. This time of preparation could be undertaken in a variety of ways. The ELCA's deaconess communities have their own system of education. Our synodical "Diakonia" program, the subject of another chapter in this book, offers a two-year course (meeting once a week for three hours) in the classic seminary disciplines of Bible, Theology and Confessions, History, and Practical Ministry (liturgy, service, pastoral care, etc.). The courses are taught by local pastors or other qualified teachers with oversight provided by the Synod through the Office of the Bishop. A rhythm of retreats, worship, and mentoring provide spiritual as well as vocational formation. There are other models. The point is that the period of training must be serious, accountable, and accessible. The bishop and synodical diaconate committee track and nurture each student's vocational growth along with his or her local pastor and other pastors and deacons.

Diaconal candidates spend a year's internship under the oversight of the local parish, its pastor, and the bishop. Candidates give about twenty hours a week of service, undergirded with regular mentoring sessions and continuing education. An examining committee under the bishop's direction certifies the candidate and pronounces the *dignus* (or *digna*) *est* on behalf of the church. Candidates are then be available for call to congregations (often their home congregations) or other ministries of service. Upon acceptance of a regular call the candidates are consecrated at the same synodical liturgy as ordinations to the ministry of Word and Sacrament.

The ministry of parish deacons includes both liturgical and diaconal service. Such dual service helps to deepen the connections between Sunday and Monday and the bodily as well as the servant implications of our liturgical actions. The deacon's liturgical service is shared with other assisting ministers from the ranks of the baptized. The one who administers the chalice at the Eucharist is also the one who brings the consecrated elements to the homebound and helps organize the parish's response to the hungry and homeless. The one who leads the intercessory prayers of Jesus' gathered community also helps organize the parish visitation of the sick, the imprisoned, the widows and orphans, together with the parish witness to issues of justice and mercy. The one who assists with baptisms also helps train and encourage the baptized to live in the world as signs of the Gospel to the unchurched. The deacon serves as a winsome lure for all the baptized to join together in the Church's ministries of *kerygma, koinonia,* and *diakonia.* Ministry to the Gospel and Ministry by the Gospel meet in the ministry of the deacon.

The deacon serves with other baptized people of God in all of these diaconal and liturgical ministries. What sets the deacon apart for consecration and enrollment on the synodical roster is the extensive period of theological training and vocational formation, the commitment to sustained and accountable service, and the offering of that service under the shepherding of the pastor and bishop.

Diaconal ministries are collegial and communal. Deaconess communities and such teachers' organizations as the Evangelical Lutheran Teachers' Association can help show the way here. Let there be ongoing theological and diaconal training. Let there be an archdeacon who represents the bishop in nurture and support of diaconal ministries. Let deacons have regular shared times with the bishop for mutual prayer and review of ministry. This cadre of available theologically trained and supervised servants has already had a tremendous impact on our synod's mission. Diakonia graduates in the

Bronx helped staff and run summer programs and ministries of mercy for the united parishes. An organized and theologically trained diaconate serving among minority persons are providing necessary resources and leadership for urban and ethnic-specific mission strategies throughout our synod. This service especially needed, given the small number of ordained ministers of Word and Sacrament from these communities. The need for a variety of Word and Service ministries is ubiquitous in our fragile and hurting world.

Ministries of Word and Service need not copy the organized diaconate of the Metropolitan New York Synod. Parishes elsewhere for the sake of more effective Gospel ministry have called and consecrated theologically trained deacons in evangelical freedom. Let a thousand flowers bloom! Other parishes and groups of parishes can support one another in these ministries. Synods and bishops, while recognizing that we do not now ordain deacons for the whole church, can yet nourish and support parish-based vocations to the diaconate by including deacons in continuing education events for Associates in Ministry and pastors; being present at diaconal consecrations; helping to link these ministries with one another; helping them seek some common criteria; and sponsoring solid theological training for all the laity. The ELCA's national Division for Ministry has been especially helpful in the nurturing of the many kinds of recognized and unrecognized ministries of Word and Service. Perhaps a seminary could offer a model program of theological training or support and help to staff existing grassroots programs. Maybe one of our twenty-nine colleges and universities could offer theological education within its teacher training curricula. The point of such heightened diaconal activity would be effective service to the Gospel and the world in memory of Jesus who came "not to be served, but to give his life as a ransom for many."

COOTIES AND JESUS

It was at an eighth-grade dance that I happened to notice Zona sitting by herself, near tears, dressed in a crinkly new white party dress. She was a strange person bereft of friends. In fact, if anyone accidentally touched her they got "Zona's cooties." In those days cooties were lethal. I had been part of her exposure to ridicule and isolation, but I couldn't stand to see her sitting there all by herself. So, God help me, I asked her to dance.

O painful remembrance! The song was "Bobby's Girl." Everyone else at the dance formed a circle around us, laughing and mocking. I stared straight down at my large, inept feet in total humiliation. When the dance was finished I made a beeline for the corner and sat down. No one came near me the rest of the evening, reminding me I had contracted a terminal case of "Zona's cooties."

The next day in school I was particularly cruel to Zona. She stood alone until we graduated. But I have never forgotten the price you pay to stand with the outcast. And that over the long haul, at least in that phase of Zona's life, that price was too high for me to pay.

Let a ministry of Word and Service remind the church of this: in a fallen world we are all Zonas—apart from God, standing alone. Diaconal people can help remind us that God in Christ has chosen to become Zona among us, the despised outcast on the cross. Let a Ministry of Word and Service help us all to recall that the mission of the church—in memory of Jesus and in the power of the Holy Spirit—is to reach out and dance with Zona. At the altar, in the midst of the baptized and their ministers, Jesus waits to stand with us again in bread and wine. The sacramental gift will remind us that the time is at hand when there will be no more Zonas, when all tears will be wiped away.

(Lutheran Forum, Lent, 1992)

CHAPTER 33
SERVANTS OF JESUS: DIACONAL PEOPLE AMONG US

SOON AND VERY SOON

> Soon and very soon we are goin' to see the King
> Soon and very soon we are goin' to see the King
> Hallelujah, Hallelujah
> We're goin' to see the King.
> (Gospel song by Andraé Crouch, WOV 744)

It is a living parable of the diaconate. It is ministry stripped to the essentials. We gather in the community room of the old Franklin Avenue Armory in the South Bronx, a huge and demoralizing shelter for homeless men run by the city of New York. Joe is playing Gospel on the old piano. He is a former resident of the shelter, Julliard-trained, who received guidance and hope through the chaplaincy of the Metropolitan New York Synod in this place. Deacon Glenn Stevenson is going from floor to floor inviting residents to the liturgy. As the congregation gathers some of the men page through Bibles Deacon Stevenson has given them at the Wednesday night Bible study he leads at the shelter. Others converse comfortably, part of what seems to be an ongoing community that has formed in this atomized corner of poverty. Some twitch nervously or stare at the floor. I prepare an altar on the table in front: laying out the linen, the cross, the gifts of bread and wine. We are ready.

The Deacon welcomes the guests, introduces the guest pastor. The Bishop and his staff are taking turns leading the liturgy this month. It is the first Sunday of Advent. In our liturgy we join the entire Church that waits in hopefulness on the Lord. We remember our baptism as we confess our sins. The singing of "Soon and Very Soon" is lively, animated. We ask God for mercy; then plead, "Stir up your power, O Lord and come!" We hear the reading of the Word of God. The pastor proclaims it. We sing in longing for the One who has been proclaimed: "O Come, O Come, Emmanuel." The Deacon prays for the church, the battered world outside, and the fragile community of the shelter. The men pray for one another by name. We share in the Family Meal of the Church. We receive a blessing and sing our thanksgiving: "Thank you Lord, Thank you Lord, I just want to thank you, Lord."

The deacon, the pastor, and the musician continue the *koinonia* of the Sacrament as we cut and share bagels and cream cheese and conversation. Stories unfold, of quotidian struggle, glimmers of hope, memories recalled, friends waiting, elusive jobs, tragedy self-inflicted or random, stories told in the shadow of AIDS and addiction and violence and poverty and racism. A fleeting community has gathered, given shape by Jesus, who draws near humanity in bread and wine and Word and neighbor. The organizer is the deacon, enabling the Church to stretch out beyond itself, turning its life toward the poor, swelling the chorus of creation in travail: "Soon and very soon."

INTO THE WATER

> In this manner he hands him over naked to the bishop or presbyter who baptizes who stands at the water. Likewise a deacon descends with him into the water and says to him, helping him to say: "I believe in God the Father almighty...." (Hippolytus, *Apostolic Tradition* 21 [c. 215]; Ethiopic translation)

In the Metropolitan New York Synod there is a great need for, and a sturdy history of, diaconal life that leads the church into the water: helping its people live out their baptismal vocations to follow and serve Jesus; to mix its life in the waters of life swirling around it; to accompany those whose lives are being torn apart into the waters of God's baptismal presence and promise. Our synod has no more unanimity about the office of deacon than any other corner of God's church, but the *diakonia* of its ministry has been pervasive. We have a history of deaconesses serving lifetimes in inner city parishes; of *Hilfswerk* that organized immigrant parishes and attended to their needs; of the creation of institutions for the aged, hospitals, social ministry organizations, orphanages; schools and teachers of children; and more recently of Stephen ministers, leaders trained in church-based community organizing; and graduates of the Diakonia program serving throughout the synod. We have not been awaiting a study on ministry to begin diaconal work. What we have eagerly awaited is the recovery of the office of deacon among us that would:

- Join our thinking and praying about ministry with the ongoing ecumenical conversation of the Body of Christ;
- Organize and inspire existing diaconal work;
- Invite and exemplify the vocation of every baptized Christian to go down into the water and serve the neighbor in Jesus' Name;
- Help the church turn its life toward the poor.

The ELCA's 1995 study of ministry was in many ways an excellent biblical, historical and theological undergirding of our collective thinking on the subject. Its proposal of an ordained diaconal ministry would have helped Lutherans to advance the cause of Christian unity. In other ways the study, and the Kansas City Assembly's decision on it, missed the point. We do not have a diaconate, with a fundamental charism to identification with the poor, recruited and empowered from the neighborhoods where the deacons live and serve. We have instead diaconal ministers needing Master's degrees. We have an office that will serve to gather and oversee many church vocations: administrators, Associates in Ministry, cantors, teachers, evangelists, and more. They will be consecrated. This is all to the good. Let a thousand flowers bloom in Christ's ministry! But in our time, in a church body floundering in its attempt to empower leadership from various ethnic communities, to have a credible mission in inner city and rural neighborhoods, to mix its life with the poor and the needs of people, to inspire to mission in a secular age, the question must be asked: "What became of the deacon?"

THE DIACONATE: TOWARD HEALTHY CHURCHES IN HEALTHY COMMUNITIES

> If I am not for myself, who will be for me? And if I am only for myself, what am I? And if not now, when? (Rabbi Hillel, *Sayings of the Fathers*, p. 25)

With the Advent liturgy at the Franklin Avenue shelter as a kind of template, let us explore some of the aspects of the diaconate in a largely urban synod:

- It is based in the mission and outreach of congregations. The chaplaincy of the Franklin Avenue Shelter is part of the outreach of South Bronx congregations into their own communities. It is run by a board of directors of pastors and laypeople from the congregations. In partnership with the synod the board called a pastor. When that pastor took another call the ministry was continued by Deacon Stevenson, who is accountable to the board and organizes the resources of the wider church to pursue this mission. The point: the deacon is connected to, and helps connect, communities of Word and Sacraments and the wider church through the synod. A revived diaconate would help make explicit the tie between the church and the community in which it would share the love of Jesus.
- It would help embody the essential unity and diaconal character of all ministry. The bishop and pastoral staff, deacon and laity all served to-

gether to lead worship at the shelter, each with a role to play, but each as servant to Jesus. We are all in the water together. Can you imagine what it would mean to the life of the church in the New York City area to have a cadre of theologically trained deacons on whom the bishop could call to help begin, resuscitate, organize, train, or staff ministries of mercy, congregational nurture, and mission outreach among us?

- The heart of the diaconate would be solidarity with the poor in the Name of Jesus. This ministry is not a form of *noblesse oblige*, the spurious exchange between the privileged and the poor. Although the chaplaincy does attend to the needs and opportunities of the residents, it does not exist to "do something for someone." We were simply there to share Jesus, and to keep company in his Name. Rather than social work, it is Eucharistic—in the sense of *con pan*, "with bread," the companionship of Jesus with his friends.
- The diaconate would help the church and its baptized servants go into the waters of the world around it. It is a simple fact that if Deacon Glenn were not serving this ministry the church would not be there. He is not alone. You will find deacons at nursing homes, shelters, soup kitchens, congregations in pastoral vacancy, continually urging the Church to get out of the boat, to walk on water—perhaps to drown—to where Jesus waits with outstretched hand.

A Modest Proposal

Our diaconal people do not come, for the most part, from national or seminary programs. Many come out of parish programs or the Diakonia program. They are local people from the neighborhoods, trained and empowered in a grassroots, "bottom-up" vocational formation. In a survey of the almost five hundred graduates of Diakonia, besides deep leadership and commitment to ministries within the parish, these were among the ministries being served in the name of the parish to the wider community: hospital and hospice ministries; community visitation of the sick and homebound; nursing home ministries; prison ministry; shelters, soup kitchens and advocacy work; neighborhood youth programs. Although some of these ministries receive remuneration, most do not.

The times call out for clarity and churchly oversight of these and other diaconal ministries. There is great frustration on the part of some pastors and diaconal ministers over issues of turf, accountability, recognition, vocational identity. Now is not the time for any synod, parish or deacon to "do its own thing." Toward such clarity I offer this modest proposal for a diaconate

in the Metropolitan New York Synod that would join the greater conversation in our church body (and ecumenically) around issues of ministry:
- First, encourage where appropriate, the participation of synodical vocations of music, administration, teaching and others that are provided for in the study of ministry and that require theological study at the graduate level.
- Second, the window of opportunity in the study of ministry that seems congruent with our life and history is that which allows for non-stipendiary and alternate-route vocations. I envision the establishment of a diaconate among us that would have as its primary charism solidarity with the poor.
- Let there be two years of training using the Diakonia model, which will assure that the vocational process will be locally and economically accessible. But let there be a direct link with the Lutheran Seminary in Philadelphia and the national Division for Ministry. This link could include courses offered in the new "seminary without walls" program jointly sponsored by the seminary and the synod; the use of seminary teachers; even direct seminary oversight of course work and offerings.
- Let there be a rigorous candidacy process linking the synod and local pastors. Let there be a track of the program in the Spanish language. Let there be explicit standards for the office of deacon and a system of oversight with ongoing vocational support. Let these consecrated deacons serve not only through their parishes, but also be available to the bishop for service in organizing ministries of mercy, support in pastoral vacancies around the synod, initiation of neighborhood evangelism and revivals, and leadership training of the ministries of all the baptized.

This proposal, modest as it is, is presently official policy in the Metropolitan New York Synod. We have a synodically authorized diaconate structured according to guidelines provided by the ELCA's Division for Ministry. As of 1998, our synod is the only ELCA synod that has a diaconate under the rubric of "synodically authorized ministries."

As we wait and plan we continue to serve. Other congregations are now serving the shelter ministry. Servants of Jesus and leaders will continue to emerge from the residents. Soon it will be time for the Bishop and staff to again take our turn. The deacon will have all things ready.

(*Lutheran Forum*, Lent, 1994)

Part Seven
"And to strive for justice and peace in all the earth."

Chapter 34
Parish Schools: Christ, the City, and the Child

> Jerusalem, Jerusalem... how often have I desired to gather your children together as a hen gathers her brood under her wings, and you were not willing! (Matthew 23:37)

> We who serve the church and hold the teaching office are certainly in a poor and lowly position, measured by the standard of the world against that of other professions. For we usually earn hostility for our labor and suffer not only haughty scorn but even hunger and want, while others are well rewarded and held in the highest esteem... But if you look at this question in the right way, no matter how miserable and despised he may be, the theologian is in a better position than all the teachers of the other professions. For as often as he performs his duty he not only does his neighbor a valuable service, which is superior to all the favors of all other men; but he also offers to God in heaven Himself the most pleasant sacrifice and is truly called the priest of the All-highest. For everything that a theologian does in the church is related to spreading the knowledge of God and to the salvation of men. (LW, A Brief Preface to the Second Psalm, vol. 12, p. 4)

A Tale of Two Children

Cecilia. She was from Ecuador and lived with her mother and little sister in a sixth-floor walk-up apartment in the Jackson Heights neighborhood of my former parish. Her little sister, Amaryllis, attended our nursery, a part of Queens Lutheran School. The family began attending our Sunday morning liturgy. During their time in our country Cecilia gave a human face to the slogan "children at risk."

Her mother. It was the plan of Mrs. Calderone that the next fall Cecilia would join her other daughter in Queens Lutheran School. She was a strong woman, who placed a high value on family, religion, education. Mrs. Calderone

---

Author's Note: These reflections come out of my experience with urban parish schools. I believe that much of what is written is also valid in suburban, town, and rural settings. I hope that the intensely incarnational reality of urban ministry translates into Christ's embodiment in all types of metropolitan settings.

was a proud woman who had worked hard to make a life for her daughters in the United States. She wanted to pass on her culture, her values to her children, as well as opportunities in this country that they would never have back home.

The city. It can be a marvelous place of opportunity and diversity. But its streets can sometimes chew up children like Mrs. Calderone's daughters and spit them out. Cecilia was soon caught between two worlds. She refused to speak Spanish at home. She cut school and ran wild and free while her mother was at work. She would often forget to pick up her little sister at Atonement, and when she did remember she would then leave her alone in the apartment. Then Cecilia began to use drugs. She and her mother fought often as their life together became a series of confrontations, truces, in an inexorable downward drift.

The final confrontation came in the living room of their small apartment. I was there with Cecilia, Amaryllis, their mother, and a police officer. The drama of a clash between two worlds had reached its climax. The police had caught Cecilia in a drug bust in the park across the street. She got off with a warning. After the officer left Cecilia bitterly spat out her rejection of her mother and her mother's values.

"You don't understand. Let me live my own life. I don't want to be some stupid old-country Spic like you. I hate you!"

Her mother lifted her hand to her daughter, then let it fall to her side. She sighed. "All right. We will leave tonight. I am sending you back to Ecuador. You will go to boarding school, wear the uniform. I will not allow you to destroy your life. How I love you! How much I want to share your life and have you share mine! But you do not care. Maybe some day you will understand how much I love you."

I drove them to Kennedy that night. On the way to the car the mother fell apart. I held her as she cried her heart out. Amaryllis closed her eyes and took her sister's hand. Cecilia watched in stony, spiteful silence. I never saw them again after that night. Cecilia was thirteen years old.

Think of Cecilia. Think of her mother. Think of the city. Think of the school in Jackson Heights that welcomed Amaryllis in a strange land. Now think of God. Jesus looked out over the city of Jerusalem and wept, speaking words similar to Cecilia's mother's: "How I would gather you, like a hen gathers her chicks, and you were not willing!" Such a mother love.

It is in the shadow of such love of Jesus and a mother that I gather the themes of parish schools: children, the city, Christian mission in education, the ministry of Christian educators. Issues raised by a life like Cecilia's come together in the life of a Lutheran school: the pain and promise of the city; strength for families; public and private education; immigration and the global and multicultural context of the Church's life; issues of justice, substance abuse, women and children at risk and so many more. But in peeling back to the core the layers of issues surrounding Cecilia's story, we find at the center the font at which this child has been baptized; and the cross, the place where Christ has come to be with Cecilia and her family. The ministry of Lutheran parish schools is cruciform. For it is at the cross that the Body of Christ gives its life for the human bodies of Christ.

Another child. Eddie. Back-to-school at Trinity in New Jersey means the return of the three-year-old choir, those young lungs screaming out, "I want my mommy, I want my daddy!" In about seven different languages (and I consider Joisey to be a foreign language too.) The four-year-olds are fine, so also the kindergarten crew. It's old homecoming week for them, they are returning to a special place in which they know they are loved. They walk the halls and rooms like country squires surveying the estate. But for the threes it's a passion play. Heartbreak city. We always have plenty of Kleenex around, not only for the little runny noses, but also for parents lurking in the hallways, feeling guilty and sad for abandoning their offspring.

So the first day of school I walk into a room and right away I can see that there are not enough laps— four screaming children, two adults whose arms and laps were already overflowing. So I pick up a wailing little fella, and he's registering ten on the Richter scale, chewing on his arm, leaving snot on my neck and shoulder. I walk him around the room and show him things on the walls, cute clowns, balloons, animals, numbers... and my little guy is getting quiet and then I hear his excited whisper..."Jesus!" He was staring at a cross on the wall. "Jesus," he whispered again.

Now I would like to say that a miracle happened here and all the crying children gazed on an image of Jesus and were quiet— like the snake Moses built in the wilderness. Forget it! Eddie rejoined the chorus later. But for an instant an image of Jesus connected with a young child's mind and heart and gave him comfort. Somewhere in his short history this child's family and church had planted the idea of Jesus in his heart, and Eddie's heart was open to the love and comfort of the cross.

The planting of the cross in the heart of a child is the true ministry of the Church. It begins at the font. It is nurtured by the Eucharist. It happens when the pastor bends low at the altar rail to bless the child. It happens when a family prays before meals. It happens in Sunday School, summer programs, youth group, confirmation class. And it happens on the bridge of a Lutheran school where the children nurtured in church and home are further tended and nourished by the teacher, a minister of the Word. The classroom. The teacher. The congregation. The home. The sacraments. The Child. In the City. We are all in this together.

THE PARISH IN THE CITY
AT THE FOOT OF THE CROSS

Little Eddie is a budding theologian, for in his desperate sense of dislocation on his first day of school he intuits what the Church confesses: only in the cross of Jesus do we see God as God truly desires to be known. Only theology shaped by the cross is true knowledge of God. The confessional form of the cross in Lutheranism is not primarily social service, or the so-called prophetic transformation of society, or ideological or sociological goals. Besides, we who claim to be Luther's heirs have no right to spout high-handed rhetoric concerning the city. Like the other Protestants we have followed our constituencies out of urban neighborhoods, taking our money with us, with one scheme after another for building mega-churches according to the "church growth" model of success. There is only one ELCA parish left in Newark, New Jersey's largest city. There are none in Paterson. Listen to the list of recent ELCA school closings (and my guess is that the LC-MS would produce a similar list): Cleveland Urban; Simi Valley High School; St. John's and St. Paulus in San Francisco; Our Savior's and Capitol High School in the D. C. area; Holy Comforter in Baltimore; Kensington in Philadelphia; Chapel of Peace in Los Angeles; Martin Luther in Chicago and more. The closing of some of the most "inclusive" institutions of our Church gives a hollow ring to lofty principles of inclusivity.

The confessional form of the cross in the inner city, in every town and hamlet and suburb, is the congregation gathered around and by Word and Sacraments where Jesus has promised to be present for the forgiveness of sins and life everlasting. Phillip Johnson, a Jersey City pastor, describes the confessional form of Lutheran commitment to the city:

> I believe that a test of 'this church's' commitment to the city and the poor is its commitment to the ministry of preaching, baptizing, teaching and serving Christ's supper in the inner cities.... If Jesus communicated in so powerful a way the universality of the love of God, he did so because he so readily brought to bear on concrete, close-at-hand life situations the particular demands of love. In the gospels the all-inclusive claims of love are made concrete in the face of the particular. The issues of love and justice are always right at the door, within one's reach. In the way of Jesus, you cannot love the poor from afar. (quoted from *Lutheran Forum* [August, 1992], pp. 32-38)

The presence of a pastor, a parish, a teacher, a school in the inner city, trained, articulate, strong, and filled with love, can be a small sign pointing to the cross. It is a clear message. We are not voyeurs of your pain. We are not arrogant enough to think we can fix your wagon or anybody else's. You are not the objects of our charity. We have come simply to be with you. The congregation is the form of our commitment to the poor, because the congregation is the form the Gospel takes in the world. And a parish school is a window for that congregation, and into it, of the life of the world around it.

Phillip Johnson is presently planning a school for his parish. He writes again:

> The inner city is home for countless forgotten and forgetful Christians, the baptized children of God, who are the victims of pastoral ignorance, neglect, exhaustion, and discouragement. They are lost to the life of the Church; their faith is like a bruised reed or barely smoking flax. They are oppressed by ignorance and superstition. They are estranged Roman Catholics who have fallen through the overstrained pastoral net. They are countless African Americans who have sunk under the brutalities of inner city life beyond the reach of their own spiritual heritage. They are immigrants by the thousands who have lost touch with their religious roots. These people, the baptized and the unbaptized, very literally may recall no hymn to sing, quote no Scripture to their children, have no pastor to call on, no community to value their gifts or to weep with them, and they cannot tell the story of their Savior... it would be hard to overestimate the radical impact on inner-city communities, if the churches shifted their major orientation from service programs directed at the poor to energetic catechesis, spiritual formation, and training for ministry among their people. To present such people mature in Christ — newly literate in the language of Scripture, empowered in and by their relations to one another, living by the faith of the Gospel, filled with the music of faith, ready to stand in the world for the truth they find in Christ — that is the healing and threatening gift the Church has to offer inner city neighborhoods. (quoted from *Lutheran Forum* [August, 1992], pp. 32-38)

When the Romans landed in Britain they pulled their boats to the shore and burned them. The message was unmistakable: We are here to stay! When the Church begins to make as its highest priority the planting and strengthening of eschatological communities of Jesus and their sturdy institutions such as schools within urban neighborhoods, then we may all see once again the power of the Cross, and our neighbors may once again believe that we have no other agenda than to be with them in the name of Jesus.

What follows are some modest proposals for giving shape to urban ministry through parish schools:

I. "That the Gospel heart of all Lutheran education, the parish community of Jesus gathered around and by Word and Sacraments, be continually lifted up and made explicit. At the center of each Lutheran school throughout the metropolis stands the Cross."
II. "That each new Lutheran urban outreach or renewal effort be accompanied by development of a school, early childhood center, latchkey program, or other institution of parish education."

The history of the church's first great mission thrust into the pagan world was not the story of lone rangers in white hats going out alone. It was communal. Patrick in Ireland, Ansgar in Denmark and Sweden, Boniface among the Teutonic tribes all brought with them Eucharistic communities to be planted in the midst of the pagan world. From the midst of these communities these pastors and bishops invited, taught, catechized, encouraged, and developed indigenous leadership. We need to recapture the sense of the congregation as a missionary community.

Several years ago I was doing consulting work for the beginnings of a community organizing effort in the Central Ward of Newark. We interviewed over five hundred people living in and around several large housing projects in the ward. They were the poorest of the poor. What we found was that there were literally no institutions in this part of the city. None. No stores, no churches (not even storefronts), no unions, no PTAs, nothing. Well, almost nothing. There were so-called "civic associations," which were nothing more than fronts for local fixers to whom people would give a retainer of money in return for small favors.

Can you imagine the impact of one parish with a school in such a place? Is it any wonder that one of the planned responses among Lutherans in south central Los Angeles to the recent devastation there is the planting and strengthening of Lutheran schools? In the parishes I have served I cannot imagine reaching out to changing neighborhoods without the schools our congregations had nurtured. In Jackson Heights, Queens, serving a parish with almost thirty different ethnic groups, we were part of a six-parish Queens Lutheran School. Queens Lutheran School serves over six hundred children, and the only ethnic group not represented on the city forms was Eskimo. In our changing blue-collar neighborhood in Bogota, New Jersey, we began a school as our response to re-rooting our parish in its place. The school has grown from twelve to two hundred and twenty children, and in the past five years we have enjoyed over one hundred baptisms, most coming through the ministry of this school. And as I said before, the wailing on opening day is a cacophony of many different languages.

What will the future hold for our cities? Strong institutions local people can call their own, or dependence on the charity of strangers?

III. "That each urban judicatory, in consultation with national development offices, establish a fund for urban education, (like the annual "bishop's appeal" or "campaign for human development" in the Roman Catholic dioceses.)"

On the right bank of the Seine in Paris, in the midst of some massive slums as unhip as the Left Bank is trendy, sits a singular church, St. Gervais. It is run by the "Community of the New Jerusalem," chartered in the mid-seventies. The basis of the community's spiritual life is simple: they believe that the inner city is an eschatological sign of God's future, the new Jerusalem. The Church of St. Gervais is open twenty-four hours a day, and for every one of those hours members of the community are in continual corporate or private prayer for the people of the city. The church abounds with programs, reaching out to the disparate constituencies of the city: tourists, shopkeepers, children, the elderly, the addicted, the home-bound, the homeless. What undergirds this pervasive presence is the community of prayer, people, and resources living in covenant with one another, the city, and their Lord.

We need such strength and communal depth for urban ministry and for our parish schools in the city. An annual appeal, accompanied by telling the stories of our schools and recruiting future teachers, could help provide a rhythm for this ministry. True, the benevolence dollar is stretched thin in our churches. Yet it has also been my experience that people share generously with institutions which are visibly successful in meeting the needs of people. A Church that says it wants to be inclusive, that says that it belongs in the cities, would be a church that loses its right to the rhetoric if it does not strengthen its most inclusive institutions. I envision reaching out to alumni and alumnae, local businesses, corporate "social responsibility" officers, and others who touch the life of our schools. This approach, of course, would require a less parochial and a more communal and accountable way of raising and disbursing these funds, much mutual conversation and planning about salary scales, scholarships for the poor, equable distribution, fiduciary responsibility and so on. But we can do it. We *must* do it or the list of inner-city school closings will continue, and neighborhoods starved for institutions to help re-knit the fabric of their communities from the bottom up will not be able to easily replace these signs of hope. Can strongly funded, effectively articulated Lutheran schools be our St. Gervais for the New Jerusalems in which we serve?

IV. "That Lutherans advocate specific urban experiments in educational choice through vouchers."

The Board for the ELCA's Division for Higher Education and Schools, which I chaired for several years, requested our Church's Division for Church and Society to join us in a study of the educational choice issue. The fine initial working paper, written by John Stumme, studies the social statements of the previous church bodies. The paper asks the right questions. It seems to go, albeit tentatively, in the direction of qualified support for educational choice through vouchers. Needless to say, the discussion our board had with Dr. Stumme covered the predictable spectrum of responses. Having heard the debates about this issue in the election year we were not surprised to find that we are not of one mind on educational choice. This issue is very divisive in New York state and city politics even as I write. My eldest son teaches in a public high school in Brooklyn and is no friend of the idea of school choice.

In my own mind I come out in favor of qualified support for the idea. Let's try it somewhere in a city where the people need all the help they can get! I think back to my intern year in Richmond, Virginia, when Judge Merhige handed down the decision that brought bussing between the City of Richmond and Henrico County to achieve racial integration in the schools. I saw "private" schools spring up all over the area with the obvious intent to segregate their student bodies. In that case I would absolutely oppose vouchers.

The Lutheran parochial school in Jersey City provides good education and a safe environment for learning in a drug-ridden neighborhood where the state has taken over a corrupt and moribund public school system. Even as this parochial school hangs on by its teeth economically it turns no one away due to financial considerations. It seems that here we come up against an ideological irony. There are a lot of white liberals who themselves already have the choice to either move to "burbs" with better schools or where they can afford a private education who would oppose the possibility of choice for the folks of this neighborhood. The people in the neighborhood of the Lutheran parochial school have no choice, especially if this beleaguered school goes under.

In an editorial entitled "Test The Voucher" in the *Herald and News* of Passaic, New Jersey we read:

> Despite intervention by the courts and a massive state effort, New Jersey's inner-city schools remain in crisis. Many urban kids who go to school simply can't learn and no one is held accountable. Newark students, for example, posted a combined score of 654 on the 1991 SAT tests-200 points below the state average.... New Jersey ought seriously to consider an experiment in the free-choice voucher system for education. The test ought to be conducted in an urban area-such as Paterson or Newark—and be of

sufficient duration for participating schools to gauge and adapt to the impact. Vouchers, education money that follows students to their schools of choice, will not solve all our problems, but they may provide an alternative for children trapped in bad schools that have absolutely no prospect of getting better. Once considered a radical scheme from the fringes of American conservatism, the voucher system has attracted more and more middle-of-the-road supporters.... Yes, urban private schools tend to be religiously oriented, but that hardly seems a drawback in the America of the 90s. In fact, it's the sense of mission that allows such schools to run scholastic rings around public institutions that cost many times more to operate...

Will vouchers drain public schools of their best students? Maybe. But there is no justification for holding motivated students hostage for the imagined benefit of a student body. Will public education be destroyed by a voucher system? Not likely. But it will have to change its focus, either to attract the students it wants or to service the students it gets. It's time we gave the people involved the chance to find their own individual solutions. Real school choice offers the tantalizing prospects of saving our children the only way they can be saved— one child at a time.

The editor and writer of this editorial, John Bendel, was for many years the chair of the board of our parish school at Trinity. His children go to public schools, but he has seen what our school means to the community and the church. He, and many thoughtful people, want to know if their church body stands with them and the schools they nurture.

V. "That Lutherans share their ministry and insights with the arena of public education."

It is also important that the Church and its schools take seriously the joint enterprise we share with all who educate the public. The most unusual expression of thanks for a speaking engagement I ever received was a bottle of 25-year-old Glenfiddich Scotch Whisky and homemade Scottish shortbread. The occasion was a symposium on the role of private and parochial schools in the education of the public. The Alexander Robertson School, a Presbyterian parochial school on 92nd Street in Manhattan, sponsored the symposium as a part of its 200th anniversary celebration. The school's beginnings were diaconal, an institution formed to educate the "ragged children" (poor) of Scottish immigrants and others in church and community. The issue was the relationship between public and private endeavors in American education. One of the panel members was Margaret Shafer, who is staff to ministries in education of the National Council of Churches. We compared notes and identified several areas in which the ministry of parochial and private schools can be shared with institutions of public education:

Excellence in education is a ministry. We support the public schools when we hold up the importance of teachers and administrators as a Christian vocation. The Church must provide spiritual and psychological support for those who serve on our behalf as educators, wherever they serve.

Parochial schools provide options in a pluralistic society (in the tradition of the *Federalist Papers*). They provide a different style, a change of scene, a fresh start for some children who may need it. Their quality enhances the overall quality of the educational offerings in a given neighborhood.

Parochial schools help the Church advocate the value of education in our bottom-line society. Education offers deeper dimensions of value than the merely practical in our consumer-oriented communal life. Education needs defenders when the question of allocation of public resources is addressed. A voucher system joins public and parochial centers of education together in an ongoing dialogue and advocacy for the best possible education for all and the resources to accomplish it.

Parochial schools have the freedom to be innovators, trying out new concepts and ideas in education. Lutheran schools have an accountability different from public schools, more freedom to serve as learning laboratories. These schools can demonstrate the translation of theory into practice to the education community before the heavy institutional commitment of the public school system is sought.

Parochial schools can share with public education the Church's commitment to community service, the place in a child's intellectual and moral development for opportunities to be responsible for others, especially those in need. In a world in which lack of clarity about values in the areas of human sexuality and substance abuse can be lethal, parochial schools can make a significant contribution to the conversation that will provide necessary guidance and vision for all our children.

Finally, parochial schools must take advantage of opportunities to develop the skills of public discourse about religion. When they help the children they educate to be in conversation with their faith; when they help them see the implications of that faith in the world around them, they reinforce the fabric of our communal life. The *eikon Christi* (image of Christ) is not parochial, but cosmic.

VI. "That programs be developed which will heighten the sense of shared metropolitan ministry and responsibility between suburban and inner-city parishes and their schools, in an age in which the powers of this world seek to divide and estrange the constituencies of the city. Example: environmental education programs in outlying areas of the metropolis, and "human environmental education" programs which showcase the vitality and diversity of the inner city."

I suppose that we already possess the instrument to fulfill what I am advocating here: The Lutheran Schools Organization. Let me just highlight here the interconnectedness of the metropolis. I remember the scuffling days of my involvement in grassroots community organizing in Queens. I remember Mayor Ed Koch walking into one of our meetings and immediately and shrewdly beginning to divide and polarize us. He began to push racial and class buttons, taking impromptu polls—"Everyone who agrees with me that the middle class are getting the short end of the stick raise your hands"— I remember some folks raising their hands while others sat in stony silence. We have had too much of the cynical politics and urban planning of those who play us off against one another. The best case history I have ever read on this subject is the book *Common Ground: A Turbulent Decade in the Lives of Three American Famiies* by J. Anthony Louckas (Vintage, 1986), which described the urban warfare in Boston in the 1970s between poor Irish and poor blacks around issues of busing, education and integration. It was a battle fought along class as well as racial lines, as the ruling class and the church took entrenched positions which allowed their polarized constituencies to leave each other's blood all over the issue. Let it not be so in the church!

It does not help to play "my ghetto's worse than your ghetto," nor to define ministry with reference to pathology alone. It also does not help if parishes and their schools in more affluent areas wall themselves off from the rest of the metropolis. Each place where ministry flourishes in city or suburb is holy turf, loved by the God of history. A school is an affirmation of particular turf, a sign of commitment as concrete as Jacob's pile of stones at Bethel. The immense pain and unjust suffering of the poorest of the poor in the inner cities does not originate only within their neighborhoods. And the solutions, capital, jobs, institutions, commitment and care must also come from the storehouse of the metropolis as a whole. We must share a common future. But each unique setting of ministry must define its own problems and its own way, each setting must gather its own strength and foster its own affirmations. Then, as equals, all sectors of the metropolis must sit down together and claim the relationships already ours as gifts of the Holy Spirit.

All I am trying to say here is that whether we belong to inner city, suburb, town, or country, we are all interconnected, we all belong to one another in the gaze of the Christ who brooded over the metropolis like a mother hen. I have begun referring to the ministry of our synod as ministry in the "metropolis" to emphasize our interconnections. So we need programs and institutionalized relationships like the Lutheran Schools Association that allow us to share our gifts with one another.

VII. "That seminary curricula and continuing education efforts include opportunities for pastors of congregations with parochial schools to clarify and grow in their role as school pastors."

One of my finest memories of time spent with Queens Lutheran School was the appearance of the Association pastors at the orientation meetings for school families. We would sit down with each new family and go over a cooperative agreement that made explicit the relationship between the church, school, and home for the child's spiritual nurture. Opportunities to strengthen the family's participation in their own parish, mutual conversation about the faith, exposure of the unchurched and the unbaptized to the faith were all afforded by these conversations. The pastor plays a key role in the life of a Lutheran parochial school. I believe that the role of the pastor described below also holds true within the overall mission of the entire parish. The pastor's role in a parish school is integrative, legitimating/empowering, and pastoral.

1. *Integrative*

Consider the many worlds that converge within a parochial school:
- The ministry of the parish: its baptismal font and altar, its ministries of service, justice and nurture in memory of Jesus
- The families of the children
- The life of the surrounding community
- Issues of education and the well-being of children and families
- The diverse cultures of its students
- Lives being torn apart by physical, mental or spiritual issues
- The faculty and their families

It is the pastor's role to be a presence in these worlds and to symbolize the presence of Christ for these disparate communities. On Monday morning the pastor is at the door, greeting the families, then dropping into each classroom to welcome children and teachers. The key words here are *presence* and *hospitality*: in the community, the congregation, faculty meetings, regular meetings with the principal, school board meetings, the homes of school families.

2. *Legitimating/Empowering*

The pastor exercises a ministry of oversight, representing the school and the ministry of its teachers and administrators to the parish, the community, the school families, the wider Church. Through newsletter articles, sermons, liturgies of installation and other Occasional Services, invitations extended to school staff to participate in the parish's liturgies and teach and proclaim the Gospel in the parish's life, and all manner of public and personal support, the pastor will undergird the ministry of the school with the depth and breadth of the things of the Church. The place of the school in the one ministry of the parish will be lifted up by the pastor continually. The pastor may be the "court of last resort" for disciplinary problems, appeals by faculty or school families, and other conflicts, always supporting the mission of the school and its ministers.

3. Pastoral

In the school setting the pastor proclaims the Word and administers the Sacraments. She will offer pastoral "soul care" for staff, children, and school families; lead worship at school liturgies and meetings; integrate the life of the school around the rhythm of the Church year; hear confessions; visit the sick; and as an *eikon Christi* serve as a continual reminder of the presence of Christ and the Church.

With the exception of primary parish oversight and administration of the Sacraments, the roles of the principal within the school and the teachers within the classrooms are exactly the same as above. In Christ, we are in this together.

VIII. "That Lutheran urban high schools and parishes participate in such programs as the PASS Plan in Paterson and Passaic, New Jersey. In this plan, local parish-based community organizations negotiate entry-level jobs and college scholarships to be awarded to inner-city students who maintain a C average and exemplary attendance in their junior and senior years of high school. The key to the plan is the monthly mentoring meetings with trained volunteers from local parishes and schools."

Here's one for our urban high schools. We are blessed in our region with such high schools such as Martin Luther, Our Savior's, and Long Island Lutheran. We are also blessed with such wonderful grassroots parish-based community organizations as East Brooklyn Churches, Queens Citizens' Organization, South Bronx Churches and other organizing efforts across the metropolis. These efforts attempt to bring together area institutions in order to develop leadership, help people define their own issues, defend their values in the public arena, gain power for full participation in the decisions that shape their lives and communities. There have been some wonderful examples of participation by urban high schools in these organizations.

The PASS Plan (Passport Awarded for Staying in School) provides concrete incentives to older youth to stay in school and away from drugs. This private/public partnership was created by the Interfaith Action Council (IAC) of New Jersey in the inner cities of Paterson, Passaic, Union City, and Hackensack. It mobilizes area banks, companies and colleges to guarantee career-entry level jobs and college tuition scholarships to graduates from the high schools of these cities. To receive employment or scholarships, the four hundred students enrolled each year in the PASS Plan must meet grade average and attendance requirements in their junior and senior years. Students attend PASS Plan meetings to receive support and training in job skills. These meetings are run by two hundred trained adult sponsors recruited from IAC member congregations.

The key to the program's success has been the grassroots participation and ownership of congregations and their leaders. The PASS Plan steering committee that governs the program is a partnership of churches, school districts, major financial institutions, companies, and colleges. Each makes substantial contributions in the form of money, jobs and other institutional support. The relationships and commitments among the various participants were negotiated by the church leaders of the IAC. Sometimes confrontational, always well disciplined, these believers living out their faith in the Kingdom of the left hand are able to make a real difference as they "seek the welfare of the city." The trained volunteers, all church members, who meet regularly with the students provide the mentoring and conversation about values and identity that foster hope and dignity in urban young people. Students from both public and Roman Catholic inner-city schools are involved in the PASS plan.

In another chapter I have described one of the members of the church I served in New Jersey as the owner of a factory in Paterson, who one day asked me to meet him at the factory to talk about Baptism with one of his employees, an eighteen-year-old father with a sixteen-year-old wife. We met in a corner of the factory and between my broken Spanish and their broken English we had a conversation about Baptism, the Body of Christ, and Christian nurture. My parishioner served as a godparent. Gabriella Maria became a child of God because of the ministry of our member who stood with the family at the font and brings them to the liturgy on Sunday. Contacts like these led our parish, a member of IAC, into participation in the PASS Plan. Social ministry emerges from the parish taking responsibility for the children it baptizes.

In a book entitled *Adolescence at Risk: Prevalence and Prevention* (Oxford University Press, 1991), Joy Dryfoos analyzes many programs now in use among adolescents in the cities aimed at such issues as alcohol and drug abuse prevention and treatment; crime; job training; and self-esteem. Of the successful programs she isolated many different factors, but two were present in every single program of merit.

The first factor is the quality of justice. Each successful program required the successful collaboration of all the institutions in the community. There was real social change in institutional relationships.

The second factor is the quality of individual mercy. Each successful program was built on one-on-one relationships between adolescents and someone who was their mentor.

Dryfoos' findings mirror the words of the prophet Micah: For what does the Lord require of us but this, to do justice, love kindness, and thereby walk humbly with our God?

IX. "That Lutheran judicatories study the cultures and needs of immigrant groups. That Lutheran schools hire staff from these immigrant groups as a sign and enabler of their evangelical hospitality and outreach."

At a recent consultation in Los Angeles about Lutheran outreach to Koreans I heard one Korean leader after another tell us what I had already come to know through experience. Among the main reasons Koreans (and many other immigrant groups) come to this country is the desire for a good education for their children. It seems to me that a church body born in a university, with a sturdy history of excellence in education, would be especially well poised to reach out to new Korean immigrants.

During my ministry at Atonement in Jackson Heights I witnessed a generation of Korean members enter the Lutheran church through our parish and its school and high school. The principal at the time, Harold Weseloh, would not only spend Sunday mornings after church helping Koreans register in our school and negotiate the problems facing immigrant kids and their families, he would also help me with other immigration issues, and together we would teach the Lutheran liturgy and theology. A Korean woman was hired as an aide in one of the classes; people in the community could relate easily to her. I remember driving the bus to pick children up from school and bring them to our after-school programs or to confirmation class, then bring them home again or to their parents' shops. At one time our parish had more than thirty children in Queens Lutheran School; many of these kids went on to Martin Luther High and performed well.

In the parish I served in Bogota, New Jersey, a generation of Hispanic folks entered the Lutheran church. We probably had more Hispanic members in church and Sunday School than most other parishes in our Synod. The key was our parish school and a strong neighborhood ministry. The neighbors change from one community to the next. But the school as a mission instrument has been a constant in my ministry.

X. "That for the sake of ecumenical clarity Lutheran communions ordain qualified teaching ministers into a Diaconate of Word and Service. Deacons represent to the church its calling as servant in the world. By struggling in Christ's name with the myriad needs of societies and persons, deacons exemplify the interdependence of worship and service in the Church's life... they exercise responsibility in the worship of the congregation... teaching... and a ministry of love" (*Baptism, Eucharist and Ministry* III).

Consideration of the teaching ministry as a diaconate may help to give an ecumenical dimension to the ongoing conversations about the shape of public ministry, as well as provide a gift to the whole church from the heart of the city, of diaconal solidarity with "the least of these." Langston Hughes, in his book *Simple's Uncle Sam*, speaks anecdotally to the tragedy of children at risk in our world. He is remembering his childhood as a "passed-around child," its loneliness and pain. He remembers so many empty houses: "If they do not have a little love for whoever lives in the house with them, it is an empty house. If you have somebody else living in the house with you, be it man, woman, or child, relative or friend, adopted or just taken in, even if it is just a roomer paying rent— even if you give them no money nor a piece of bread and not anything— if you got a little love for whoever it is, it will not be a empty house. But if nobody cares, it is an empty house. I have lived in so many empty houses full of peoples, I do not want to live in a crowded empty house no more."

"God bless the child who's got his own," goes the old blues song. We live in a world of empty houses and abandoned children, fracturing families and latchkey adolescent lives. A majority of the poor and malnourished and sexually and physically abused in this country are children. Children from the most stable homes face confusing choices with potentially lethal consequences, the deteriorating quality of education, and other societal pressures. It strikes me how diaconal is the teacher's vocation these days. Think of the powerful image, the powerful icon, that the teacher represents— the one who holds Eddie and teaches Amaryllis, the architect of space at the foot of the cross at which children hear: "You belong!" The teacher who spends time with the children of poverty; who practices the pedagogical craft with imagination, art and the gift of building community; who links children with their baptismal identity and the fullness of God's love in the dying and rising Christ; who in the tradition of St. Lawrence presents these children to the whole Church as its great treasure. The teacher as an *eikon Christi*. An image, a presentation of Christ.

Not all persons who presently teach in Lutheran schools or are rostered as "Associates in Ministry" would qualify as deacons. Let there continue to be varieties of commissioned and consecrated ministries for the sake of the Gospel. But some theologically trained men and women who are ready to live their lives in the public ministry of Christ's church would be candidates for the office of ordained ministry of Word and Service as teaching deacons.

A Teacher's Kid

My father was a teacher in a Lutheran parochial school. In the Gospels Jesus is called "rabbi" thirty-nine times. Growing up in the home of a teacher in a parish school I came to understand why.

CHAPTER 35
TO TAKE CARE OF THE BODY: SOCIAL MINISTRY AND EVANGELISM THROUGH THE PARISH SOCIAL MINISTRY COMMITTEE

> When faith leads to action in outward affairs, that which takes place is spiritual in the midst of the carnal. Everything our bodies do, the external and the carnal, is called spiritual behavior, if God's word is added to it and it is done in faith. (Martin Luther, *Luther on Vocation* by Gustav Wingren [Muhlenberg Press, 1957])

The annual Christmas program of the nursery school of my former parish in New Jersey is always a Cecil B. DeMille production. The students file on stage and stand on pieces of tape marking each one's spot. Behind each piece of tape is a rhythm instrument. At a certain time in their song the children turn around, pick up the instruments and bang away with the piano. This year, the kids had practiced their routine so thoroughly that they performed like the U.S. nursery drill team.

Show time! The children strut onto the stage and onto the tape. They sing their lungs out. Then they turn around on cue and grasp their instruments and flail away with abandon. Except that this year there is one problem: the little girl next to Anthony has taken both her castanets and Anthony's tambourine. She is whaling away in rhythm heaven. Anthony comes up empty-handed and his face registers pure panic. He looks behind him: Nothing! His face screws up as if to cry.

If we are going to talk about social ministry, then the look on Anthony's face tells us all we need to know about the point of such ministry. That moment of panic, dislocation, fear, abandonment plays itself out in myriad ways, over moments or lifetimes. Anthony's is the face of the alcoholic's downward drift, the homeless family living in a car in Hackensack, the IBM manager in Poughkeepsie losing his job, the abused and brutalized women and children in our heartless world, the starving Somali, the person next to you in the pew who has learned the meaning of the lump in the breast or lymph node, the one going through divorce, the one raising children alone. The object of social ministry is Anthony, the poor—the *anawim* of the Hebrew Scriptures, folks living on the margins of vulnerability— or any of us on our bad days. Anthony. A face abandoned and ready to cry.

He sees Melissa next to him shaking his tambourine. He reaches for it and she pulls away. He strikes out at her but misses. He pulls his hand back again. He's going to deck her.

"Anthony!"

His face registers recognition. The calling of his name by a familiar, trusted voice brings him back to himself.

"Anthony! Fake it!"

He smiles, relieved and secure. He does a Milli Vanilli and shakes his hands and body to the music without the tambourine. As if his instrument were in his hand. With one word from a servant of the church, the Community of Jesus keeps company with a frightened child. It is the church which first called forth Anthony's name in Baptism.

This moment of simple grace reveals much concerning social ministry. Anthony's need was addressed through a relationship. In all ministry, relationship matters. Too often what passes for social ministry or social service is performed by strangers who despise or use the poor, giving charity which is despised by the strangers receiving it. In the church love flows out from those willing to share their lives and their community with the stranger. Anthony's relationship with his teacher was enabled by the church's willingness to fashion a sturdy institution that would join children and their families to the competence, compassion and outreach of a parish community. And in a bottom-line age in which we think we can fix everybody's wagon, this boy's lack of an instrument was not remediated but his need was addressed by a love willing to stand with him in the midst of his confusion and weakness.

A brief look at the church in Scripture and history reveals that the church is forever organizing itself to address human need within the household of Faith and into the world beyond. From Stephen and his six fellow deacons to their successors today, faithful social ministry is not something tacked onto the church's agenda, a sideline for bleeding hearts. It is central to the Gospel and to the one ministry of the communities gathered around and by the Word and Sacraments. The social ministry committee can be the means for parishes to be voices calling out to all the world's Anthonys in the Name of Jesus.

Some Areas of Responsibility for the Parish Social Ministry Committee

1. *The social ministry committee will see evangelism as its primary task.*

For Lutherans social ministry and evangelism are one. By this remark I do not mean having the poor "sing for their supper." There is a difference between hustling people and genuine hospitality. Renewed parishes will take responsibility for the unchurched and the poor in their neighborhood. Each program of social service or social change will include a credible invitation to participate in the life of the parish.

I think of Ricky and his mother, whose story I told in Chapter 1. Evangelism begins with the recognition that they have names; Ricky, Maria, they have names. The hands God puts around them, in a drab rundown motel of losers and the poor, are yours. It was a rite of passage for our parish when Ricky and Maria were baptized, joining social ministry with the gracious invitation of Jesus to include all within the Body of Christ. In the way of Jesus Ricky's and Maria's baptismal certificates give them a home in the household of the parish.

2. *The social ministry committee will attend to the needs of those within the household of faith.*

This task means taking responsibility for the great public and political sacramental acts of the Church. When we baptize we do not leave the children at the font. We follow them to their schools, where it matters greatly to us if they are safe and can learn. We care whether they will abuse alcohol and other drugs, whether they will have a shot at a good job and decent housing, whether they will be formed in their baptismal faith as fellow priests living the Gospel in the world. When we feed people at the Table we care about those who cannot be with us, remembering the homebound and hospitalized, those in prison, those absent for a variety of reasons. The social ministry committee helps define what kind of a community we will be. The sick are visited. Meals are brought to the sick one's family. A meal is served after funerals. Children are tutored and challenged. Physical and economic needs of members are addressed. Transportation is provided to the liturgy and other occasions. The social ministry committee will learn how to assess the needs of its fellow members and help organize the fabric of the parish to address such needs.

3. *The social ministry committee will oversee the parish's participation in ministries of social service and the corporal works of mercy.*

In the church I most recently served in New Jersey this meant the joining of the parish—and then our ELCA mission cluster of congregations—

to the county-wide Inter-Religious Fellowship for the Homeless. Our social ministry committee organized our participation in IRF, which included the staffing of local shelters, administration of transitional housing, dinners for the homeless, and advocacy efforts. When we purchased the house next door to our church and used it to shelter homeless families in a transitional housing program, this committee helped administer efforts to help the family get back on its feet, including medical help for the children as well as the searches for jobs and permanent housing. The committee members also provided invitations and access into the life of the parish, including our parish nursery school, summer programs, Sunday School, and Spanish-language outreach. Finally, the social ministry committee provided training and encouragement for caregivers in these programs.

4. *The social ministry committee will oversee the parish's participation in ministries of social change through a parish-based community organizing effort.*

Community organizing is the discipline that helps a parish, family, neighborhood develop the power to sit at the table where decisions are made that shape their communal life. These grassroots organizing efforts can be found all across the country: in Appalachia; on the farm; in suburban and inner-city neighborhoods. First-rate community organizations contain the following elements:

- Collective leadership effectively trained
- A broad base rooted in institutions rather than in individuals;
- Commitment to forming intentional links among the money, people, and values of these institutions to sustain their effective participation in the public arena;
- Commitment to acting on a variety of issues, helping their people face the real world in its varied challenges;
- Commitment to building power for its people, parishes, families, and neighborhoods;
- Commitment to acting on their beliefs and values, to bringing a vision of justice to decisions about the common life.

Both the city and blue-collar suburban parishes that I have served have benefited greatly from our participation in community organizations. These benefits have included:

- Alliances with other groups on issues important to us.
- Training grounds for our congregation's leaders, continued spiritual formation as beliefs are enacted in the life of the world. Leaders learn how to listen and draw out new leadership, run meetings, negotiate, raise money, and many other organizational skills.

- Positioning the activity of the parish in the thick of the action, in a world of doubt and struggle where people starved for meaning can come into contact with the love and concern of God's people. People are hungry to be part of a noble vision making a difference in the world. Community organization supports evangelism for a church willing to make a strong public witness.

The accomplishments of these organizations are many and varied: Nehemiah homes in Brooklyn; renewal of neighborhoods; improvement of public education; victories in the war on drugs; affordable housing; influence on local, state and national policy. But just as important have been the modest victories with which I am most familiar: saving a building on 92nd Street in Jackson Heights; breaking ground for twelve units of affordable housing in Bogota, New Jersey; the formation of a charter school in the south Bronx. The social ministry committee can shepherd the parish's involvement in community organizations, rooting the life of their people in the bricks and mortar, institutions and neighbors of their turf, signs of God's commitment to human history and its redemption.

5. *The social ministry committee will organize the response to appeals* for disaster relief, advocacy efforts, and other social ministry opportunities addressed to the congregation by their synod, national church body, ecumenical agencies, or local emergency task forces. Let me list three examples of how parish social ministry committees have helped organize effective response to the immediate needs of others in situations of disaster.

Several congregations traveled to North Dakota, bringing much-needed supplies and help to victims of floods. This partnership was personal, parish to parish.

As a result of Hurricane Mitch in 1998, 70% of the members of Cristo parish in Freeport, Long Island (a Latino mission congregation of the synod) were directly affected. Most of the members lost property, and 23 relatives of Cristo's members died in Honduras. Responses to this disaster were immediate because of the network of parish social ministry committees. One congregation, Resurreccion in Hempstead (another Latino mission congregation) sent a delegation with its pastor to help in the aftermath of Mitch.

I led a delegation from our synod to visit our companion synod, the Northwestern Diocese of Tanzania. We saw the devastation of floods caused by El Niño and the extreme poverty of our companions. This past year drought has caused massive hunger in Tanzania. The pastors of our companion synod had not been paid for four months. An appeal through the social ministry committees of our synod yielded over $10,000, enough money to bring every pastor current in their salary (the average salary of a Tanzanian pastor is $56 per year).

6. *The social ministry committee will raise funds and help administer the pastoral discretionary fund.*

Through this fund the congregation answers the knock on the door of stranger or friend in immediate need. The fund is pastoral because folks whose lives are being torn apart are also suffering psychic pain and loss of dignity. The congregation and its pastor are, or ought to be, people you can seek out when there is nowhere else to go. Whether the fund is used to help an elderly member get over a hump with a month's rent so she can stay in her place, or the family out of work whose child is funded to remain in the parish school, or another night in a motel for a family on the skids, or Christmas gifts for children or the stranger on the street, this fund becomes a way for a congregation to answer the question: What kind of a parish do we want to be? The use of the fund in our parish in Bogota, New Jersey, was always accompanied by an invitation to be a part of the Family of Jesus, and by an invitation to work on the root of the problem. The social ministry committee became very effective in linking need with resources. And many of the homeless and hopeless did find their way to our altar and the Bread of Life.

7. *The social ministry committee will provide opportunities for training and spiritual formation for parish members involved in social ministry.*

Bible studies on aging, hunger, and other issues engaged by the ministry of the parish will undergird these efforts in the Word. The action\reflection model of deeper learning has been particularly effective in the parishes I have served. After a stormy meeting with the mayor about the proliferating drug traffic in the neighborhood the members who participated pray together and study the Jesus story about the paralytic being let down through the roof in Mark 2. After singing Christmas carols in a nursing home the parish youth group reflects on their experience through the story of Anna and Simeon and the baby Jesus (Luke 2:25 ff.) Support groups are started for single parents in the parish school and Sunday School, and for the bereaved in congregation and community. Members about to serve dinner for the homeless for the first time are trained not only by those who already work with the poor, but also with Scripture stories that relate the compassion of Jesus to "the least of these."

In short, it will be the task of the parish social ministry committee, along with the pastor and other ministers, to use the ministries in their oversight as means to increase the faith and effectiveness of the people of God.

8. *The social ministry committee will link the concerns of the world and its people with the liturgy of the Church.*

Through announcements and prayer requests the committee members will bring the practical and human concerns of "seeking the welfare of the city" to each liturgy. Deacons and assisting ministers will be people who are active in the congregation's ministries of compassion, so that there is coherence between service at the altar and in the world.

One of the most powerful examples of this congruence took place one day in my former parish when we linked the table of the altar with the kitchen table in the house next door that we had purchased to provide shelter for homeless women and children. Our effort to house these children of God caused controversy in the congregation—several members left the parish—and community—zoning laws multiplied as the town fought this ministry. Our resolve to begin this ministry in the face of deep and visceral opposition was cemented when we connected the tables. After we had received Holy Communion at the altar we processed to the house. The acolytes and crucifer carried the cross and torches as the entire congregation followed them out the door and around the corner. The procession went to the kitchen table where the cross and torches illumined groups of members who prayed at the table for the mothers and children who would be living in the house. We then returned to the altar to hear the benediction and the command: "Go in peace, serve the Lord." The social ministry committee planned this Eucharistic experience.

Lutheran social ministry will remain centered in Word and Sacraments, extending them into the world, giving shape to Jesus in the ebb and flow of human life. Its witness in the world will point to the destiny of every corporal act of mercy, every corporate act of social justice: "Then I saw a new heaven and a new earth... and I heard a loud voice from the throne saying, "See, the home of God is among mortals. He will dwell with them as their God... he will wipe every tear from their eyes. Death will be no more."

(*Lutheran Partners*, January 1994)

Chapter 36
Requiem

> Matthew 2:1-12: "When they saw that the star had stopped, they were overwhelmed with joy...."

The star led the strangers to the outcast, the child hunted by society in order to be killed. They followed the star at great risk. Their joy at following the star was all they knew. It seemed they had been born to follow the brightness of its rising.

My cousin, Thomas Bouman, recently died of AIDS. He was a distinguished scholar, father, husband, and faithful Christian. He fought hemophilia all his life and lived in a wheelchair, enduring countless operations and medical procedures. He was one of the first heroes of my life, enduring his affliction without complaint. His grit and determination overcame so much in his lifetime, yet we were never aware of the effort of his living because of his acceptance of its terms. Within those limits Thomas constructed a deeply compassionate, joyful, and generous existence. He had glimpsed the light of the star.

I was angry when Tommy died of AIDS. I can arrive at no explanations of God's dealings with humanity that give me any particular insight into pain of this kind. In a fallen world in which King Herod hunts down and kills baby boys, incomprehensible suffering has always been with us. But the star has risen in the East, illuminating the One who came to be with us, who went to the cross and burst from the tomb. I know that Thomas' family clings to that resurrection light by faith. So do you and I.

I have watched several people die from AIDS and have conducted the liturgy at their funerals. We see through a glass darkly, even as we follow the star. As those who have seen the light, there is much we can learn and share about HIV and AIDS.

First, this disease is lethal and pervasive. It strikes all segments of humanity. Those who have seen the light must continue to warn one another that unprotected sex and drug abuse can kill. It is not loving nor wise to withhold knowledge, support and presence from those who may be susceptible to "at-risk" behaviors. The church that follows the star must not walk in darkness.

Second, the disease isolates those who suffer and their loved ones. We have put a stigma on HIV infection. My cousin's wife had trouble finding a funeral business willing to bury her husband. The AIDS sufferers I have visited describe loneliness and terrible hunger of the soul. We must remember that those who followed the star were seeking to hold and behold one who had been sentenced to death by Herod. Those with AIDS have told me that sometimes a willingness to touch the shoulder, hold the hand, or share a hug can do much to penetrate the terrible loneliness of being too often treated like pariahs. You cannot get AIDS from hugging a human being, sitting next to a child in school, donating blood.

Third, I reject the notion that some people with AIDS are victims and others are getting what they deserve. AIDS sufferers with whom I have shared ministry have included the wife of a drug abuser, a homosexual man, a drug addict. Each one is a child of God. Christ died for each one. Those who follow the star belong where life is at risk. Risk is where Jesus is always to be found in Scripture. Ministry with those who suffer from AIDS— and their loved ones— is like any other ministry in which God meets people. Guided by the Holy Spirit, the believer is strengthened by Word and Sacraments and the community gathered around them, and receives forgiveness of sins and assurance that nothing in all creation can separate any of us from the love of the One upon whom the starlight fell.

It is the season of the Christ-Mass, the Divine intrusion into the darkness of our culture of death and silence. The star burns brightly in the praise and mission of Christ's church. It shone for the strangers from the East. It illuminates the church with resurrection brightness. It burns for you— for your future and those you have loved who have died in Christ. It burns for those with AIDS and all their loved ones. It shines for Tommy, who has seen how brightly shines the Morning Star.

(From *The Faces of Advent/The Faces of Hope*,
a devotional published by the
Metropolitan New York Synod, 1996)

Chapter 37
A Tale of Three Houses

> Communities formed by a truthful narrative must provide the skills to transform fate into destiny so that the unexpected, especially as it comes in the form of strangers, can be welcomed as a gift...The primary social task of the church is to be itself-that is, a people who have been formed by a story that provides them with the skills for negotiating the danger of this existence, trusting in God's promise of redemption (Stanley Hauerwas, *A Community of Character* [Notre Dame, IN: University of Notre Dame Press, 1981], p. 10).

Eva's Shelter

Eva's Shelter is a refuge for homeless women in a poor section of Paterson, New Jersey. Chris, the lead singer for a punk-rock group called "The Chains," came with me to Eva's Shelter one night to deliver food and money raised by the band in a benefit concert. Chris was a new member of our parish. Touched by a sermon that mentioned the plight of New Jersey's homeless, he had made the mistake of asking, "What can I do?" Punk rock and homeless women, a marriage made in heaven. The shelter was in an old parish house surrounded by decrepit buildings, boarded stores, cold rainy streets. The shelter and feeding program are run by an ecumenical coalition in the area, a witness to Christ's compassion for the city. The shelter is named for Eva, a neighborhood widow whose personal care for the hungry and homeless was continued by the shelter. We knocked on the door and then looked down at the mail slot as it opened and a female voice yelled, "Who's there? Get down here where I can see you." I crouched toward the mail slot and revealed my white clerical collar. We heard at least five locks snap open. We carried in the boxes of food and handed over the money we had brought. We were invited to stay for coffee and brownies. Before I could sit down at the table a young lady with horn-rimmed glasses, matted, scraggly black hair and copious amounts of jangly costume jewelry came over to me.

"Are you Pastor Bouman?" she asked.

"Guilty as charged," I answered, edging away from her.

Then I recognized her as someone who had come to the door of our church after she had been burned out of the Paterson hotel room by a fire that had made her and over a hundred others homeless, and had killed several. I remembered giving her some food, a little money, an hour of my time. It seemed she had aged a decade in the year since I had seen her. She was a forceful sort, a trait to which I attributed her continued survival. She showed me a rosary she had taken off one of the victims of the fire and asked me to bless it. I did. She asked for money and cursed me when I told her I was tapped out.

I sat down at the table in front of a cup of coffee and fresh brownies. My friend Chris was in deep conversation with the shelter's director about the homeless in North Jersey, stretching his eighteen-year-old horizons. I looked at my companions around the table. One was very young and completely blissed-out. One was sullen, glaring from the corner. One had a dull, sweet face and smiled at me every time I looked at her. When she spoke she uttered incoherent babble. One sat regally, straight-backed, wearing an old hat, the kind with lace coming down the front. By morning all of them would be back on the street.

Another bedraggled woman was let in out of the night. I watched the scramble that resulted as the women went to the beds to reclaim their turf for the night. The new arrival put her bags on the last unoccupied bed.

The parish that I served in Bogota ministered to many homeless people; our parish house provided interim housing for homeless families at one point, preceding the congregation's purchase of the house next door for this purpose. We at Trinity in Bogota, New Jersey, got around. I was moved by the general cheerfulness and cleanliness of Eva's place. There was evidence in the form of flowers and touches of paint and soap that the shelter was a place where human beings cared about their sisters. The people who ran Eva's were compassionate, with an admixture of unromantic toughness. They were not slumming with the down-and-out, but living their faith in servant love. This shelter represented the stretching-out of the caring of many congregations in the Paterson area.

I was also touched by my young rock-and-roll friend, looking for his place at the foot of the cross, so different from so many of the indifferent, strung-out, selfish people in this emerging generation.

For these women it was just another night in Paterson, seeking shelter, hanging on, finding a bit of hearth where they could, mostly just getting by. The so-called thousand points of light were barely piercing their long darkness.

For me it was not just another night, but an epiphany of sorts. Eva's shelter, the people who run it and support it, and places like it in America of the approaching millennium are reminders that the heart of all ministry is solidarity with the poor. There was something Eucharistic about coffee and brownies with the homeless and a pushy street lady scrounging for a buck. Eating and drinking with Jesus. His real presence.

It was time to go. Chris and I said good-night. One person did not want to let go of my hand. We took one last look at Eva's Shelter and stepped out into the cold, wet streets of Paterson.

WHERE AGNES LIVED

Agnes. A lifelong member of our church and community, she was eighty years old. She lived alone in an old frame house. She had no place to go where she could continue some measure of independent living. We helped her search for over a year. Her home as well as her inner and outer health deteriorated badly. She died when the house burned down one night, probably as the result of her own neglect.

With Agnes on our hearts, the leaders of our congregations resolved to interview every older adult living alone in our town during the Octave of Prayer for Christian Unity in 1988. Over two hundred and fifty elderly neighbors told us on that occasion that housing was their primary concern. An ecumenical committee was formed to research and advocate for housing options. The group consulted with the Interfaith Action Council, a North Jersey community organizing effort that includes the Meadowlands Mission Cluster of the New Jersey Synod. The IAC helped to provide the training, wider context, and support for the ecumenical effort in Bogota. By the time of the 1989 Octave for Christian Unity, our local congregations made a public call for three specific housing options:

- A tax deferral program that would use the equity to pay the taxes on a senior's home.
- An accessory housing ordinance that would involve the renovation and creation of an additional affordable housing unit in the home of low income seniors. Where there had been one dilapidated dwelling, there were now two good units of housing.
- The creation of new units of affordable housing for the elderly.

Over the next two years Bogota's parish leaders conducted negotiations with government and private sector leaders. With the aid of the Interfaith Action Council's housing partnership, the group identified banks that were willing to participate in a loan pool to help create affordable accessory housing. The county housing authority pledged to put up seven thousand dollars per unit for the creation of accessory housing. Freeholders, assembly committees, bankers, the Bergen County executive and many others appeared before large public meetings in Bogota churches and pledged their support. Our parish leaders gave testimony and monitored countless local meetings with the mayor and council as the accessory housing ordinance took shape. And meetings with the New Jersey Department of Community Affairs as well as the Bergen County Housing Authority helped lay the groundwork for new senior citizen housing.

In November of 1991, before a gathering of over 150 senior citizens at one of the Bogota churches, the following housing options were officially announced with joy:

- The creation of a tax deferral program with the county freeholders and a local bank.
- The successful passage of the first accessory housing ordinance in Bergen County.
- The unveiling of plans and drawings for twelve units of affordable senior rental housing to be built in the neighborhood.

The successful efforts of our people to secure modest but tangible results in their quest for justice in the housing market bring home several points. First, the grassroots, "bottom-up" approach assured that the people had ownership of the proposals from the beginning. This is why the NIMBY, or "not in my back yard," syndrome did not happen in Bogota on the accessory housing issue. The link with the Interfaith Action Council provided local people with the training, analysis, power, and ability to confront and hold decision-makers accountable. Finally, these efforts were a parable of ecumenism anchored in a rhythm of prayer and liturgy, an ecumenism that puts legs on those prayers toward the neighbor and the struggle for justice.

THE HOUSEHOLD OF FAITH

The two houses that I have described represent points on the continuum of the church's social ministry: social service and social change; ministries of compassion and ministries of justice and advocacy. What unites them is their genesis within communities of Word and Sacraments. They flow from the prayers, study and proclamation of the Word, liturgies, sermons, baptisms, Eucharists of the communal life of the household of faith. Chris visited a shelter in Paterson because he listened to a sermon and witnessed the baptism of a homeless child. Our parish fought for justice in housing for the elderly because our Eucharistic ministers had spent many hours sharing the Sacrament with Agnes and other homebound neighbors and had listened not only to their needs, but to Christ's words of promise and command in the Eucharist. The Church must continuously press the connections between social ministry and advocacy and their genesis in the Apostolic faith of communities of Word and Sacrament, and their relationship to the inexhaustible grace of the dying and rising Christ poured out on all sinners.

Our efforts to stand with the poor, to transform systems of domination and corruption, to engage in corporal acts of mercy are not messianic. The Kingdom, as Luther's catechism reminds us, comes indeed without our efforts. Many of today's political and liberation theologies are flawed by misdirected deification of human longing and effort. All human activity in the Kingdom on the Left comes under judgment. It is proximate, provisional, but also a sign of the Messiah's nearness.

The household of faith is the place where Eva's Shelter and Agnes' house meet at the pulpit, the altar, the font. These houses and their people are the particular places in which believers find God's presence and live in obedience to God's commands. Ministry in the community offers ways for our parishes to "seek the welfare of the city," (Jeremiah), and affirm the carnal, intimate particularity in which God is always present in and to the world. Social ministry can be an affirmation and sign of the community's faith in the Lord of history. Such ministry locates the eschatological activity of Word and Sacrament communities in the midst of this time, this place, these neighbors, these homes and shelters, these hurts, these present opportunities. It is the practical living-out of the implications of Baptism and Eucharist for the life of the world.

(*Lutheran Partners*, November\December, 1991)

Chapter 38
Give Me That Stranger: The Ministry of Word and Sacrament Communities in the World

> When faith leads to action in outward affairs, that which takes place is spiritual in the midst of the carnal. Everything our bodies do, the external and carnal, is called spiritual behavior, if God's Word is added to it and it is done in faith (Martin Luther, *Luther on Vocation* by Gustav Wingren [Muhlenberg Press, 1957]).

Ite, Missa Est

The liturgy of the Church on the Lord's Day is not a private catered affair, but a public action celebrated in the midst of creation. If that is true, then the final words of the liturgy are not a dismissal, but a commission to continue the liturgy in the quotidian routines, joys, and sorrows of human history. "Go in peace, serve the Lord." And the people respond, "Thanks be to God," as they bear forth the Real Presence that has reentered the rhythms of their lives. *Ite, missa est.* The Mass is over. Get out of here and continue the Mass. And the people say, Amen! But the Church's Amen! is public. Evangelical. Compassionate. The tabernacle of Christ's presence is the world, the cosmos.

A parish renewed in the Gospel is a parish determined to live its life in the midst of the world.

A true parable about the public Amen! of the church. Edgar is, by anybody's standards, a strange character. He lives alone near the New Jersey parish that I used to serve, in a welfare motel better known for drug addicts and prostitutes than for old men who walk two miles to a church in Bogota. For some reason he adopted our church and there are times when he pushes our understanding of what we mean when we say that all God's children are welcome. He seems a good man, with a true and honest faith, although a bit rough around the edges. Some of the social graces have been rubbed away from years of trying to survive in an inhospitable world, and to those who do not know him he can be kind of scary. On occasion he can get loud and demanding and, if the truth be told, my heart sank on Palm Sunday when he was waiting in the sanctuary for me after a full day of liturgies, First Communions and pastoral conversations of much pain and sorrow in the sacristy and narthex. I knew that when Edgar waited for me he wanted a ride, and he usually wanted some of my time as well as some other bits and pieces of what I could produce to help him survive.

This is my confession to the reader: I wanted the Amen! to be over. *Ite missa est.* The Mass is over. Get out of here. Amen!

On the drive back to Edgar's motel he talked my ear off and I prayed for patience. Yet something strange and wonderful began to occur as I pulled into the parking lot of the run-down Motor Inn. A door opened and an elderly woman emerged. She knocked on another door and another elderly woman emerged. They limped to our car. Others waiting at the edges of the parking lot followed. They had been waiting for us. I was in someone else's church now. For the first time I noticed that Edgar's hand grasped a bunch of palms. The first lady was by the door.

"Did you bring them?"

He got feisty, the man can really be a jerk.

"What do you think, I would forget you? Get out of here!"

But Edgar with all his rough edges was also the only person who had ever passed for a pastor in this backwater parish of broken souls. The ELCA won't be building any successful megachurches here. But I tell you, there could be no more fertile soil for "church growth" than this concrete parking lot and its waiting children of God.

Then he smiled and gave her a palm branch through the window. She tried to kiss him and he pulled away. But this lady knew her pastor. She clutched her piece of palm, as if she had just been given the most precious gem and called the gathering group over to the van. I could only watch in awe as the palms from our liturgy at Trinity were distributed among the down-and-out who waited for the Amen! of the church in the shadow of the George Washington Bridge. Edgar got out of the car.

"Bless us!" he commanded me. I got out of the car, blessed their palms, placed my hands on each forehead and pronounced the benediction. If I had had bread and wine in my possession I would have fed them right there. I got back in the car as my feisty friend began to carry on.

Another confession: I was grateful to leave him. But as I pulled out of the parking lot I caught a glimpse in my rearview mirror of the continuation of our Sunday morning Holy Week liturgy as a grumpy old man passed out the palm branches to more arriving children of God who are mostly forgotten and despised.

Ite, missa est. It is my conviction that somehow the continual renewal and reformation of this particular parish will have something to do with turning its life—a life rich in liturgical faithfulness, serious ongoing engagement in the Word, evangelical fervor, and confessional integrity-toward a motel of burnouts and the deep corporal and spiritual needs shared by all humanity. Faithful parishes everywhere are called to continue the Incarnation with their own specific equivalents of the welfare motel.

To Take Care of the Body

> Joseph went to Pilate, pleaded with him and cried out:
> Give me that Stranger
> Who since his youth
> Has wandered as a stranger.
> Give me that Stranger
> Upon whom I look with wonder,
> Seeing him a guest of death.
> Give me that Stranger
> Whom envious folk
> Estrange from the world.
> Give me that Stranger
> That I may bury him in a tomb,
> Who being a stranger has no place
> Whereon to lay his head.
> Give me that Stranger
> To whom his mother cried out
> As she saw him dead:
> "My Son, my senses are wounded
> And my heart is burned
> As I see you dead!
> Yet, trusting in your resurrection,
> I magnify you."
>
> (from the Eastern Orthodox Holy Saturday Liturgy)

How lovingly Joseph took care of the body of his Lord. And the women on that early Easter morn, how faithfully they returned to the tomb to anoint the body. Care of the body is our first instinct when a loved one dies.

We close the eyes. Wash and cover the limbs. Prepare for burial. We take care of the body. Easter, resurrection hope, begins with a word. Disoriented, grief-stricken, as we all are when a loved one has died, Mary of Magdala does not even recognize who it is that is standing before her in the early morning garden. She is intent on details of post-mortem care. When you're dead, you're dead.

"Tell me where you have laid him that I might carry him away."

Take care of the body. Yet with a single word Jesus begins to take care of His body in the world.

"Mary." He calls her by name.

"Rabboni." She replies.

A Body for the risen Christ is being formed.

It begins for each of us with a word. At Baptism the name of the Triune God is spoken over our own names. The church, the Body of Christ, is re-incarnated over and over again at each Baptism. We become the Body. Take care of the Body. What we have come to call the social ministry of the church echoes the intent of Joseph of Arimathea and Mary of Magdala. Give me the Stranger. Give me the body that we may take care of it. Far from being a species of social work a technique for problem-solving, an arrogant "prophetic" voice, or a technical autopsy of this world's pain, the ministry of the Body of Christ to the bodies of Christ is a continuation of the announcement of Jesus' resurrection from the dead.

Theses for Parishes Renewed in the Gospel
There is only one Gospel ministry.

There is no such thing as "social ministry" in the sense of some specialized activity of the Church that is somehow different from all else which the Church does, prays, is. All ministry is about the Gospel: "God was in Christ, reconciling the world to himself."

If my former parish in New Jersey follows the Holy Spirit to a ministry of presence at nearby welfare motels, it is only one part of the effort of this parish to gather around the means of grace a community of believers and bring them into relation to the dying and rising Christ. All other goals, laudable and vital though they may be— social justice, economic growth for poor neighborhoods, power for the powerless, social service— are derived from the self-understanding of a community gathered by and for the Word and the Sacraments. And all activities of such communities of faith, including what we have come to name "social ministry," return to the continual reference, judgment, and inspiration of this Word and these Sacraments.

The doctrine of the Two Kingdoms must be taken with utmost seriousness by Lutherans engaged in social ministry.

The Kingdom of God, as Luther said, comes indeed without our efforts. Our witness to Jesus' resurrection through our ministry to the battered and abandoned neighborhoods and bodies of our world is not messianic. Many of today's political and liberation theologies are flawed by misguided deification of human capabilities and "transforming" efforts. All activity of the Kingdom of the left hand comes under judgment as provisional. It fleshes out the positive significance of the fifth and seventh commandments in terms of responsible care for our neighbor's body and goods. It joins the Kingdom on the Right in lived-out witness to the resurrection of Jesus from the dead.

Lutheran social ministry in the Kingdom of God's left hand will fashion communal and ecumenical responses to community issues so that people may participate in the shaping of their own history.

This thesis means, I believe, that Lutherans ought to take a hard look at the possibilities of the discipline of community organizing. Ministry with integrity engages people at the core of their beliefs, their vision, their imagination. This involves power, responsibility, and the deepening of both interpersonal and political relationships.

Consider an abandoned house on 92nd Street, around the corner from the church that I served in Jackson Heights. The residents of 92nd Street asked their local parish to help them with the problems posed by empty buildings like this one. Jackson Heights, Queens was a troubled community in the early 1970s, experiencing rapid ethnic change, economic stagnation, drugs, crime, and a serious arson problem. It was a dreary litany, played out in neighborhoods across the country, magnified in later years by the trauma surrounding the verdict in the Rodney King case in Los Angeles. In neighborhoods like these families feel threatened and churches hold on for dear life.

The most immediate threat to this block of 92nd Street concerned this abandoned building. There had recently been fires in buildings like this one and nearby blocks were scarred by arson, deterioration, and abandonment. The place was a haven for derelicts and addicts who harassed the neighbors. The building was an unlit match ready to ignite and destroy the entire block. It was also a powerful symbol to the neighbors of their powerlessness.

The residents asked their local congregation if they could help them do something about the abandoned building in their midst. I was the pastor. This wasn't about global issues of apartheid, world peace, or saving the planet. One building, one block, local families were looking to their neighborhood church to "seek the welfare of the city."

How do congregations usually respond when confronted with such a request? Let me list a few of the traditional ways in which a parish becomes involved in "social ministry."
- The pastor can take some personal action. A phone call. A speech. An interview with a local newspaper reporter. The leader has the comfort of her convictions. 92nd Street still has its abandoned building. The "insider" approach is reactive and builds no power or civic competence among the people.
- The parish can refer to resolutions passed by synodical and national conventions and "social statements" passed by their national embodiment of the Church. In the ELCA we pass a lot of these. And there is a place for "a word fitly spoken" (Proverbs) with theological precision at opportune moments. But our beleaguered neighbors were asking us to act—and act quickly—on our statements and resolutions. Very few churches know how to move from "talking the talk" to "walking the walk." Without action these statements and resolutions are a form of cheap grace.
- The parish can get some people together and raise a little hell, stage a demonstration or confrontation with those it thinks hold power. Activists love this approach. Fellini could have filmed our attempt at this. We summoned the powers that be to a meeting in our church basement in the wake of a rash of muggings. They sent community relations experts whose only job was to absorb us. Every local loudmouth and eccentric showed up along with the politicians and their canned speeches. We never negotiated with anyone who could make a decision. The muggings continued.
- Participation in electoral politics. But what if your candidate loses?
- Caring for the immediate victims. This is the usual and compassionate response of congregations and the social service agencies of the church. When the neighbors are mugged by junkies hanging out in the abandoned building we will visit them in the hospital. We can counsel the addicts who shoot up within the building's walls. When the building finally burns, taking half the block with it, we can provide food, clothing, shelter, relocation for the victims. Caregiving is an approach congregations must never abandon. But does it exhaust the possibilities of biblically informed parish ministry?
- Finally we used the discipline of community organizing.

At the time of the neighbors' request our parish had been a member of a community organization of over twenty parishes representing 75,000 families called the Queens Citizens' Organization. I shared the 92nd Street neighbors' request with our QCO parish leaders. They had learned how to dig through city tax rolls to track down the owners or managers of real estate. The research of several parish leaders with 92nd Street neighbors discovered that title to the building was held by the City of New York in default of taxes. Because of our participation in a borough-wide QCO antiarson campaign we knew whom to hold accountable for buildings such as the one on 92nd Street. The parish leaders contacted his office and secured a promise of immediate demolition or sealing of the building.

It was then time to involve the rest of Atonement Church and the residents of 92nd Street in the process. Our parish participants were commissioned at a liturgy using the rite of Affirmation of Baptism. Our Sunday School children distributed leaflets to every door on 92nd Street inviting the residents to a meeting at our church to discuss the matter. Almost 90% of the residents showed up at the meeting. They were given a choice by the city between demolition and sealing. The discussion was animated and touching. They were thrilled to have a little piece of their history within their own competence and direction. Some residents were speaking to one another for the first time. And the church became the focal point of a burgeoning sense of community. They voted for the sealing-up of the building. Once the building was secured a new owner was found. In a building where muggers and addicts once lurked and the threat of fire was palpable, curtains are now hung, children go out the door to school, another family makes its dwelling, as a small sign of hope on a strong block, 92nd Street.

Our leaders reported the results back at the time of the liturgy and our faith community gave thanks in prayer, testimony, doxology. QCO leaders from other parishes and the 92nd Street neighbors were invited to be a part of that celebration at our liturgy. Social ministry, leadership development, ecumenical witness, social justice and evangelistic hospitality were all gathered into the liturgy of the people gathered around Word and Sacraments. Implementing the global tasks of peace and justice begin in renewed local parishes of Word and Sacraments who organize in order to demonstrate their love for their neighbors.

For Lutherans social ministry and evangelism are one. The ministry of a renewed parish will take responsibility for the unchurched and the poor in its neighborhood.

Edgar from the motel is legion. He and his comrades come to the doors of churches and parsonages in every community across the United States and Canada. The homeless, the poor, the con artists and the cons, the eccentrics, the mentally ill, and the lonely. They call forth corporal as well as spiritual acts of mercy. They remind those like me, committed to organizing communal responses seeking power for social change, that ministry is always at its heart individual, particular. Here are some basics of social ministry for congregations committed to responsibility for the poor and unchurched in their neighborhoods:

Open the door. Being present and available in the name of Jesus is the first charism of social ministry.

Invite the person in. Continue the hospitality of the Eucharistic Family Meal. Ask about their well-being and listen respectfully to the answers. Everybody human has a story she or he is dying to tell. There is an opening for ministry in the hospitality that respects human dignity and invites people to tell their stories.

Respond. The first time I always give some form of aid no matter how repugnant the person or how outrageous the spiel. The response is not always monetary— it can be food, a scholarship for a family's child in our school, a job referral, whatever. The first time I always respond.

Invite people to move to the root of their problem. Remember that you are committed to faith in the power of the Gospel and its embodiment in the Christian community to turn around any and all wayward or tragic situations in the power of the Holy Spirit. Ask the person: Do you want to change your life? Or, do you want to find long-term help to cope with your situation? If they do, invite them back for further conversation and continue the relationship. Here is where the many contacts of pastor and parishioners come into play: local, state, and social ministry agencies; job placement programs or employment opportunities; shelters for the homeless or abused, Twelve-Step programs; other services known to the parish social ministry committee— whatever it takes to truncate a downward spiral. Remember Jesus' words: "Stand up, take up your own bed, and walk."

Extend a clear invitation into the life of the parish. Invite the person to the one square meal a week that is Life itself. For too long we have separated the love and charity of our Christian witness— social service agencies and institutions— from their origin in communities of Word and Sacraments. People do come when they are invited. It is mystifying to me that the churches can speak volumes about the need to "get the Church into the world" and then fail to at least invite the frail and fragile of the world into their midst.

Along the way we come to know our limitations and human finitude. One pastor or parish cannot eradicate every human need. But we can open the door. We can respond with whatever little of time and resources we can spare. And we can invite in the name of Jesus.

Renewed parishes know the importance of continual prayer. We can pray for each person God sends to us by name. There is strength and comfort in putting the bodies of these strangers— and always your own— into the hands of the Stranger who promises through the Psalmist that even if the journey reaches the depths of Sheol, the Lord is already there answering the door. Let Lutheran social ministry be a midrash on the words of Luther: We are all beggars, that's for sure.

Lutheran social ministry will return frequently to its baptismal foundation. It will extend the Eucharist into the world. It will remain rooted in the Word.

In an earlier chapter I have described a meeting with the mayor. Let me now link that meeting to Baptism:

I had just left my wife, who was in the hospital to give birth by Caesarean section in the morning. I arrived late to a meeting with Mayor Koch of New York City. The sight took my breath away. The auditorium was filled with over 1500 delegates from the churches of the Queens Citizens' Organization all gathered around large vertical signs identifying church and neighborhood. I went over to the familiar faces gathered around the sign of my parish, Atonement Lutheran, Jackson Heights. We had voted on local issues to bring before the mayor. We had recruited and trained fifty people for our delegation. The meeting was stormy. The mayor tried to take over the meeting and evade the issues; he ended up walking out. The political fallout and protracted publicity were intense; church folks were news for days. But we had achieved what no one will ever give us as a handout— respect. Quietly, over the next several months, and after further, less tense meetings, the mayor delivered the commissioners of sanitation, police, transportation, and others to negotiating sessions in Queens. A host of local community issues were solved at these meetings. A wary but respectful and dignified relationship between the mayor and the parishes of QCO had been forged. The meeting with the mayor was political in the Aristotelian sense. We had a say in our lives, some control of our history, in the name of the God of history and of creation.

The morning after that meeting in February of 1978, our daughter Rachel was born. Three Sundays later the body of Christ performed another political act, as public and earthy as a meeting with the mayor. I baptized Rachel in the Name of the Father and of the Son and of the Holy Spirit. The act of baptism is an act of responsibility for the body of the child. We extend the font to meetings with the mayor. Issues of education, drugs, jobs, are baptismal issues. They are about Rachel and all the baptized children of God. We will follow the children of all ages whom we baptize. We will follow them into the world. We will nurture their faith and their bodies.

The politics of the Body of Christ continues as the Eucharist is celebrated. The act of celebrating the Lord's Supper is an act of responsibility for the bodies of those we feed, and for those without food. It is a political act; we follow the Eucharist out into the world. One Sunday, in the church that I served in New Jersey, we went from our altar and marched down Palisade Avenue to St. Joseph's Roman Catholic Church. The priest led his people out the door after their Mass to a table that we had set up in front. Together, our people signed petitions concerning unfair utility bills and affordable housing. It was all one liturgy, from pulpits to altars to public witness, the Body of Christ strong in the world through renewed parishes.

The witness of renewed parishes in the world is eschatological.
Sometimes I think the biggest growth industry in the Church is meetings about social ministry. There are housing conferences and homeless marches. There is consciousness-raising about many issues. There are many strategies and competing initiatives. Programs and outreach objectives come and go. We lobby the government and the wider Church about a host of issues. We deliver papers at conferences and draft statements and resolutions. Some of this is helpful, even crucial to the tasks of the Church—and some of it is foolish.

But let us never forget that the classic Lutheran form that social ministry takes in the world is the parish, a people mature in Christ, nourished by Word and Sacraments and willing to lay down their collective and individual lives for the sake of the Gospel. They are a present sign of the future destiny of the neighborhood. And they have a plan.

> Then I saw a new heaven and a new earth; for the first heaven and the first earth had passed away, and the sea was no more. And I saw the holy city, new Jerusalem, coming down out of heaven from God, prepared as a bride adorned for her husband. And I heard a loud voice from the throne saying, "See, the home of God is among mortals. He will dwell with them as their God; they will be his peoples, and God himself will be with them; he will wipe away every tear from their eyes. Death will be no more....

The song of the renewed parish, sung in the midst of the world, is this: "Maranatha. Come, Lord Jesus. Amen."

(*Lutheran Forum*, Una Sancta Issue, Reformation, 1992)

Conclusion

Conclusion
Apocalypse Now!

> The first criterion of success in any human activity, the necessary preliminary, whether to scientific discovery or to artistic vision, is intensity of attention or, less pompously, love. (W. H. Auden)

There is a palpable spirituality in the land on the eve of the third millennium. The intensity of our attention is going in many directions. For many it will be a time of summing up, of making assessments, of lofty thoughts about the goal— if any— of human history. For some the shadow of the millennium will provoke ecstatic or "otherworldly" spiritual impulses. People will root around in Revelation, check the signs of the times, and harbor apocalyptic visions. There will be greater intensity in this culture's critiques of any spirituality which sinks us deeper into the material, as in organized religion or texts or dogmas. The millennium hints to many in this present age that God will not be boxed in or contained anywhere in a church, in this history or flesh. In the words of Father Divine, the Harlem preacher of the 20s, there is no "tangibilification" of God. And there has already begun the millennial malarkey of Promethean spirituality: the perfection of the human, of the self. As if, at 12:01 in the year 2000 we will have arrived. In all of it there is, in Frank Kermode's term, "The sense of an ending." And people fear chaos above all.

In the midst of the great spiritual hunger, expectations, millennial party reservations, and transcendent visions we remember why it is that we mark time as we do. We hear a young unwed mother sing a song of growing life inside her womb. Literal tangibilification. God in the belly. Magnificat.

Her song is an invitation to remember that the celebration of the millennium is a celebration of the Incarnation. That God is with us. That the intensity of attention of our millennial spirituality is carnal, earthy, human. We have been marking our time since a woman delivered a baby, believing that human history is precisely the transcendent place of our spiritual deliverance and companionship. The Magnificat, the soul praise of God, is the wonder that in Mary's womb humanity has been elevated into the intensity of attention and love of the holy God.

The song, as all great art, begins with the heart skipping a beat in an awesome vision. She needed to hear "Don't be afraid" when the angelic vision was accomplished! Her reaction to hearing the Gospel of the nearness and transforming relevance of God is similar to that of the shepherds and all disciples. She goes in haste to share it. Far from transporting her out of the world and into millennial visions of transcendence, it places her across the kitchen table with kin, Elizabeth. True millennial spirituality sinks deeply into relationships, the creating of community around our life's stories. She tells her story. Elizabeth blesses her: for the new life in her womb and for her faith: "Blessed is the fruit of your womb.... Blessed are you who believe there would be a fulfillment of what was spoken to you by the Lord." Faith and communal spirituality rooted in human stories are pillars of millennial hope, and the heart of faith is Jesus, God's response and presence to all millennia.

Mary in turn blesses God. At the dawn of the first day of the first millennium she translates the Gospel into what it means for everyday people: the hungry, the empty, the poor. She is translating religion into life, tradition into relevant hope. She is mixing creed ("The promise he made to our ancestors, to Abraham") with society ("from generation to generation"). Millennial incarnation spirituality is countercultural, strewn with Lukan reversals: the proud are scattered; the powerful brought down... the lowly lifted up; the hungry filled... the rich sent away empty.

Our congregations are placed on Mars Hill — Mars Hill, that place in Luke's second book where Paul continues Mary's sermon" — with opportunities to make a powerful witness in these days turning toward the millennium. They offer community rooted in the Word and Sacraments in a world of unmoored, deeply personal spirituality that leaves people empty and hungering for more. Our congregations are ethical communities offering tangible opportunities for service to and with the poor, a servant spirituality rooted in Servant Jesus "who thought equality with God not something to be grasped, but emptied himself...." Our congregations can teach and catechize because we know that faith is not just subjective, a cul-de-sac leading into the dead end of the self. It is not faith in faith. "My soul magnifies the Lord, and my Spirit rejoices in God my Savior." It is faith in Jesus Christ. We can witness to the mooring of this faith to things outside of the self: to texts, to the witness of generations, to carnal things like bread, wine, water. We can teach and live what the Holy Spirit does, binding us to the revelation of God in Christ through the means of Grace.

We celebrate the millennium by burrowing closer into humanity, by moving closer to the breach in the walls of the city described by Isaiah, by singing Mary's song full of Lukan reversals and by living it. As intensity of attention heightens toward the millennium, let congregations and their many ministries invite the world to consider the incarnation of Jesus, and let us sing together Mary's song. Magnificat.

THE ENDLESS ALLELUIA

The parish is where the Church hunkers down to incarnate the Word of God in the inspiration of the Holy Spirit. From the "oikoumene" households of the primitive church depicted in the book of Acts and the Epistles, through the planting of Eucharistic communities in the midst of the pagan world by Ansgar, Boniface, Patrick and others, to the nascent gatherings of today's mission developers, the parish has been the unique form of the Church's evangelical presence in the world. For Lutherans the community gathered by and around Word and Sacraments is the confessional form of the Incarnation.

The walls of the congregation are permeable. By "parish" we mean not only the gathering of the family of believers around Word and Sacraments but also its setting, its turf, its surrounding neighborhood. The family of believers gathered around Word and Sacraments is an eschatological sign of the Reign of God in the midst of its neighborhood. I have long admired the ministry of faithful parishes in our synod and their ability to give leadership of the best parish practice shaped by evangelical and catholic theological and ecclesial commitments. Their settings are different, their programs are diverse, but the presence of Jesus and the Apostolic Tradition infuse everything they do. Worship and the world intersect with integrity as these parishes — and you on your good days — move toward the breach with the Gospel. You are the light spoken of by the prophet: "Then shall your light shine...."

I was recently invited to preach back home at the parish in which I grew up, Grace Church in River Forest, Illinois. It is a large church in a substantial suburb. The occasion was the monthly series of Bach cantatas. My sermon was to accompany Bach's Easter cantata, BWV #4, "Christ lag in Todesbanden." My faith was nurtured, my theological convictions formed, my sense of the centrality of Word and Sacraments given to me by the parish of my youth. I found that at its heart ministry was no different in River Forest, Illinois than in Queens, New York City or Bogota, New Jersey, in a parish in the Metro-New York Synod or a parish in first-century Corinth.

The text of the cantata gives no answers, just assertions. It begins with a beautiful orchestral sinfonia. Its flowing beauty is deceptive because the cantata is about the *duellum mirabile*, the strife between life and death that brought our salvation. The choir in fugue-like interchange and gradual crescendo asserts that Christ lay in the strong bands of death. Then, as if that doleful assertion mattered not at all, the choir simply asserts, in joyful acclaim, over and over again, "Alleluia, Alleluia, Alleluia...." So goes the rest of the cantata, wavering between death and life, despair and victory, each given their due, but always the last word belonging to the endless "Alleluia." At the closing chorale the final "Alleluia" is declared with stunning clarity.

"Your light shall shine." The tune may change its key from the ruined ancient streets of Jerusalem, to the Lower East Side to River Forest to Gustavus here in Manhattan. But the song remains the same. In the words of a 5th-8th Century Latin text in the 1940 Episcopal hymnal:

> Sing Alleluia forth in heartfelt praise,
> You citizens of heaven, O sweetly raise
> An endless Alleluia.
>
> Then let the holy city raise the strain,
> And with glad songs resounding wake again
> An endless Alleluia.
>
> Such song is rest and food and deep delight
> To saints forgiven; let them all unite
> In endless Alleluia.
>
> Almighty Christ, to you our voices sing
> Glory for evermore; to you we bring
> An endless Alleluia.

From the parish for the life of the world.

www.ingramcontent.com/pod-product-compliance
Lightning Source LLC
Chambersburg PA
CBHW031238290426
44109CB00012B/342